Food & Philosophy

To our mothers

Please see the other titles in the Epicurean Trilogy, conceived by Fritz Allhoff:

 Fritz Allhoff, ed.,
Wine & Philosophy:
A Symposium on Drinking and Thinking

 Steven D. Hales, ed.,
Beer & Philosophy:
The Unexamined Beer
Isn't Worth Drinking

"*Food & Philosophy* is a book we're very happy to keep at our bedside for late-night reflection and indeed inspirational 'food for thought.'"

Andrew Dornenburg and Karen Page,
authors of *Becoming a Chef*

Food & Philosophy

Eat, Drink, and Be Merry

Edited by Fritz Allhoff and Dave Monroe

BLACKWELL PUBLISHING
350 Main Street, Malden, MA 02148–5020, USA
9600 Garsington Road, Oxford OX4 2DQ, UK
550 Swanston Street, Carlton, Victoria 3053, Australia

First published 2007 by Blackwell Publishing Ltd

1   2007

Library of Congress Cataloging-in-Publication Data

Food and philosophy : eat, think, and be merry / edited by Fritz Allhoff and Dave Monroe.
    p. cm.
    Includes bibliographical references and index.
    ISBN 978-1-4051-5775-9 (pbk. : alk. paper) 1. Food. 2. Philosophy. I. Allhoff, Fritz.
II. Monroe, Dave.

    B105.F66F66 2007
    641.3001—dc22

                                                                        2007017481

A catalogue record for this title is available from the British Library.

Set in 10.5/13pt Sabon
by Graphicraft Limited, Hong Kong
Printed and bound in the United Kingdom
by TJ International Ltd, Padstow, Cornwall

The publisher's policy is to use permanent paper from mills
that operate a sustainable forestry policy, and which has been
manufactured from pulp processed using acid-free and
elementary chlorine-free practices. Furthermore, the publisher
ensures that the text paper and cover board used have met
acceptable environmental accreditation standards.

For further information on
Blackwell Publishing, visit our website:
www.blackwellpublishing.com

Contents

Contents

Foreword

Odessa Piper

Do we eat to live, or do we live to eat? It is time to file that query away in someone else's century. Our "Eureka" moment arrives with this question: can we, will we, start eating as if our world depends on it? If you doubt it, just pick up a newspaper. Many of society's most profound challenges could benefit from a better understanding of our food ways, from how we select it, grow it, distribute it, eat it, and ruminate on it to, ultimately, how we assign meaning to it.

The academics, cooks, and humorists who have contributed to this book have a common denominator: they are each in their own way quite passionate about food. Their writing ranges from rigorous discourse in the philosopher's tradition – through well-footnoted scholarship – to highly unorthodox perspectives. I get the sense they are a fun-loving and generous lot, people you would like to share a long and interesting meal with. There are hold-outs who still "eat to live" and will argue that we should not consider food to be anything more than a commodity, a temporal pleasure, one of the seven sins, or worst of all, "trendy." In their essays, they challenge our thinking about food and ask us to go deeper in these explorations.

These essays advance the idea that food – and its attendant arts of growing, preparing, and degustation – holds the power to restore meaning and proportion to a society that is hell-bent on consumption for consumption's sake. The authors question why we should insist on relegating food to the lower orders of meaning, even as our mechanized world continues to drift further from the center. They examine some of the obviously absurd machinations of our relationship with food, to the absurdly obvious solutions right in front of our face. The juxtaposition of topics – including indigenous food ways and GMOs, Epicureanism and restaurant criticism, eating disorders and fast food, picky eaters and food as art – offers something for everyone, even while begging the question: who else could benefit if our food ways were invested with greater conscience and consequence?

Taken in total, I hear a declaration for the reenchantment of food. It has long been my sense that a daily dose of real food – fruits and vegetables intact with their trace miracles – that ineffable component of wholeness, can fortify our search for meaning and deepen our capacity to live. Many of us have come of age with the catch phrase "small is beautiful." We are starting to realize that small is also powerful, as evidenced in fields as diverse as organic farming, indigenous medicine, and micro-lending. To my way of thinking, an abundant accumulation of countless small solutions could demonstrate how humanity might yet sustain its place within the Earth's communities of life.

While you graze among these essays keep in mind what the writer and philosopher Alexandre Dumas said: "Man does not live by what he eats, but by what he digests." So chew these words slowly and enjoy going back to the buffet. We can have it all. We can celebrate what we love about eating while we learn to eat in a way that allows our species to thrive. And while we are at it, eat to live another day, at least to ponder life's deepest questions.

Acknowledgments

First, we would like to thank all of the contributors. Many of these people we have only communicated with by phone or email (though, of course, we hope that changes!), yet they already feel like friends. We appreciate the quality of their work and, of course, their willingness to slough through our seemingly unending barrage of editorial feedback; they all did this with great attitudes. We both recognize their efforts and marvel at the quality of their finished essays. It is also worth appreciating how diverse they are: they come from across a range of professions, ranging from academic philosophers (or other academic disciplines) to various facets of the food or related industries.

Second, we would like to thank our publisher. Blackwell Publishing has, from the start, demonstrated exceptional enthusiasm for this project. In particular, we acknowledge Jeff Dean, Danielle Descoteaux, and Jamie Harlan. Jeff has been especially helpful, and we thank him for his constant feedback and entertainment of our inane and seemingly (for him) never-ending emails.

Third, we thank each other: we are lucky enough to be good friends and all the more so for being able to "work" together on a project like this.

Finally, we thank you, the reader: enjoy the volume! And eat good food. And *think* about it.

Fritz Allhoff, Kalamazoo, Michigan
Dave Monroe, St. Petersburg, Florida

Setting the Table: An Introduction to Food & Philosophy

Fritz Allhoff and Dave Monroe

Socrates: *True enough. I was forgetting that they'll obviously need salt, olives, cheese, boiled roots, and vegetables of the sort they cook in the country. We'll give them desserts, too, of course, consisting of figs, chickpeas, and beans, and they'll roast myrtle and acorns before the fire, drinking moderately. And so they'll live in peace and good health, and when they die at a ripe old age, they'll bequeath a similar life to their children.*

Glaucon: *If you were founding a city for pigs, Socrates, wouldn't you fatten them on the same diet?*

Plato, Republic 372c3–372d5[1]

Within the pages of this anthology, the reader will find a smorgasbord of essays written about a range of topics connecting what we eat with some very interesting and, in many cases, important philosophical concerns. We have arranged our authors' contributions thematically, in the hopes that readers can, as with *à la carte* menus, select essays that appeal to their philosophical palates. Of course, as with all bountiful spreads, we encourage readers to partake in every offering, as each essay is uniquely delightful and intellectually worthwhile. We hope that, as a result, readers will find their appetites whetted for further such discussions.

Our aims in producing this anthology are twofold. First, the editors and contributing authors – who appreciate the value of philosophical rumination – hope to show foodies, gourmands, chefs, and others who treasure food that critical reflection upon what and how we eat can contribute to a robust enjoyment of gastronomic pleasures. Relatedly, the second aim of our combined effort is to draw *philosophical* attention to *food itself*. Historically, philosophical discussions of food have been subordinate to gaining insight into other philosophical issues. Occasionally, talk of eating has served as a metaphor for other "nutritive" endeavors, like the acquisition of knowledge. Other times gastronomic concepts (e.g., taste) were adopted to specify certain classes of value judgments, most notably in aesthetics and philosophy of art. Alternately, we find philosophical conversations of what and how we eat embedded in arguments aimed at elucidating deeper, but only loosely related, points.

Such is, for example, the case with the epigraph quoted above. Socrates and Glaucon do not discuss diets with an eye toward establishing conditions for ideal culinary habits. Rather, the context in which this argument occurs is an investigation of *justice*. This seems clearly to be a case in which food is important only as an aspect of some larger issue. While this is not universally true of all food-oriented philosophical discussion (one thinks of notable exceptions like Brillat-Savarin), it seems to be the dominant historical attitude. Recently, however, there has been an increasing number of attempts to throw philosophical light on this underappreciated, if ubiquitous, aspect of human life. This anthology is a continuation of this movement; we support the thesis that food is, and ought to be, a proper object of philosophical reflection in its own right.

One might say, then, that this anthology, and the movement within which it is situated, starts from a suggestion drawn out of Glaucon's protest to Socrates. Human beings eat for more than mere sustenance; we are also reflective creatures with an apparently unique capacity for *taste*. To give food a just, properly nuanced, philosophical treatment requires sustained investigation: we are, as Glaucon indirectly observes, more than mere pigs, so discussion of our diets calls for more sophistication. Because we are reflective, we ought to think about what ramifications our diets may have for other people, animals, or the world at large. Perhaps we should ponder our capacity for gustatory delight, and attempt to pin down what qualities make food *good,* in addition to nutritive. The faculty of taste, and its associate objects, might raise interesting questions for theories of perception and certain views of the mind. One may also wonder about the extent to which cultures determine food preferences, and so on. As mentioned, there is a cornucopia of interesting philosophical issues related to food; these are but a nibble of the topics here explored. Oddly, in contrast to the wealth of issues there is a relative dearth of philosophical literature, save perhaps in the fields of environmental ethics and aesthetics. Thus, *Food & Philosophy* serves up another course of timely food-oriented thinking, and one that attempts to broaden the discourse.

To this end, we have included authors from diverse but relevant backgrounds, all of whom take a reflective stance toward food. Many of our contributors are active academic philosophers, but the reader will also enjoy, and glean insights from, essays by professional chefs, food writers and critics, sociologists, and anthropologists. We are delighted to have assembled this range of perspectives, especially in the case of our culinary professionals. The thoughts of those who daily work with the subject matter should not lightly be set aside, and we take their inclusion as a mark of distinction. After all, who better to talk about food than those for whom it provides a craft and way of life?

We thank the reader for joining us at the table we have set. We are pleased that you have decided to share our aims and spend time ingesting our cooperative project. While the essays in this volume may not satiate you, we are confident that your palate for philosophy and food shall be enriched. This is our most profound hope: that you will find delight in further thinking philosophically about the contents of this volume.

*   *   *

In the second part of this introduction, let us offer you a tour of what is going to happen in this volume, as well as to gesture toward some of the issues that will be covered therein. As you probably saw in the table of contents, the volume will be "served" to you as a meal, and one replete with five courses at that! We hope that you find it satisfying, though, unlike at a fine restaurant, we would not object if you still hungered for more after it is all over.

We start with a foreword by Odessa Piper, who is a highly acclaimed chef. In opening the volume, though, we did not *just* want a chef with a high profile, but rather someone whose work and culinary ideals bear some sympathies to this project; we feel fortunate to have had her agree to participate. Piper grew up in New England, and went on to work on a farm in Canaan, New Hampshire that practiced sustainable agriculture. There are certainly philosophical and ethical elements to such approaches, and these were deeply influential on Piper's culinary art. She went on to open L'Etoile – in Madison, Wisconsin, in 1976 – which was part of an important movement in food to create local cuisine using only local ingredients. (Another well-known example of this movement is Alice Waters' Chez Panisse in Berkeley, California.) Drawing from her experiences and approaches to food, we think that Piper provides an excellent start to the volume.

After the foreword, we move into the first of our five courses: the appetizers. We decided to start with "Food in Culture & Society" as the essays in this unit really do set the stage for the rest of the book. Whatever else food is, it is inherently social and cultural. The food that we eat does not appear from nowhere, but rather derives from historical contexts and is shared with those in our communities; these communities provide us with our dining companions, as well as provide the infrastructure through which food is grown, distributed, and purchased. In some cases, of course, these "communities" can be quite large (as when orange juice is sent around the world from Florida) or, in others, quite small (as when we buy food at local farmers' markets).

We start with an essay by Michael Symons, which talks about Epicurus, whose name has grown to be synonymous with passion for eating and drinking; in addition to casual usage, we even see his name attached to "products," such as epicurious.com, which is one of the most popular online recipe resources. Symons talks about the influence of Epicurus, as well as some interpretative issues and traditions that attach to his work. Next comes an essay by Lydia Zepeda, who is a professor of consumer science at the University of Wisconsin, Madison. Zepeda is interested in decisions that American society has made about food, both in terms of *what* we eat, and also in terms of what we are willing to pay for it. She presents her case with substantial empirical data across the twentieth century, as well as international comparisons. Third, we have an essay by Jen Wrye, which considers vegetarianism as a social choice. While vegetarianism is often defended on moral grounds, Wrye is also interested in the social contexts through which such decisions are made as well as various conceptual and theoretical issues underpinning vegetarianism. Finally, we have an essay by Sheila Lintott, which is about eating disorders. Obviously, there are social pressures that contribute to the proliferation of eating disorders, but Lintott discusses some of the aesthetics that underlie these pressures; she even invokes Kant, but we have encouraged her to be gentle therein. Thus concludes the appetizers.

Next, we present the first course: "Taste & Food Criticism." Again, we wanted to start with some of the cultural and social issues pertaining to food, but then we might notice that, once food is "underway" in some sense, people then start *talking* (or writing) about it. Some of these people say that food is good, or else that it is bad. Some of them say that certain food is better than other food. And so on. Well, how is this all supposed to work? Why do *those* people get to render commentary on the merits of certain foods? Do they enjoy some sort of privileged stature for some reason? Maybe they have *special training* and this training therefore entitles them to make the sorts of claims that they make. Or else maybe they simply can *taste* things that others cannot; we all have various taste thresholds, and some people are just *better* at tasting. (This is not necessarily good for them, though, as they might end up tasting the bad stuff more acutely as well.) On the other hand, maybe none of this is right and taste is just wholly subjective. If this latter line is true, then what should be the status of food criticism? These issues go back at least as far as the great philosopher David Hume, and constitute a serious and ongoing philosophical debate.

In the first essay of this unit, Michael Shaffer talks about the sense of taste. Philosophically, the perceptual mechanisms underlying taste have not received much attention – in fact, nearly all of the literature on perception has focused on vision, almost completely to the exclusion of other sense modalities – and Shaffer wants to remedy this. He argues that taste is *not* some sort of special expertise, but rather that those whose opinions we esteem as rather better at *describing* the sorts of things they are tasting; Shaffer thinks that the perceptual experiences of most of us are actually quite similar, but that our ability to translate those experiences into language can be widely divergent. Next comes Jeremy Iggers, who is a restaurant critic for the *Minneapolis Star Tribune*. Iggers is interested in the phenomenon that many of the restaurants given the lowest marks by critics are, in fact, the most popular among consumers. This is especially apparent if we consider "branding": restaurants like Burger King and the Rainforest Café enjoy tremendous public appeal, yet seemingly lack any important culinary merit. *Why* is this? Iggers considers two options: either taste is subjective and the restaurant critic is therefore irrelevant, or else taste is not subjective and the public therefore makes poor choices about what it eats. While we will not give away his conclusion here, the reader might try to guess it from his above-mentioned job title. Last, we have an essay by Fabio Parasecoli, who is an editor for the Italian food and wine magazine *Gambero Rosso*. As with Shaffer, Parasecoli hungers for a better understanding of the perceptual mechanisms that underlie taste. In this essay, Parasecoli talks about some of the neurological and physiological features that give rise to taste, as well as some of the ways that food can be manifest in memories and how those memories go on to affect future perceptual experiences.

Next comes the second course: "Edible Art & Aesthetics." In this unit, we look at some of the aesthetic issues that attach to food. Most generally, we can ask *whether* food can be appropriately considered as an object of aesthetic import. We talk about paintings or symphonies being beautiful, but not about food; or, when we do talk about food being beautiful, we are usually talking about its *visual*, as opposed to gustatory, appeal. Why is this? *Should* food be considered an object of art? If so, what are some of the important questions that we need to tend to therein?

This unit starts with an essay by Kevin Sweeney, who is especially interested in whether taste, as a sensory modality, can ground claims of aesthetic judgment. As mentioned above, we uncontroversially attach beauty to objects of vision and hearing. However, many great philosophers, including Plato and Kant, have argued that the objects of taste can *not* be proper objects of art; Kant, in particular, argued that taste too readily admits of subjectivity to properly ground aesthetic judgments. Given the rise of modern gastronomy, we might wonder whether food has earned its proper place in aesthetic discourse, or else whether these traditional skepticisms should hold. Next comes an essay by one of the volume's co-editors, Dave Monroe, who is interested in a specific challenge to the aesthetic status of food: its consumability. If you think of other objects of aesthetic worth (e.g., paintings), the relevant aesthetic practice (e.g., viewing them) is certainly not destructive. Other aesthetic objects (e.g., symphonies) can at least be reproduced later and, again, are thereby not destroyed in the process of appreciating them. Food, however, seems different insofar its destruction (through consumption) is *precisely* how we garner our appreciation of it. *If* aesthetic objects must (somehow) persist across time, then this might give us reason to think that food cannot be a proper object of aesthetic merit. Monroe considers whether this conditional is true, as well as whether food necessarily fails in the relevant manner. Third, we have an essay by Carolyn Korsmeyer. Korsmeyer is interested in some of the language that we use to describe food and, in particular, with seeming-opposites like 'delightful' and 'disgusting': how could *both* of these words attach to the same culinary objects? Consider, for example, *foie gras*, which some people champion and others detest. *Why* is this the case? One option is to have a radical subjectivity of taste wherein the same things, quite literally, taste good to some and bad to others. While this might sometimes be the case, Korsmeyer argues that the proper analysis has to do with *how* people are tasting: whether with their minds or else with their palates. Ultimately, she thinks that some of the disgust that we feel toward some objects might either be mitigated or exacerbated by the cognitive stance that we take toward the objects of our consumption. Finally, we offer an essay by Glenn Kuehn; this is clearly one of the most fun contributions to the volume, particularly as it concludes with a recipe for cheesecake! Kuehn argues that a central part of the aesthetic practice of food is the interaction that it fosters among us and the way in which it can stimulate communal growth and inquiry; he goes on to defend this vision by appeal to the work of John Dewey.

Whether appropriately or inappropriately named, dessert consists in "Eating & Ethics"; this title is not meant to disparage the importance or centrality of ethics but, well, this is just how the courses were going and this is where ethics was most at home in the volume. There are undoubtedly many ethical issues that attach to food, some of which were alluded to in the first unit on "Food in Culture and Society." Most generally, we can ask what *should* we eat? Organic? Free-range? Locally grown? Vegetarian? Foods that are not genetically modified? However we answer these questions, those answers will necessarily display our ethical commitments; whatever the answers, we could always ask *why* the answers are what they are, and such a procedure would obviously be begging for some sort of moral invocation. Or, at least, a prudential one, which might amount to the same thing. This unit, then, surveys many of these topics and provides some guidance therein.

We start with an essay by Roger King, who talks about some of these broad ethical issues and how they connect with eating. In particular, he notices that eating places consumers in a wide network of relationships to plants and animals, soil, farmers and farm workers, and corporations, as well as to community, tradition, and future generations. What and how we eat configures and reconfigures these relationships, and therefore ethical questions necessarily arise when talking about eating. Next up is Matthew Brown, who considers picky eating as a moral failing. As he points out, we are quite used to people saying things like "I would never eat that," and we usually take claims to be unproblematic (often to the chagrin of an embarrassed host). However, Brown thinks that they *are* problematic because he thinks that we all have moral obligations toward openness, self-knowledge, accommodation, and gracefulness; he further thinks that these obligations can be observed by having an open mind toward a wide range of foods. The third essay of this unit is by Paul Thompson, who discusses the ethical issues that attach to genetically modified foods. Endearingly irreverent, Thompson makes the case that we should be able to eat whatever we like, though he offers various hazards and pitfalls pursuing genetically modified diets, as well as assessments of how those hazards and pitfalls should bear on the choices that we make about foods. Finally, we have Linda Jerofke, who writes about the moral elements of hunting and of consuming game meat. In her essay, Jerofke considers arguments both for and against these practices, both from traditional hunting and anti-hunting camps, as well as from other groups, such as Native American populations.

We are extremely excited about the last unit, wherein we have essays from chefs; we call this "Compliments of the Chef." While we have hoped to make this volume accessible to non-philosophers, it is worth noting that almost all of the above essays have come from academics (though this includes disciplines other than philosophy). Even in the cases where contributions have come from non-academics (e.g., Parasecoli and Kuehn), these have nevertheless been people with substantial training in philosophy. Our chefs, however, do not necessarily have any background in philosophy, though they have all done an admirable job relating their craft in philosophically respectable ways.

First, we have an essay by Jennifer Iannolo, editor of the online food magazine *Gilded Fork*. Iannolo distinguishes between levels of 'sensuality,' arguing that more profoundly enriching gustatory experiences than those we normally have are possible, and preferable, once we adopt a reflective and appreciative attitude toward what we eat. Her essay is especially tantalizing and delicious, as she illustrates her thesis by appealing to ways in which our attitudes about sexuality and pornography mirror our approaches to eating. Next we have an essay by Christian Krautkramer, in which he argues that the standards governing cooking in restaurants and in the home considerably differ. Home cooks, he argues, have a special duty to their guests generated by the direct relationships of love and friendship between cook and diner. This fosters what he calls an "inclusive fraternity" of the kitchen – in the home, we come together to share both food and fellowship. On the other hand, the professional chef has a different set of duties, which result from obligations to the profession and, as Krautkramer argues, to the food itself. Thus, the restaurant kitchen, given a general lack of personal connection between cook and diner, becomes an "exclusive fraternity" of professionals. The third offering in this section is by Mark Tafoya, the executive chef for *Gilded Fork* and a culinary entrepreneur. He brings to light ways in which food and dining can play a role in bridging cultural gaps, thereby acting as a means of diplomacy. The "diplomacy of the dish," as he puts it, takes place in two ways. First, we can come to appreciate others by learning to enjoy their food. Second, we forge bonds and bridge diplomatic gaps by coming together to eat – a practice with a long history in human affairs. Tafoya's discussion is fleshed out by many wonderful examples. Rounding out this section, and indeed, our anthology, is a jointly authored essay by a husband-and-wife team of Colorado-based chefs and food bloggers, Aki Kamozawa and H. Alexander Talbot. They insightfully discuss the need to balance three considerations in culinary art: inspiration, taste (flavor), and aesthetics. In the course of showing why these conditions are important to a well-rounded cuisine, they draw upon experiences with various cooking methods, techniques, and ingredients. Thus, we readers become aware not only of the important balance of inspiration, taste, and aesthetics, but also of how chefs are able to bring these together.

Finally, we conclude with an afterword by Woody Allen. This was an essay originally published in *The New Yorker* and, in addition to being hysterical, probably mentions more philosophers than any other essay in this volume. While we hope that the essays herein will be fun and engaging, it is worth appreciating the fact that philosophy need not be too serious, and Allen does an admirable job in making this apparent; it seemed an appropriate resting point for the volume.

In closing, we hope that you enjoy this volume as much as we have enjoyed putting it together. We also hope that it helps you to think philosophically about food and about eating. Bon appétit!

Note

1   Plato. *Republic*. Trans. G. M. A. Grube. Indianapolis: Hackett, 1992.

Appetizers

Food in Culture & Society

Food is a central activity of mankind, and one of the single most significant trademarks of a culture.

Mark Kurlansky, American writer

1

Epicurus, the Foodies' Philosopher

Michael Symons

"How could you be so interested in food when half the world is starving!" The silliness of such a criticism presumably sticks out more these days. But the apparent self-contradiction was less obvious back in March 1984, when epicurean interests were relatively written off. Scholars might respectably devote themselves to the economics of sugar production, the genetics of pig breeding, the nutritional measurement of populations, the ethnography of gatherer-hunters, and the politics of Third World hunger, but not stray towards meals as such, and certainly not the pleasure of their own stomachs.

The criticism was made at a lively dinner party, and the host specifically challenged my organizing of the First Symposium of Australian Gastronomy a few days later. Her objection only unlocked further fervor. We needed more food talk, not less. We could discuss both dinner parties and Third World hunger. We needed our conference. In the event, the two days of gastronomy and gourmandise brilliantly confirmed Brillat-Savarin's advice that such gatherings should combine food theory and practice. With the participation even of a couple of gastronomically inclined academic philosophers, we had begun confronting the mystery of meals.

Exhilarated, I resolved to take the question into the enemy camp, as it were. I would undertake a PhD to understand the intellectual embarrassment at our own dining. Indisputably, our existence depended on meals. We spend much time at, preparing, or paying for them. They connect people with one another, even across the oceans, and with the natural world. So why was the table scorned, and especially the enjoyment of it?

The first finding was, of course, that the intellectual disdain was far from universal, and also softening. Some sharp London journalists, led by renegade philosopher Paul Levy, had already used the word 'foodie' in *Harpers & Queen* in August, 1982, even if the "new sect which elevates all food to a sacrament" was so tiny that all the foodies knew each other. Within academia, too, some well-credentialed thinkers were already working in the area. Following anthropologist Claude Lévi-Strauss, the then fashionable structuralists dressed up meals as "culinary triangles", "binary oppositions", and "grammars", an approach soon rivaled by more materialist scholars such as K. C. Chang and colleagues, Jack Goody, Sidney Mintz, Marvin Harris, and some of the French historians identified with the *Annales* school. The first significant academic journal in the area, *Food & Foodways*, would appear in 1985.

In wider reading, I looked into the ancient Greek philosopher, Epicurus, whose name had been appropriated for epicureanism as either irreligion and debauchery or, more positively, the display of refined sensibilities. Modern interpreters pooh-poohed any suggestion of the allegedly ascetic Epicurus' own lower-case 'e' epicureanism. However, I was forcibly struck that, contrary to the conventional wisdom, Epicurus announced that he had based his philosophical system on the "pleasure of the stomach." The more I investigated his system, the more I became convinced that here was the foodies' long-neglected philosopher, still suffering from the strictures of the much too high-minded academic tradition. Soon I had persuaded a few fellow foodies to restore the Epicurean tradition of monthly philosophical banquets in Adelaide, South Australia. Once we adopted a relatively formal structure of someone delivering a paper, before dining and general conversation, these events seemed appropriately to honor Epicurus' memory, and his request that such dinners should continue. More than two decades of further study and experience have only confirmed the correspondences between Epicureanism and epicureanism. Both value the material world, the senses, empiricism over ideology, pleasure within limits, friendship, and celebratory dinners.

Within recent Anglophone culture, foodies have not always represented a reputable philosophical position. They have not always articulated a political, theological, economic, or other framework. They have remained largely besotted with gastronomic consumerism. Yet serious food scholarship has been multiplying, including within philosophy. With more recognition, the epicurean conversation has begun extending from its natural home, the table, to take on the world. Especially when coming *from* meals, rather than *to* them, so to speak, thinking foodies can usefully develop Epicurus' big picture, which is astonishingly consonant with a modern liberal's. This chapter urges food philosophers to embrace their hero.

"The Garden"

Epicurus is thought to have been born on the island of Samos in 341 BCE. He studied and worked in other centers before settling in Athens in 308 BCE, dying there about 270 BCE. He arrived relatively late among the ancient Greek philosophers, implicitly developing and responding to Democritus, Plato, Aristotle, and others. He established a school called the Garden, because the community grew food on the outskirts of the city. The group studied, published, slept, and ate in a nearby house within the city wall in a respectable district known as Melite. While Epicurus was something of a cult leader, the school was known for egalitarian attitudes toward women and slave members. Two centuries after Epicurus, Cicero was impressed that the house still "maintained a whole company of friends, united by the closest sympathy and affection."

Epicurus sought to provide answers to all worries, and his system is generally accepted as both wide-ranging and internally consistent. His scientific theories included convincing versions of atomic physics and natural and social evolution. He took an empirical approach to knowledge, requiring not merely observation, but tentativeness. His moral system took off from his hedonism – so that right and wrong did not come from on high, but proved themselves by the everyday contentment they produced. He was a deist in that his gods were not concerned with human affairs. His numerous related insights included the ubiquity of limits, so that death was an end, and therefore "nothing to us." The quest for wealth and power was especially fruitless, and likely to bring inconvenience rather than happiness, so that he recommended the security of living unknown.

His attempted social revolution, upsetting prevailing structures of both thought and relationships, spread widely through the Roman Empire, with numerous Epicurean groups being mentioned and writers identifying with the ideas. The New Testament preserves hostile references to the belly worshippers, and the movement eventually suffered at the hands of Christian authorities, so that all Epicurus' numerous books are now lost. Historians piece his scheme together from fragments, classical commentaries, and the surviving works of followers, notably the scientific poet, Lucretius. Epicurus retained influence within the Western tradition, especially during the intellectual revolutions leading up to, and including, the Enlightenment. His name also became associated, socially and politically, with liberalism.[1]

So much is generally accepted, and is sufficient for Epicurus to be considered as a serious, materialist philosopher not without interest, although not nearly of the same rank as Plato and Aristotle. But perhaps he has been relatively underestimated because his ideas emerged from meals.

The Meal at Yport, 1886

Epicurus gave pointers for reassurance during periods of personal crisis. According to an abridgement once widely known as the "Fourfold remedy," and as recorded by Philodemus of Gadara (and translated by Gilbert Murray), a person should never forget:

> Nothing to fear in God.
> Nothing to feel in Death.
> Good can be attained.
> Evil can be endured.

For another quick impression, which sets such advice within a wider philosophy, modern interpreter John Gaskin opens his collection of ancient writings, *The Epicurean Philosophers* (1995), with a summary:

> All that is real in the universe is an infinity of void space, and an infinity of primary particles in random and everlasting motion. Such is the physics of Epicurus.

The ethics have a like simplicity: all that is needed for human happiness is a life among friends, a body free of pain, and a mind free from fear and anxiety.[2]

Note the lack of any direct reference to food in either of these thumbnail sketches. Nonetheless, for a third encapsulation, consider the picture on the cover of Gaskin's modest paperback. The oil painting shows a dreamy meal under an apple tree in the French countryside in the late nineteenth century. Dappled sunlight catches nine or ten guests with glasses of red wine in their hands. The long white tablecloth is scattered with decanters, bottles, plates, bowls, cutlery, and a large joint (possibly a roast turkey), and a young girl leans on the table, having just picked Flanders poppies and daisies. The cover uses a detail (about one-third, eliminating the bride and groom) of Albert Auguste Fourié's painting, *The Wedding Meal at Yport* (ca. 1886).

The book designer might well have made a snap choice of cover, improving the composition of a not entirely distinguished artwork. And yet the private, restful meal seems to encapsulate Epicurean philosophy, or at least its sensibility, more accurately than a sculpture of Epicurus' head, which is often used in books as if to indicate a great mind. While, in common with other scholars, Gaskin fails to make clear the centrality of the table, I like to think that the book designer glanced at Gaskin's two succinct paragraphs, speaking of friendship and happiness caught in nature's swirl, and intuitively recognized that Epicurus based his philosophy on meals.

The ancient scheme – interweaving ideas about the natural world, the reliability of knowledge, and the anxieties of everyday life with practical recommendations – was not only taught around the table, but, I propose, had also been discovered there. Epicurus made one or two direct and many indirect references to this. He was known at the time as the belly-centered philosopher. All circumstantial evidence of his method and his findings confirms that Epicurus used his eyes, ears, nose, and feelings of anxiety and repose to observe the world, and then communicated results to companions for further discussion. Confronting the conventional scholarly prejudice, foodies need to know that a table under an apple tree, well-disposed guests, food, drink, and conversation have long provided solid foundations for a successful worldview.

The Age-Old Calumnies

Belonging to the next generation of Athenian philosophers, Chrysippus said that Epicurus followed in the steps of Archestratus, a scholarly gourmet (after whom Alain Senderens's great Parisian restaurant L'Archestrate was named in the 1970s), who traveled the ancient world in search of the delights of the belly, recording his findings in a lost text. In another characterization by a close contemporary, Damoxenus has a cook in his comedy *Foster Brothers* boast that he had studied at the Garden, explaining that Epicurus was a very good cook, because he learnt from nature. The later Roman poet Juvenal spoke of "cultivating one's kitchen-garden, like Epicurus." In other words, Epicurus was viewed in ancient times as a gardener, cook, and cookery writer, not only as an influential teacher.

Whatever his precise practical skills, Epicurus should certainly not be denied any love of food, despite recent scholars' attempts. More than two thousand years after Epicurus, Karl Marx wrote his doctoral dissertation in praise of this "greatest representative" of the Greek Enlightenment. Marx was particularly impressed by Epicurus' concept of the atomic swerve, which seemed like a universal motor of change that might even explain something like free will. Marx was yet to escape Hegelian idealism in favor of materialism, and so denied the importance of meals for the ancient system, concluding: "The principle of Epicurean philosophy is not the *gastrology* of *Archestratus* as *Chrysippus* believes, but the absoluteness and freedom of self-consciousness – even if self-consciousness is only conceived in the form of individuality."[3]

Twentieth-century scholars produced sporadic translations, introductions, and analyses of Epicurean physics, ideas of the gods, hedonism, and so on, and in every case either clearly distinguished Epicurus from lower-case epicureanism or just ignored the possibility. After recording 20 explicit denials, I gave up keeping a list, but to cite an influential student early in the century, Cyril Bailey claimed that the original Epicureans ate "nothing but bread as a rule with the occasional addition of a relish." This for him was well "removed from the living of an 'epicure'." Similarly, Epicurus "was no Epicurean sensualist," John McDade explained in his introduction to a more recent, gift-book version of Epicurus' "Letter to Menoeceus," retitled *Letter on Happiness*. "The use of the term 'Epicurean' in the English language to mean 'out-and-out hedonist' is, then, both unfortunate and mistaken."[4]

Those endeavoring to redeem Epicurus have rarely questioned the authenticity of his statement: "The beginning and root of all good is the pleasure of the stomach; even wisdom and culture must be referred to this." Surely this alone is clear confirmation of the importance of meals for the philosopher. The ancient compiler of gastronomic sources, Athenaeus, included the quotation along with another from Epicurus' collaborator, Metrodorus, who wrote to his brother: "Yes, Timocrates, devoted to the study of nature as you are, it is indeed the belly, the belly and nothing else, which any philosophy that proceeds according to nature makes its whole concern."[5]

Escaping from such evidence has required scholarly contortions. Two-thirds of the way through a relatively thorough textbook, J. M. Rist revealed: "We are now at the point where we can consider one of Epicurus' most notorious sayings, which has come down to us from many ancient sources and has been much misunderstood." When Epicurus said that the beginning and root of all good was the pleasure of the stomach, this was "paradoxical," and "exaggerated by the Epicureans themselves for polemical reasons." Epicurus meant "not that eating is fun, but that the beginning and root of all good is not to be hungry and not to be thirsty." So, according to Rist, Epicurus recognized the necessity of eating and drinking, and that was that.[6]

While Epicurus certainly recommended a simple life, everything had its limits. "Frugality too has a limit, and the man who disregards it is in like case with him who errs through excess." He left such other morsels as: "those have the sweetest pleasure in luxury who least need it." The important thing was not to become a slave to desire: "We think highly of frugality not that we may always keep to a cheap and simple diet, but that we may be free from desire regarding it." As he also explained: "Most men fear frugality and through their fear are led to actions most likely to produce fear."[7]

The most emblematic activity of the original Epicureans became their banquets on the twentieth of the Greek month. The banquets were sufficiently distinctive to warrant a lost book by the

Cynic satirist Menippus, and for Epicureans to gain the nickname *eikadistae*, "Twentyers." A partly obliterated text from the later Epicurean, Philodemus, suggested that Epicurus' custom was to "celebrate this feast of the 20th with distinguished companions after decorating the house with the fruits of the season and inviting everyone to feast themselves." The head of the Academy in the second century BCE, Carneades, reproached Epicurus for having wasted time anticipating and recollecting pleasures, and for keeping a gastronomic record, as if in an official journal, on "how often I had a meeting with Hedeia or Leontion," or "where I drank Thasian wine," or "what twentieth of the month I had the most sumptuous dinner."[8]

Epicurus upheld the value of companionship, and one of his principal doctrines was that "Of all the things which wisdom acquires to produce the blessedness of the complete life, far the greatest is the possession of friendship." He presumably recognized that friendships were formed and maintained at meals, and that collaborators were additionally helpful with the tasks of food production and preparation. According to Seneca, Epicurus considered with whom was more important than what one ate. He advised: "You must reflect carefully beforehand with whom you are to eat and drink, rather than what you are to eat and drink. For a dinner of meats without the company of a friend is like the life of a lion or a wolf."[9]

Epicurus observed that some people wanted to become famous and conspicuous, thinking they would thus win safety from others. Instead, people were trapped by their own celebrity and power; they lost their freedom. Epicurus saw greater rewards in seclusion, extolling the "immunity which results from a quiet life and the retirement from the world." With advice to escape the "prison of affairs and politics," he offered the simple injunction: "Live unknown." Yet this did not stop him founding a highly successful missionary movement. Epicurus and members of his school published many books and letters, although their main method of communication would seem to have been across the dinner table. Living unknown surely meant reserving socializing largely to private meals. The networking power of conviviality is how I interpret one of his so-called Vatican Sayings: "Friendship goes dancing round the world proclaiming to us all to awake to the praises of a happy life."[10]

The Gastronomic Default

Leaving Epicurus aside for the moment, and relying on minimal observations, what might foodies believe? If they started thinking at the table, where might it lead? What might diners at the *Meal at Yport* decide about the world, or at least what might those who identify with the dappled tableau work out?

Experience would probably teach attentive diners that good food in good company can be immensely satisfying. They can feel at one with the world. This is what life is all about, they might reflect, even if only rhetorically. They might also learn the benefits of moderation, given that over-indulgence brings discomfort. In confronting the stomach's definite limit, they might contrast this with the endless fantasies of more figurative forms of greed, especially for wealth and power. Such prandial discoveries are at least plausible.

Quickly tiring of dining alone, gourmands would come to treasure companionship. Not only is friendship both pleasant and necessary, but it is typically maintained at the table. We often make and keep friends by sharing meals. There is no great loss, and much good humor, in serving others first, in looking after your neighbor. Hosts can positively glow with generosity. That is, on a social level, foodies seek out companionship and manage it using unstarched guidelines, a sensible etiquette that adds up to a view of ethics. Supplying the table necessitates social mechanisms, too, so that not only potluck dinners demonstrate that the ostensibly selfish needs of the stomach are most effectively served communally.

At some ontological level, observant gourmets might be humbled by nature – by white peaches, by champagne, and, more generally, by season, *terroir*, and careful cultivation. Reflecting that the roast turkey (or whatever awaits on the Yport table) was only recently gobbling, they might detect a gobble-and-be-gobbled world. Nature is not so much dog-eat-dog, but layered and interdependent. In this metabolic universe, the sunlight makes the wheat grow, and the seed turn into bread, while the poultry finds missed and spilled grain, before being sacrificed, and so on. Thoughtful diners might decide that ecological cycles conserve matter, which supports some idea about the indestructibility of primary particles. Diners might also sniff out, literally by olfactory means, some notion of atoms.

Attentive diners have probably already found themselves learning through observation, satisfaction, and conversation rather than through ideologies and dogmas, and are not overawed by political and religious authority, preferring reclusive reassurances. Through their gardening, purchasing, cooking, and sharing, serious foodies have developed a workable understanding of the world, a broad set of findings, encompassing much, and all connected through the table.

This somewhat systematic set of viewpoints, which might be termed the foodie or epicurean default, would be relatively culturally independent, given that every individual confronts the same demands of hunger, collectively met within the one metabolic universe, and teaching elementary ideas about moderation, the golden rule, and so on. These table-top tenets mesh noticeably with those of Epicurus and also of many other meal-oriented commentators before and since.

Accordingly, in praise of gastronomic simplicity, Epicurus wrote to an unknown recipient: "Send me some preserved cheese, that when I like I may have a feast."[11] Being satisfied by a piece of cheese has been said to prove that Epicurus was not an epicure. On the contrary, the same request has been recorded by any number of unquestioned foodies. The inventor of 'aristology' (study of dining), Thomas Walker, wrote in his weekly London newspaper, *The Original*, in 1835: "Some good bread and cheese, and a jug of ale, comfortably set before me, and heartily given, are heaven on earth." As a more recent example, the culinary theologian Robert Farrar Capon praised "the plainest things in the world, prepared with care and relished for what they are." A good cheese, he wrote in *The Supper of the Lamb* in 1969, might "recall man to the humbleness of his grandeur and the greatness of his low estate . . . May you be spared long enough to know at least one long evening of old friends, dark bread, good wine, and strong cheese."

The various types of belly worshippers have been vilified in much the same ways. Epicurus defended his own epicurean tendencies in the "Letter to Menoeceus":

> When, therefore, we maintain that pleasure is the end, we do not mean the pleasures of profligates and those that consist in sensuality, as is supposed by some who are either ignorant or disagree with us or do not understand, . . . For it is not continuous drinkings and revellings,

nor the satisfaction of lusts, nor the enjoyment of . . . luxuries of the wealthy table, which produce a pleasant life, but sober reasoning, searching out the motives for all choice and avoidance.[12]

That unquestioned gastronomer, Jean-Anthelme Brillat-Savarin, made much the same defense in a prefatory "Transition," strangely included towards the end of *The Physiology of Taste* in 1825, going on to explain the root of such misrepresentation:

This equivocation has been instigated by intolerant moralists who, led astray by their extravagant zeal, have pleased themselves to find excess where there was but an intelligent enjoyment of the earth's treasures, which were not given to us to be trampled underfoot.[13]

E/epicureans have long had to confront a deep-seated antagonism within high Western culture. This is what I sought to understand in my PhD research, helped by my discovery of Epicurus and his gastronomic hedonism, and further investigations of the entrenched philosophical antipathy from idealists. Epicurus was a definitively materialist philosopher, another of his Vatican Sayings advising: "We must not violate nature, but obey her."[14] Likewise, the foodies' preoccupation with physical reality makes it hard for them to escape the charge. It was no coincidence that the eventual arch-materialist Marx retained his early sympathy for Epicurus. It was not surprising that many academics, in defense of high culture, looked down on the stomach. The entrenched marginalization of both Epicurus and foodies has to be understood in the context of the hostile view, especially as represented by the classical and highly influential idealism of Plato.

The Seductions of Plato

The awe-inspiring philosopher of higher things, Plato (ca. 427–ca. 347 BCE), consistently denounced any serious interest in food. His distaste was the obverse of his adulation of a supposed "world of forms." For Plato, this other world was the real one, and ours a shadowy copy. His or perhaps a follower's *Seventh Letter* provides a neat introduction through a contemplation of a circle. The underlying argument is that human representations of circles are always inadequate. Even the most careful drawing is never perfect. Verbal and mathematical descriptions only point to the real thing. We seem to have a closer example in our heads, given how we know, or think we know, what a circle is. However, a circle in our heads can hardly be the real circle, which seems to require some kind of metaphysical existence. Through constant debate and reflection, Plato believed, philosophers reached out for the perfect, eternal, and ultimately unattainable circle. Plato often advanced this argument, notably when beautifully analyzing love in *The Symposium*: the lover ideally abandons mere physical lust to strive for real, sublime (platonic) love.

Plato worked hard at depicting a hierarchical model of the world, where ideas were supreme. By contrast to the wonderful realm of reason, food and drink reeked of the transient, inadequate, inferior, material world of the senses, bodily pleasures, and humdrum, non-philosophical activities. Anything to do with the stomach was inferior and to be shunned. Feeding reduced people to the level of animals, and the appetites needed strict controlling. According to his often-quoted attack in the *Gorgias*, cookery masqueraded as an art, but was only a "kind of knack gained by experience . . . a knack of . . . producing gratification and pleasure," fitting under the heading of "pandering." Sometimes Plato's depiction was dualistic, with the world of forms contrasted with this lower world, and sometimes tripartite. Among his recommended three social classes in the *Republic*, the upper class were philosopher-kings, the middle class their enforcers, and the lower class were preoccupied with the production and preparation of food. As another example of the three-way division, in the *Timaeus*, he observed that our head, where the soul resides, is closest to the heavens, and that the heart with its passions came above the disruptive stomach, home of the appetites, below. The soul "lifts us from earth towards our celestial affinity, like a plant whose roots are not in earth, but in the heavens," Plato declared.[15]

One of the twentieth century's most influential thinkers, sociologist Emile Durkheim, claimed to provide a scientific account of Plato's world of forms. In the *Elementary Forms of the Religious Life* in 1912, Durkheim explained pure knowledge in terms of a *conscience collective* – in French, and often translated as the "collective consciousness." This is any society's shared mental pool of know-ledge. That is, the perfect circle sought by Plato could be viewed as not the circle in my own head, but the circle in all our heads. Lying beyond us as individuals, it can seem more transcendent. Importantly, the world of forms emerged out of activity in this one, and post-Durkheimian social science might describe the circle as a "social construct." Children are brought up drawing circles, talking about circles, and running around in them, until they have learned what everyone might be referring to. Durkheim further stressed that the widespread and deep-seated adoption of the notion of the circle gave it a somewhat illusory solidity or social facticity, as he called it.[16]

Plato had been an acute observer, but had elevated circles and other archetypes to an entirely other universe, rather than recognizing their place within this one. Plato's glorification of the philosophers' stock-in-trade, the use of rationality in quest of sublime truths, would have been of even more cultural benefit if it had not been at the expense of this-worldly, sensual experience and immediate, prac-tical endeavor. Plato's arguments might have more appeal these days, too, if they were not so elitist and even authoritarian, which was Karl Popper's charge in *The Open Society and Its Enemies* in 1949.

Epicurus is often viewed as responding to Plato virtually point for point. He reinverted Plato's world (as Marx would do with Hegel's), making the opposite case at every level, physically, ethically, and epistemologically. The secret is that, for Epicurus, the belly ruled the mind, rather than vice versa. Head and stomach should perhaps work together, although materialism is hard to avoid if we believe, along with Epicurus, that philosophy has ultimately to serve prac-tical needs. So, rather than pursue knowledge for its own sake, Epicurus wanted useful knowledge, which helped remove unneces-sary personal burdens. In place of Plato's endless striving for unattain-able truths, Epicurus respected the limits to knowledge, similar to those limits that made nonsense of quests for glory and riches: "The wealth demanded by nature is both limited and easily procured; that demanded by idle imaginings stretches on to infinity." Of immediate interest to gourmets, Epicurus up-ended Plato by distinguishing the finite hunger of the stomach from endless desires, including for new taste experiences, which he blamed on the "ungrateful greed of the soul."[17] That is, an epicurean was to obey the stomach, rather than the soul's hunger for novelty, which would never be satisfied.

Plato's theoretical antipathy to meals requires further study and rebuttal. Moreover, an unconscious Platonism, letting the head or culture speak louder than the stomach, has to be guarded against. Take the case of nutrition, which is ostensibly an empirical science. Yet, in listing vitamins alphanumerically, in enumerating desirable nutrient levels and in prescribing geometric pyramids, it can seem to relate health to some rational truth rather than decent meals. Even within food studies, scholars have often given too much weight to food choices as mere signs and expressions of social or cultural conditions. These include not only the structuralists' deliberate treatment of eating as a language, but also statements along the lines that the upper-crust drink champagne to demonstrate their social superiority. The deceptiveness of this approach is brought out when inverted, as if people could be said to eat gruel to show they were poor.

One defense of so-called objective idealism, as exemplified by Plato, might be that it stresses a common culture. At least the tendencies towards authoritarianism admit a genuine concern with social cohesion. Against this, Epicurus' emphasis on the individual's physical and mental wellbeing has arguably been at the expense of the commonweal. This relates to the accusation that modern foodies pursue self-interest, "when half the world is starving." One possible defense for epicureans lies along the liberal lines that all people should be left to serve their stomachs, unmolested. Furthermore, the liberal suspicion of governments can be extended to wariness about the undermining of the free market by increasingly global corporations. An argument might be made that starvation has generally been generated by organized plunder, stimulated by the drive to economic growth, rather than by leaving others to pursue their own pleasure within natural limits.

Perhaps the freedom of the individual is a worthy political demand, but it hardly explains the workings of society. A more active defense of the epicurean position might be to point out that the drive to satisfy the individual stomach is the basis for society. Most forcibly, sociologist Georg Simmel explored in a 1910 essay on "The sociology of the meal" the apparent paradox that the material selfishness of the stomach became the strongest reason for society and for the highest sentiments. Epicurus had a similar argument in mind when declaring that self-interest was a sound basis of friendship: "All friendship is desirable in itself, though it starts from the need of help."[18] Epicurus preferred the less formally organized, more individualistic, face-to-face kinds of social engagement that extended out from the companionship of the table. He would seem to have conceived a more networked structure of society than Plato's corporate model, with philosophers at the head. In serving their stomachs, foodies develop a firm belief in the conviviality not only of the immediate meal but also the wider society. While large-scale organizations – both public and corporate – have often promoted technological and social innovation, epicureans can point to the often superior efficiency of more informal networks operating in a street market, for example.

Epicurus set out a sensible philosophy that diners might still identify with. He belonged to the cluster of positions often known as materialist and standing over and against the anti-food, idealist philosophies, archetypically Plato's. Associating with some kind of epicurean position, foodies do not need to seem merely self-indulgent and philosophically stunted. They join well-established and noticeably liberal traditions. In a final extolling of the foodies' philosopher, the same cultural shifts that have made room for food philosophy over the past one or two decades have also made it highly relevant.

Diners Strike Back

By the 1980s, second-wave feminism had demonstrated the unsettling androcentricity of advanced Western culture, including within the academy. The global mixing of cultures had encouraged postcolonial and multicultural challenges. Popular culture became a legitimate object of study. With the implosion of the Soviet Union in 1991, Marxism went right out of fashion, too. Given major reevaluations of these kinds, intellectuals showed uneasiness with any unduly ambitious or all-encompassing theoretical perspective, questioning so-called grand theory and high cultural canons. Such openness, or perhaps loss of nerve, attempted a smile as postmodernism.

On the positive side, the loosening of academic draw-strings made room for hitherto scorned or neglected topics, and disciplines with names ending in '-ology' and '-onomy' were joined by those ending with 'studies', and not just women's studies. Cultural studies shook up the humanities by finding value in the previously overlooked. And food studies emerged, most noticeably during the 1990s.

On the negative side, this shift came with complaints about loss of meaning, vertiginous doubt, relativism, and trivialization. If nothing were important any more, then it did not matter if an interest in food were intellectually lightweight. True, food journalists have been preoccupied with the latest ingredients and smartest restaurants, and celebrity chefs their various *trucs*. Culinary historians such as Alan Davidson – one of the original 'foodies' discovered by Paul Levy and colleagues – explicitly rejected more philosophical and sociological approaches. Still other scholars referred food back to more 'important' areas, so that meals merely appeared in the works of great novelists or demonstrated women's social position, for example.

Yet meals can provide not merely physical but real intellectual substance. Food studies are prima facie far-reaching, crossing into virtually every territory. Meals are not easily sectioned off, but bring people together with other people, the wider economy, and the natural world. Finally, the thought of Epicurus demonstrates that the "pleasure of the stomach" can lead, at least according to the present author, to fully-fledged natural, social, and epistemological investigations. Epicurus might have justified his philosophy as promoting personal contentment, and yet this necessitated answers to life's big questions. A belly worshipper's love of conviviality went dancing around the globe. Of particular relevance, Epicurus' thought was empirically grounded in everyday experience, and so provides a response to recent tendencies towards relativism. The circle is no mere social construct, but is based in the real struggle of material existence with its wheels, pots, seasonal cycles, and so forth. Equally, his materialist epistemology stood against absolutism. His propositions are thus also timely in that postmodern intellectual openness only seemed to invite a resurgence of various fundamentalisms, starting off with claimed economic imperatives of market capitalism.

Materialist philosophies, especially that of Epicurus, can come to the aid of foodies and, conversely, the fascination with stomachs has implications for philosophy. Food philosopher Raymond Boisvert's webpage declares his hope that "philosophers could actually begin to grasp philosophizing as a 'human' rather than a 'mental' activity." With a reconsideration of Epicurus as an epicurean, philosophy might deepen from words about words into words about the world.

His gastronomically based scheme inspired many effective thinkers behind progressive shifts in Western thought – Karl Marx has been mentioned, and Thomas Jefferson might also, to name but two. The main principles developed by Epicurus have been tested by time; his atomic physics remains good; his evolutionary theories still work; his emphasis on natural limits is urgently required; his ethical suggestions make sense; he proffers distinct answers, and yet remains suitably tentative.

The attempted quarantining of Epicurus from the epicureanism that carries his name helped shield Western thought from the deeper implications of sharing meals. Far from being trivial or immoral, the epicurean impulse can lead to a wide-ranging and highly workable framework. Socrates announced that he differed from other people in that they lived to eat, whereas he ate to live. Yet eating is living, and living is eating. While the authoritative Western bidding has long been that considerations of food and eating are unworthy, the tables need turning. Philosophical diners can strike back.

Notes

1   An enthusiastic account is provided by DeWitt, Norman Wentworth, *Epicurus and His Philosophy*. Minneapolis: University of Minnesota Press, 1954.

2   Gaskin, John, ed. *The Epicurean Philosophers*. London: Everyman, 1995; Philodemus p. 77; "Introduction," p. xxiii.

3   Chapter 5 of Marx's doctoral thesis, entitled "On the Difference Between Democritean and Epicurean Physics."

4   Bailey, Cyril. *The Greek Atomistis and Epicurus*. Oxford: Clarendon Press, 1928: 224; McDade, John. "Introduction" to Epicurus, *Letter on Happiness*. Trans. Robin Waterfield. London: Rider.

5   Athenaeus, *The Deipnosophists*, vol. 5. Trans. C. B. Gulick. Cambridge, MA: Harvard University Press (Loeb), 1933, p. 546 (standard classicists' reference: XII, 546).

6   Rist, J. M. *Epicurus: An Introduction*. Cambridge: Cambridge University Press: 104–5.

7   One basic collection of surviving writings, Bailey, Cyril, *Epicurus: The Extent Remains*, Oxford: Clarendon Press, includes these quotations on pp. 117, 89, 127, and 137 (classicists' shorthand: *Vatican* LXIII, *Menoeceus* 130, Stob. *Floril.* XVIII, 14, Porphyry *ad Marc.* 28).

8   These two overly neglected banquet references come from Festugière, A. J., *Epicurus and His Gods*, trans. C. W. Chilton. Oxford: Blackwell, 1955: 70, n. 56; and Plutarch, *Moralia*, vol. 14. Cambridge, MA: Harvard University Press (Loeb), 1967: 546 (*Non posse* 1089C).

9   Bailey, *Extant Remains*, p. 101 (*PD* XXVII); Gaskin, *Epicurean Philosophers*, p. 69 (Seneca *Ep Morales* XIX, 10).

10   Such sentiments are often repeated, and examples appear in Bailey, *Extant Remains*, pp. 99, 115, and 139 (*PD* VII, *PD* XIV, *Vatican* LVIII, Plutarch *Adv Col* 1125D, *Vatican* LII).

11   Bailey, *Extant Remains*, p. 131 (Diog. Laert. X, 11).

12   Bailey, *Extant Remains*, p. 89 (*Menoeceus* 131–2).

13   Jean-Anthelme Brillat-Savarin, *The Physiology of Taste*. Trans. M. F. K. Fisher. New York: Counterpoint, 1949: 363–4.

14   Bailey, *Extant Remains*, p. 109 (*Vatican* XXI).

15   Plato, *Gorgias* 462–3; *Timaeus* 90A.

16   Durkheim spelled out the argument elsewhere, including "The dualism of human nature and its social conditions," in Wolff, Kurt H., ed., *Emile Durkheim, 1858–1917*. Columbus: Ohio State University Press: 325–40.

17   Bailey, *Extant Remains*, pp. 99 and 117 (PD XV, Vatican LXIX).

18   Simmel, Georg. "The Sociology of the Meal." *Food & Foodways*, 5(4), 1994: 333–51; Bailey, *Extant Remains*, p. 109 (Vatican XXIII).

2

Carving Values with a Spoon

Lydia Zepeda

Tojuan non tlenon tikua kion
("We are what we eat" in Nahuatl)

Our bodies are the cumulative manifestation of our personal, societal, and policy choices with respect to food, agriculture, and land. We *are* what we eat. Our ever-increasing consumption of calories in general, and empty calories in particular, is a key cause of the rise in obesity, heart disease, type II diabetes, and other preventable illnesses. We are indeed digging our graves with our spoons. Some blame personal responsibility for the obesity crisis. Others see those affected as victims. This essay argues that rather than one or the other, personal choice is influenced by the context that we as a society have created. The solutions therefore must extend beyond personal choice by recognizing that we need to change the context in which our choices are made for our behavior to change.

At the extreme, food-related illnesses could be viewed as the inevitable culmination of 10,000 years of civilization or perhaps as a self-correcting means of natural selection. As individuals, we seem to have lost the ability to recognize when we are satiated. From a policy perspective, we also seem to be unable to adjust to knowledge and change. We have the greatest scientific knowledge about nutrition in history. Yet our policies and our behaviors do not reflect this. Instead they promote an energy-dense diet and a sedentary lifestyle. The consequence is that we, and our children, are getting fatter,

Lydia Zepeda

having more diet-related health problems, and spending ever-increasing amounts on health care and attempts at weight loss.

There is a clear path of how we got here, but it is not inevitable. The US has worked very hard to achieve the distinction of spending the smallest proportion of our income on food of any country. Clearly, the most important characteristic of food for us is that it is cheap. Although we are less and less inclined to spend time in food preparation, we do not value those who feed us highly either. We pay those who grow, prepare, and serve our food among the lowest wages in our nation. Why this is so reflects both our history and our values as a nation.

The Value of Food in Our Society

What we are willing to pay for says a great deal about who we are. It identifies what we value in both absolute and relative terms. My father told me that the one vote that always counted is how you spend your money. I suppose he was a bit skeptical that anyone counted the ballots in the South Texas community where he grew up. However, he was certain that the merchants were counting the money in their tills. He viewed every dollar spent as an affirmation not only for products and services bought, but how they were made and sold and by whom.

My father understood the structure of the US economy and our role in it. Our purchases are the main driver of the US economy; we *are* the US economy. Food is one of the many things we purchase to form our economy. In the US, food makes up a surprisingly small part of our expenditures. This is not true for much of the rest of the world, nor was it true for us historically.

Researchers comparing 114 countries found that the average US household spent the smallest proportion of expenditures on food at home, beverages, and tobacco (less than 10 percent).[1] For comparison, other high-income countries spent 17 percent of their household budget, while households in middle-income countries spent 35 percent, and households in low-income countries spent over 52 percent. Clearly, poor people spend a higher percent on food because their incomes are low, but even among the richest countries we spend the smallest proportion on food. Food in the US is relatively cheap in comparison to every other country in the world.

To gain a sense of why that is so, it is instructive to look at how our personal expenditures have changed over time. In 1901, the average US household had 5.3 people and spent 43 percent of its budget on food and alcohol. In 2004, the average US household had 2.5 people and we spent less on food eaten at home (7.7 percent of expenses) than what we spent on social security and pensions (10.2 percent). Our expenses rise to 15 percent of our budget if we include food away from home. The increase in expenses for food away from home, from 3 percent in 1901 to 42 percent of all food expenditures in 2004, is the only reason that our food expenditures are as large as they are. What is surprising about the US is that the proportion we spend on food does not change much with income; the amount varies from 12 percent for the richest households to 16 percent for the poorest. The upshot is that even the poorest among us spend a smaller proportion of our income on food than the average amount spent by all other high-income countries.[2]

Therefore, in global and historical terms, food in the US is cheap. This seems logical for a country that has a lot of land, yet people spend a much higher proportion of their income on food in Canada, Russia, Australia, or Brazil where land is plentiful. One could attribute cheap food in the US to the combination of land, water, and climate, but we know that historically food in the US was expensive. Cheap food was hardly inevitable given the chronic historical labor shortage, at least from the Euro-American perspective. The labor shortage was addressed successively by explicit policies supporting slavery, immigration, and mechanization.

Our national policy was motivated to make food cheap and plentiful. It has been tied inextricably to our policy of territorial expansion, occupation, and removal of indigenous peoples and their rights. Food was a critical issue in US history; early colonists and pioneers routinely died of starvation and malnutrition. Often this was due to lack of understanding about the environment they were in and by trying to impose a foreign system of agriculture. The attitude was not one of adaptation, but of conquest. Territorial acquisition was the precursor to drawing settlers from the Eastern US and Europe who were required to farm and produce food to secure title. Food production of commodities was the "price" of gaining occupied land. This food ensured stability not only in the territories, but the process could not have been sustained had not a surplus of food been available to sell to the East. The food fed Easterners, who in turn sold Westerners the products they could not produce but needed to survive in the territories. The policy of homesteading was crucial not just to secure territorial expansion, but to produce the cheap food needed to fuel the industrial revolution.

A Policy of Cheap, Energy-Dense Food

So how did we transition from a country where food was scarce to being plentiful and cheap? Or at least certain kinds of foods are plentiful and cheap. For about 150 years, US agricultural policy has had as its goal the production of cheap commodities.[3] This quantity goal was set when food was relatively expensive and when we knew little about nutrients. The objective was to make sure stomachs were full. Given the expansion of the US territories and movement west of farming, foods had to be able to travel long distances. They had to be standardized so as to make exchange easy and efficient. The emphasis was therefore on grains and beef.

A key element in the process was the role of technology development in mechanizing US agriculture, in developing varieties of plants and animals suitable for monoculture, and in standardizing products to facilitate trade. Chemical means of fertilization and pest control further enhanced the ability to farm commodities. All of this would have been impossible without public resources. Publicly funded land grant universities and federal grants supported much of the research and development of the technology to industrialize agriculture and the food industry. Public monies also paid for the rural infrastructure (electrification, roads, dams, water projects, etc.) that permitted industrialization of America's agriculture. These public policies and funds served to subsidize and promote the production, commodification, and industrialization of energy-dense foods.[4]

Later, the US government made payments in the form of price supports and loan deficiency payments for crops. Almost all of it was for grains, oilseeds, and cotton. None have been for fruits and vegetables. We justify price supports and loan programs to help keep farmers in business. However, the occupation of farmer and rancher is expected to have the largest numerical decrease of any occupation between 2004 and 2014 despite being less than 1 percent of the population.[5] The justification for the current farm programs is misplaced; they have not been effective at helping farmers stay in business. Further, if agricultural policies and programs were justified from a public health perspective, the types of crops supported would look very different: less animal feed, no sweeteners, less starch, and much more fruits and vegetables. No doubt this would impact how the landscape looked.

The consequence of our agricultural policies is that we got exactly what we paid for. We produce an abundance of calories, particularly meat, feeds, fats, and sugars. We have and continue to be food exporters, but domestically we are eating more of this cheap, high-calorie food. In 1970, we ate 2,234 calories per person per day. In 2003, it rose by over 500 calories to 2,757 per day.[6] Most of the increase was due to increased consumption of fats and oils, grains, sugars, and sweeteners. Thirty percent of the calories we eat are empty calories: sweets, desserts, soft drinks, alcoholic beverages, salty snacks, and fruit-flavored drinks.[7] In terms of calories we consume nearly as many from soft drinks alone as from fruits and vegetables.

The predictable result of eating more calories is that we are fatter. Almost two-thirds of us are overweight and about a third of the adult population is obese. The average US male is 5'9" and weighs 191 pounds, and the average US female is 5'4" and weighs 164 pounds.[8] Being heavier has its costs. The US Department of Health and Human Services puts the medical costs of obesity and overweight at $117 billion annually.[9] More importantly, we could live longer and live better if we changed our eating habits; poor eating habits play a major role in half of all deaths.[10]

We want cheap, plentiful food and we certainly have it in the US, but we are not taking into account the indirect costs to get that food or the costs we incur by eating it. More importantly we are using public monies and public policy to create an environment that facilitates poor eating habits. We use public money to ensure that high-fructose corn syrup, animal feeds, oils, and grains are cheap and plentiful. Food manufacturers use these low-cost ingredients to produce and sell us foods that we eat too much of. We then use mostly private money to try to lose weight, and a combination of public and private monies to cover the costs of health care that are a consequence of our unhealthy eating habits. From a public health perspective the system we have created makes no sense. For an individual or family to buy a healthier diet we have to spend more money because we have constructed a system in which energy-dense foods are artificially cheap.

The Role of Technology and Social Change

While plentiful land and government policy have played a role in what we eat, technology and social change have also had a big impact on what and how we eat. Technological advances are behind the increases in the production of key crops and livestock. Much of the improvements in breeding, machinery, chemicals, and genetic engineering were developed at public land grant universities with public funds. Much of the food science technology was also developed with public funds at land grant universities. The technology has focused on extracting components of food for food processing, as well as new methods of preservation and storage. Food components are extruded and mixed to create new foods, many of which are "convenient," "tasty," and loaded with empty calories.

In many ways, the emphasis on refined and convenient foods has its roots in the pioneer heritage of the US. Foods needed to be compact, storable, and energy-dense to survive the journey west as well as the winters. Food was merely fuel that needed to be prepared as rapidly as possible. Flour, beans, salt-pork, and lard were staples. The cuisine was filling but not particularly healthy. The notoriety of chuck-wagon cooks implies that food of this era was not particularly tasty, either. The lack of variety in ingredients did little to encourage culinary prowess, food appreciation, or preserve ethnic food traditions. The US is a nation built on commodities: large quantities of homogenous foods. Is it any wonder that we are the founders of fast food?

A limited number of commodities and canned foods were the backbone of our urban food systems. We even had explicit policies to undermine the transplanting of food knowledge. Many of the vast numbers of immigrants at the turn of the century were forced to learn American cooking techniques as part of the government acculturation policy. One can only imagine what Italian immigrants, as one example, thought as they were being shown how to cook American food. What is evident today is that immigrants continue to bring their food traditions to the US, raising the quality and choice of foods we eat by doing so.

The Depression, of course, reinforced the emphasis on providing cheap, energy-dense food. Current farm programs have evolved from government policies developed during the Depression. Much of the rural infrastructure was built using labor from make-work programs. World War II added greater incentives to produce cheap, energy-dense food to feed troops. Our food policies were single-minded in emphasizing quantity of food.

The post-World War II years brought not only economic growth and increased food availability: they brought about social change. Prior to the 1950s, many women worked on farms and in factories and those who stayed at home were involved in provisioning food and services for their households. During the 1950s, incomes were sufficient to permit many more women to stay home. In combination with the labor saving household devices there was an increased preference for and availability of processed foods. Women's time was freed from housework and cooking by technology and ensnared in competitive consumption on a much broader scale than Thorstein Veblen had ever imagined in his treatise on "conspicuous consumption" and the ruling class.[11]

The US diet during the 1950s and 1960s often looked like the US diet from before: meat, potatoes, a vegetable, and perhaps some form of fruit for dessert. However, the sources of the food were more likely to be commercially canned, packaged, frozen, or instant. TV dinners were developed, and any food that could be made instant was: milk, mashed potatoes, orange drink, and so on. Serving sizes grew. Desserts became more elaborate as frozen and packaged offerings increased. We demonstrated our wealth by serving more meat and desserts that had traditionally been expensive, and less bread and potatoes.

Industrialized deskilling, a common manufacturing practice, spread to the kitchen. The few cooking skills and food knowledge that survived the commodification inherent in America's agricultural policy declined further from lack of use. There was no need to recognize whether food was fresh or ripe, as it was canned, frozen, or pre-packaged. There was no need to put up your own foods; you could buy them. Cooking increasingly drifted towards heating up things. Perversely, much of the attention on cooking in women's magazines focused on utilizing prepared foods (e.g., frozen foods, canned soups, etc.) in new and often complicated combinations. It was cooking with all the work, but none of the skill or flavor.

Women apparently found their lives as unsatisfying as their cooking, and the women's movement gained momentum in the 1960s and 1970s. Rather than valuing "women's work" or seeking a more equitable distribution of household work, the focus became increasing opportunities in the workplace. The oil crisis, inflation, and a rising divorce rate added economic impetus for women to join the workforce.

As labor force participation of women rose, the sharing of household chores did not increase commensurately,[12] so women had less time to prepare meals. However, scarcity did not raise the value of home cooking; food preparation was further diminished and deskilled. With the help of microwaves and increasing dependence on food eaten away from home, even greater emphasis was placed on convenience. In addition, rising incomes fueled a boom in demand for more variety of food and more meals out.

Changes in lifestyles have also contributed significantly to our changes in diet. We are much more able and more likely to live alone, especially if we are older. And advances in medical science have raised life expectancies such that there are more and more older people. But these folks were born prior to World War II, growing up during years of relatively better diets despite shortages. How will life expectancies change among those born and raised in the era of junk food? It is known that obesity – particularly childhood obesity – lowers life expectancy. One predictable impact of our poor diets is that life expectancies will start to decline.

Eating in the New Millennium

These trends continue into the 1990s and 2000s with greater demand for variety and meals out, even among the poor. Eating fast food, pizza, ready to eat cereal, and microwavable anything is now the norm. Portion size grew even further. Timing and location of our eating has changed as well. We snack more and eat fewer meals. Where we eat has changed; we eat in cars, in front of televisions, computers, while on phones, but only a third of families eat their main meal together every night.[13]

Our craving for variety appears to be limited to the color and design of the packaging or the message of the advertising rather than the flavor or the ingredients. The trend in demand for 'ethnic' food is as self-deceptive as our survey responses that we want healthier foods. We do not want real Mexican or Italian food, we want Americanized versions covered in processed cheese. We actually eat more butterfat per capita today than our parents or grandparents did; however, we eat it in the form of cheese and ice cream, while they ate it mostly as fresh milk, cream, and butter. We prefer foods that are sweet, creamy, and salty, but avoid fruit, cream, and adding salt. One has to wonder if the real things would be more satisfying than their extruded and prepared imitations. Would we eat less if we ate the originals?

While consumers may say they are interested in the quality, freshness, and healthfulness of our food, this is not consistent with what we are actually doing. Perhaps we are embarrassed to be candid. Perhaps we are in denial. The truth is, even within a context that makes energy-dense food cheap and convenient, we seem to be working very hard to eat more food that is less healthy for us. Old habits are hard to change.

We claim to be too busy to eat proper meals or to prepare food. However, the average US adult spends about 75 minutes a day eating as a primary activity and additional time eating as a secondary activity. However, we spend only about 30 minutes a day in food preparation and clean-up, and five times that amount watching television.[14] We seem to be making some clear choices about what we are willing to do with our time as well as our money.

Of course, there have always been dissidents. There is a small sector of the population eschewing empty calories and seeking higher quality, healthier foods. Organic food sales are rising, but interestingly much of the recent growth is in prepared foods and beverages. And while one could argue that a soda made with organic sugar is somewhat better for the environment, the argument that it is healthier for people is unconvincing.

Valuing Those Who Feed Us and
Those We Feed

Everyone eats. Given its fundamental function, what we eat and how we eat manifest our individual and collective values. What then does this tell us about who we are and what we value? What does the food we buy say about how we value those who feed us? What does the food we prepare and how we prepare it say about our regard for ourselves and those we feed?

Reflecting our personal and societal goals to spend minimal effort and money on food, is the increasing willingness to pay others to cook for us. The US employs nearly 10 million people in food service and food preparation.[15] These jobs are generally low paying, high stress, often physically demanding, and have rapid turnover. Youth aged 16 to 19 make up a fifth of cooks and food preparation workers, and one fourth of all food and beverage servers. Little education is required and much of the training is done on the job. Median wages for waiters and waitresses are $6.75 per hour (this includes tips), while fast food cooks earn on average $7.07 per hour. Clearly, we place very little value on those who are preparing and serving us food.

Nor do we place much value on those who grow and process our food. Current earnings in food manufacturing are 22 percent below average manufacturing wages.[16] We value the over 650,000 farm workers in the US growing and harvesting our food even less; they make on average $7.70 per hour.[17] We simply do not value food highly or the people involved in feeding us.

Nor are we willing to put much effort or money into those we feed. What we feed our children affects their health and wellbeing. The rise of childhood obesity is perhaps the most recognized health outcome, but it is not as though non-obese children have very healthy eating habits either. Obesity is simply the most evident health consequence of our eating habits. Using data from 13,000 US 7th through 12th graders, researchers found that only 38 percent ate two or more servings each of fruits and vegetables *per week*.[18] In other words, the overwhelming majority of our youth are not eating in a *week* the minimum *daily* recommendations for fruits and vegetables.

When educators are asked about improving children's nutrition, about half felt that their school was making some effort to improve the quality of meals and snacks available. However, only 30 percent felt that parents were supportive of these changes.[19] Parents are more inclined to direct their concerns towards the impact of others; 76 percent of parents are worried about the negative influence of other kids on their children, but fewer parents (68 percent) think that they themselves should be responsible for teaching good nutrition and eating habits to their kids, while only 40 percent feel they have accomplished this.[20]

How is it possible that a third of US parents do not feel responsibility for teaching their children good eating habits? Is the food system simply so broken that it is impossible to do so? Do the parents lack the knowledge and skills? After 100 years of culinary deskilling and 150 years of commodification of food, both are likely. Evidence of children's eating habits and food-related health problems indicates that the 40 percent of parents who think they have taught their children healthy eating habits are either woefully ignorant of what their children are eating or of what healthy eating is.

Digging Ourselves Out with a Spoon

The tremendous increase in scientific knowledge about nutrition has been accompanied with the largest change (for the worse) in eating habits. If we are so knowledgeable, why can we not stop our over-eating and poor eating habits? We need to modify not just nutrition information, but public policies to foster better choices.

There is no doubt we have the knowledge, much of it funded through public sources, to eat healthier. The technical experts have solid data and clear recommendations. Much of the information could be presented very simply and effectively, such as the "five a day" program. However, that campaign has been rendered obsolete by new, higher standards despite the fact that the average American does not eat five servings of fruits and vegetables a day.

Most of the dissemination of nutrition information is neither clear nor concise. For example, the old food pyramid was veiled in euphemism; never actually stating that one should avoid sodas and junk food. The new pyramid is even more obtuse and requires an explanatory reference booklet. There seems to be little intention to actually inform. Perhaps this is because the dissemination of nutrition information is at odds with public policies that continue to support a food system of energy-dense foods. Government nutrition programs aimed at providing access to foods for the poor and nutrition standards for school lunch and breakfast programs also are designed to support antiquated agricultural polices rather than promote accepted scientific nutritional guidelines.

The culmination is that we are simultaneously making energy-dense foods cheap through public policy and pushing these foods onto the most vulnerable among us: the poor and the very young. One of the consequences of cheap, energy-dense foods is that obesity rates are higher among the poor.[21] African Americans and Hispanics are much more likely to be poor than white Americans, and they also have a higher incidence of obesity. Healthier foods such as fruits and vegetables are often more costly. It is cheaper for low-income households to buy energy-dense junk food made from the agricultural products subsidized by US agricultural policy, paid for by US taxpayers, and subsidized again in food programs aimed at the poor and young.

In order for people to change their behaviors, to have a choice, we need to change the terms of our agricultural policy so that it is based on public health. At the very least we need to stop subsidizing the production of the energy-dense foods that are killing us. A rational agricultural policy would encourage the production of foods that are healthier for us and that we do not eat enough of because they are expensive: fruits, vegetables, and whole grains.

Let Them Eat Cake

Eating directly affects our wellbeing as well as that of our society. How we raise, process, distribute, and consume food affects the environment. Food is our connection to the natural world. The need to eat places requirements on us; it is a rhythmic reminder that we are part of a natural system that requires sustenance.

Historically, we have developed a policy to promote the production and availability of cheap, plentiful food in the US. Cheap food has always been fundamental to political stability. People revolt when they are starving. But the convoluted result of our policy to subsidize, both directly and indirectly, energy-dense food is that we are literally carrying out Marie-Antoinette's directive. Cake and other processed foods are cheap; raw foods, and fruits and vegetables, are expensive. People are no longer starving in the US; indeed, our problem with food is that we eat too much and eat too many empty calories. Food is killing us, and the poorer we are, the more at risk we are. But even though poor eating habits are related to higher mortality, "give us vegetables" does not have quite the power to rally people as cries for bread. It is too easy to blame individual choice for food-related health problems. After all, no one forced us to eat junk food; they just made it incredibly easy and cheap.

Notes

1   Seale, Jr., J., J., A. Regmi, and J. Bernstein. *International Evidence on Food Consumption Patterns.* Washington, DC: US Department of Agriculture, Economic Research Service, Technical Bulletin Number 1904, October 2003; at www.ers.usda.gov.
2   US Department of Labor – Bureau of Labor Statistics (BLS), *Consumer Expenditures in 2004.* Washington, DC: BLS Report 992, April 2006.
3   Tillotson, J. E. "America's Obesity: Conflicting Public Policies, Industrial Economic Development, and Unintended Human Consequences." *Annual Review of Nutrition* 24 (July 2004): 617–43.
4   Cawley, J. "Markets and Childhood Obesity Policy." *The Future of Children* 16, no. 1 (2006): 69–88.
5   US Department of Labor – Bureau of Labor Statistics (BLS), *Occupational Outlook Handbook: Tomorrow's Jobs*, December 20, 2005; at www.bls.gov/oco/oco2003.htm.
6   US Department of Agriculture – Economic Research Service, "US Food Consumption Up 16 percent since 1970." *Amber Waves* (November 2005); at www.ers.usda.gov/AmberWaves/November05/Findings/USFoodConsumption.htm.
7   Block, G. "Foods Contributing to Energy Intake in the US: Data from NHANES III and NHANES 1999–2000." *Journal of Food Composition and Analysis* 17 (2004): 439–47.
8   Gay, L. "Record Levels of Food Available, Eaten by Americans." Scripps Howard News Service, November 22, 2005; at www.knoxstudio.com/shns/.
9   US Department of Health and Human Services, *Statistics Related to Overweight and Obesity*; at www.win.niddk.nih.gov/statistics/index.htm.

10 Frazao, E. "High Costs of Poor Eating Patterns in the United States." *America's Eating Habits: Changes and Consequences*. US Department of Agriculture, Economic Research Service, Food and Rural Economics Division, Agriculture Information Bulletin No. 750, May 1999.

11 Veblen, Thorstein. *The Theory of the Leisure Class*. New York: B. W. Huebsch, 1924.

12 Bonke, J. *Choices of Foods: Allocation of Time and Money, Household Production and Market Services*. MAPP working paper no. 3, ISSN 09072101, September 1992.

13 Klapthor, J. N. "What, When and Where Americans Eat in 2003." Institute of Food Technologists news release, August 22, 2003; at www.ift.org/cms/.

14 US Department of Labor – Bureau of Labor Statistics (BLS), *American Time Use Survey – 2005 Results Announced by BLS*. Washington, DC. BLS news release 06–1276, July 27, 2006.

15 US Department of Labor – Bureau of Labor Statistics (BLS), *Occupational Outlook Handbook: Chefs, Cooks and Food Preparation Workers*, August 4, 2006; at www.bls.gov/oco/ocos161.htm; US Department of Labor – Bureau of Labor Statistics (BLS), *Occupational Outlook Handbook: Food and Beverage Serving and Related Workers*, August 4, 2006; at www.bls.gov/oco/ocos162.htm.

16 US Department of Labor – Bureau of Labor Statistics (BLS), *Table B-3. Average Hourly and Weekly Earnings of Production or Non-supervisory Workers*, September 1, 2006; at www.bls.gov/news.release/empsit.t16.htm.

17 US Department of Labor – Bureau of Labor Statistics (BLS), *Occupational Outlook Handbook: Agricultural Workers*, August 4, 2006; at www.bls.gov/oco/ocos285.htm.

18 Harris, K. M., R. B. King, and P. Gordon-Larsen, "Healthy Habits Among Adolescents: Sleep, Exercise, Diet, and Body Image." Paper presented at the Conference of Indicators of Positive Development, Washington, DC, March 12–13, 2003.

19 Center for Health and Health Care in Schools, *Nutrition, Physical Exercise, and Obesity: What's Happening in Your School? 2005/2006 Survey Results*, 2006; at www.healthinschools.org/sh/finalresults06.asp.

20 Public Agenda, "From Self-Control to Good Eating Habits: Parents in New Survey Report Limited Success in Teaching Their Kids 'Absolutely Essential' Values." News release, October 30, 2002; at www.publicagenda.org/press/press_release_detail.cfm?list=49.

21 Drewnowski, A. and N. Darmon, "The Economics of Obesity: Dietary Energy Density and Energy Cost." *American Journal of Clinical Nutrition* 82 supplement (2005): 265S–73S.

3

Should I Eat Meat? Vegetarianism and Dietary Choice

Jen Wrye

The majority of vegetarians in the West share a universal experience of being asked why they refuse to eat animal flesh. This common question reflects the fact that animal derivatives, and meat in particular, have always been preeminent food items for most people in the world. Their dominance is an indication of both their consumptive utility as well as emblematic significance. If this is the case, how can we explain the ongoing decline in the number of people who consume meat and a rise in the number of people who adopt a vegetarian lifestyle? Surely the decision to become vegetarian suggests a material comfort that provides individuals with a multitude of non-meat food options. However, vegetarian dieting simply cannot be reduced to a matter of individual preference, even if this is the common perception. Certainly, being vegetarian requires that individuals choose to actively abstain from meat eating. Yet there remains a strong symbolic component to this diet that cannot be denied or elided; a strong pull to something that seems larger than a simple decision. In this essay, I will explore the relationship between the individual and social components involved with the choice to become vegetarian. I argue that the vegetarian diet is best understood by considering the ways in which individuals negotiate their preferences and tastes inside the larger representational structure of vegetarianism.

Jen Wrye

Understanding Taste

Taste is a somewhat ambiguous term since it refers both to the actual flavor of an item as well as our judgment of it. In a society of plenty, taste most obviously denotes notions of choice – choosing according to preferences or likes and dislikes. The magnitude of how we consume these items cannot be diminished. The shift toward postmodern society requires attention to new modes of social organization and social life. In other words, within the context of consumption, personal taste or choice emerge as critical issues. In affluent societies, to what extent are choices free or controlled? Can we abandon any notion that our choices and preferences are systematically regulated or organized – that excessive and differentiated supply creates unsystematic demand?

While it is commonly assumed that individuals choose to become vegetarian of their own accord, many food writers talk about the social nature of taste. This belief that choices and tastes are somehow socially constrained requires consideration of who is imposing boundaries or how they are imposed. At the very least, this implies some conception of "communities." Academics have written extensively about communities – those organized according to class, race/ethnicity, gender, immigration status, and so on. Pierre Bourdieu is perhaps the greatest proponent of the view that tastes are shaped according to community affiliation and membership, noting that social class comprises the preeminent form of social organization. In his influential book *Distinction*, Bourdieu studies the ways in which upper- and lower-class tastes are generated and reproduced in relation to the realities of social class in mid-twentieth century France.[1] He organizes his view around the notion of 'habitus.' The habitus is the learned environment of a person and encompasses the entirety of individuals' existential environment. While the habitus is robust, it is not all-compassing. Therefore, the strength of the habitus is that it allows for a range of possible actions, but only those which fall within its constraints.

As mentioned, Bourdieu believes social class to be the greatest factor in determining tastes. But social class, following from his notion of habitus, includes economic as well as cultural capital. In fact, they comprise each other. Moreover, tastes, by which he

46

seems to refer to the knowledge of and the desire for particular commodities, are necessary elements in the process of forming and reproducing class. Taste is deeply embedded in class cultures. He writes:

> The habitus is both the generative principle of objectively classifiable judgments and the system of classification (*principium divisionis*) of these practices. It is in the relationship between the two capacities which define the habitus, the capacity to produce classifiable practices and works, and the capacity to differentiate and appreciate these practices and products (taste), that the represented social world, i.e., the spaces of lifestyles, is constituted . . . the habitus is not only a structuring structure, which organizes practices and the perception of practices, but also a structured structure: the principle of division into logical classes which organizes the perception of the social world is itself the product of internalization of the division into social classes.[2]

Taste, therefore, functions to make, embed, and reinforce the social distinctions that separate the upper from the lower classes. Consumption practices are generated by the habitus and the hierarchy of taste is a reflection of a regulated class hierarchy.

Somewhat in line with Bourdieu's argument, other researchers have argued that food creates communities in and of itself. Bourdieu's focus on ideas recognizes that practices of consumption reinforce distinctions in social class. However, the scope of his study seems to impose limitations on communities, while shared food habits themselves may bind people together. Thus, while food-related activities may reinforce existing community relations, they also have the power to generate new social groups beyond simple commensality. This is exemplified by the movement toward "countercuisine" and "ethical eating," where individuals choose and reject foods according to a specified set of criteria, including healthfulness, the treatment of workers, or the food's source, to name a few examples. Selective eating does more than confer a particular individual self-conception. Rather, people will systematically organize, sometimes into cohabitative collectives, to live and eat according to their protest. Some of those drawn to identifiable eating philosophies may share what Bourdieu would identify as a social class. But food activists from different cultures and social classes may also forge strong relationships around food.

A second puzzle present in Bourdieu's writing is the tenuous place of the individual. He does not insist that individuals cannot make any choices or that social class is absolute. Rather, he maintains the choices people supposedly make according to their own preferences can be anticipated if we know their social background. Bourdieu rightly contextualizes choices within the limits of access (class) and links the "individual" to the "society" and the "private" to the "public." But in doing so, the latter subdues the former despite some evidence that the shift toward postmodernity has brought with it increasing freedom for individuals and the demise of structured class culture. Drawing on Anthony Giddens, Deidre Wicks claims shifts in consumption practices may be linked to the discourse of "life politics", which represents a shift away from the politics of inequality associated with the modern period.[3] Life politics is concerned with processes of self-actualization. Since people are anxious about who they are in relation to changing external circumstances, the choices they make concerning what they consume become a means of expressing self-identity. In light of this, decisions surrounding our different preferences might be seen as highly individualized, private, and personal.

This position surely provides some insights. But it too easily ignores consistency in consumption patterns between members of the same social group. It would be more useful to recognize that the situations in which commodities are consumed are not stagnant and echo shifting social conditions; that our consumptive behavior is neither fully determined nor wholly free. This is especially true of vegetarian eating. What is frequently conceived as an individual choice has larger social implications. In order to comprehend the relationship between the private, individual choice of diet and public, collective, structured food ideologies, an understanding of vegetarian dieting is required.

What is a Vegetarian Diet?

What does it mean to be vegetarian? Or even vegan? Technically speaking, a vegetarian is a person who eats no flesh, or more popularly, any entity that has a face. However, matters are more complicated.

What do we mean by flesh or even eating face-possessing beings? Should we follow this prescription exactly or can vegetarians eat products derived from animals? These are significant questions, since the way in which these terms are defined sheds light on the extent to which vegetarian dieting can be seen as a matter of mere personal choice or as being connected with something much larger, such as a matter of collective identity. In fact, the idea of what may or may not count as a vegetarian diet has sparked pointed defenses of a more strict definition against the perceived growing trend toward broadening it.

Vegetarian dieting has a long history across the world and its Western influences can be traced back as far as ancient Greece. Prominent vegetarian figures spanning several thousand years, including Pythagoras, Leonardo da Vinci, Harvey Kellogg, Albert Einstein, and even ex-Beatle Paul McCartney, have become important role models for justifying and identifying with this dietary choice. However, vegetarian eating must be further understood in the context of increased "niche" diets. Since the 1960s, specialized dietary movements, particularly those related to health, have increased dramatically among individuals in the West. While many such food fads quickly vanish, some, including the vegetarian movement, have remained strong. Additionally, modern problems such as ecological degradation and escalating animal exploitation have generated important responses, which further recommend an understanding of what constitutes the vegetarian diet.

Despite varying viewpoints of what constitutes a vegetarian diet, one can point to some preliminary definitions. "Traditional vegetarians" do not eat any animals at all – including poultry or fish, which follows from the technical definition provided above. Yet, there are further subcategories, such as lacto-vegetarians, ovo-vegetarians, or lacto-ovo-vegetarians, who eat no flesh but will eat some animal products; in this case, milk and eggs, respectively. On the other hand, vegans fall into one of (loosely) two categories: dietary vegans and ethical vegans. The former group does not eat animals or animal derivatives, but may rely on animals' bodies in other commodities. The latter group refrains from eating or using any animal product, including milk and dairy items, eggs, honey, wool, leather, and cosmetic products. They may even avoid services, including medical procedures, that involve animal testing or animal products.[4] However, there is some evidence that even this characterization fails to account for many purported vegetarians' eating patterns. For instance, some vegetarians will eat fish or seafood but refuse all other animal flesh. According to George, eating vegetarian apparently covers the consumption of poultry as well, as evidenced by her contention that people may be " 'semivegetarians' – those who eat dairy products and eggs, as well as a little fish and chicken, but no red meat."[5] In keeping with these categorizations, being vegetarian for many individuals refers to the consistent but not constant rejection of food items derived from mammals.

Carol Adams has been the most vocal opponent of such loose descriptions of vegetarian dietary practices, which she claims sanitizes being vegetarian:

> What is literally transpiring in the widening of the *meaning* of vegetarianism is the weakening of the *concept* of vegetarianism by including within it some living creatures who were killed to become food. Ethical vegetarians complain . . . their radical protest is being eviscerated. People who eat fishmeat and chickenmeat are not vegetarians; they are omnivores who do not eat red meat. Allowing those who are not vegetarians to call themselves vegetarians dismembers the word from its meaning and its history.[6]

Notably, the vegetarian diet she envisions is "animal free," including their bodies "as well as dairy products and eggs" (p. 21).[7] Despite the importance of rejecting dairy and eggs to her vegetarian position, she does not seem to prohibit from the category of vegetarian those who consume such commodities. Her general refusal to avoid categorically excluding lacto-ovo-vegetarians from the group called vegetarian can be explained by her attempt to mount a broader critique. Indeed, what distinguishes Adams from some others writing on the subject is that she aims to explicate vegetarianism as an ethical position rather than simply as a diet, even if she does draw the line at animals' bodies. Her work thus draws on the larger symbolic elements of vegetarianism whereby animals occupy a tenuous and largely exploited place in human life.

As this discussion has shown, knowing what comprises a vegetarian diet is not a simple task. Many individuals seemingly negotiate the terms of their diets in ways that make the particular character of vegetarian choice difficult to pinpoint. Nevertheless, I hope to demonstrate that this preference requires greater contextualization and attention to the reasons people remove meat from their diets.

Eliminating Meat: Vegetarian Diets and Vegetarianism

Accounting for why people are eliminating meat from their diets requires some consideration of whether increasing numbers actually *are* giving it up. There is some debate as to whether this is true, and the evidence is far from conclusive. Notwithstanding the type of definitional problems elaborated above, some research indicates that the number of vegetarians is increasing. Beardsworth and Keil estimate that the proportion of self-defined vegetarians in the UK is between 4 and 6 percent and between 3 and 7 percent in the USA.[8] They also note that membership to the British vegetarian advocacy group, Vegetarian Society, jumped from 7,500 to 18,500 between 1980 and 1995, while the ASPCA approximates the number of vegetarians at roughly 15 million. Yet some measures indicate that people's self-identification as vegetarian may not substantiate the claim that more people are actually eliminating meat from their diets, since abstaining from meat and being a vegetarian may not be coextensive, given definitional ambiguities. While the UK has seen a reduction in meat consumption, mainly in response to massive meat food scares, the quantity of meat consumed in North America has increased. The USDA reports a steady rise in meat consumption between 1970 and 2002, noting that total meat consumption (mammals, foul, and fish) increased nearly 9 percent to 200 pounds per person during the period.[9] What has shifted gradually is only the type of meat consumed – from pork to beef and now from beef mainly to poultry. This data seems to cast doubt on claims that a vegetarian trend is obvious.

Nevertheless, per capita increases in the amount of meat consumed do not specifically correlate with the number of people who abstain from meat eating. Rather, it could be that the people who continue to eat meat are simply consuming more of it. The proliferation of meatless dishes available today may provide some clues. One need only take a quick survey of restaurant menus and grocery store shelves to notice an abundance and growing number of vegetarian menu options, meatless convenience food options, and meat surrogates (soy hotdogs or burgers, for example). Certainly this indicates that both a market and demand exists for such commodities, even if it does not strictly imply there are more "real" vegetarians. Of course, some omnivores may be simply eating meatless dishes more frequently. Nevertheless, such an example at least suggests that vegetarian staples are rising in popularity and that overall the Western vegetarian meal and perhaps even the diet is no longer the territory of a few, but has become something approaching a mass movement affecting millions of people.

But around what are people organizing? What reasons do people have for eliminating meat from their diets? I have already alluded to some of these reasons. The four leading motivations for adopting a vegetarian diet appear to include concerns over (1) the healthiness of meat eating; (2) the environmental degradation surrounding meat production; (3) the suffering and death of animals; and (4) the palatability of meat or the way it "tastes" in the broadest sense. This is by no means an exhaustive list and reasons usually overlap. What is significant is that there are a range of justifications for avoiding meat and animal products, which might suggest we should abandon any expectation of comprehending vegetarian eating. Yet this conclusion would be misguided. I propose that the best way to examine the vegetarian diet is through the lens of vegetarianism. Eating is both a personal and social activity. Vegetarians, including "semivegetarians," abstain from meat and therefore reject an entire food category. Thus vegetarian dieters respond to something about meat. In so reacting, they acknowledge a force that is particular to meat. This does not reflect personal preference or individual taste, but rather a larger body of ideas related to meat. As Julia Twigg maintains "in developing its ideas, vegetarianism has not operated in isolation, but has drawn on themes already present in the dominant culture's attitude to meat."[10] Thus, vegetarianism is a reaction to attitudes about meat. I contend that it is the "taste" of meat, as a motivating reason, which connects the vegetarian diet with the larger structure of vegetarianism. Meat's taste and vegetarians' reactions are important because these are visceral and particular responses, yet ones which link with other more reasoned and calculated decisions.

A useful starting point for this discussion concerns the symbolic meaning attached to meat in contemporary Western culture. Most agree that meat is a powerful symbol which can be seen as fitting into the broad structure of meaning that underpins culinary tradition. Twigg provides a framework that attempts to explain meat's predominant place by drawing attention to a hierarchy of status, power, potency, and desirability among foods.[11] Her codification orders items according to their edibility or inedibility. She locates red meat near the top of this potency hierarchy, with white meat and fish below it, other animal products like eggs and cheese below these, and vegetable foods lowest of all. These higher items become central dishes that make "a meal." Others have also commented on the importance of meat to the Western diet. In her examination of contemporary Western restaurant menus and family meals, Mary Douglas argues that meat is the principal dish around which the meal is formed.[12] She suggests that the order in which we serve foods, and the foods we insist on being present at a meal, particularly a formal one, signal a taxonomy that mirrors and reinforces our larger culture. She claims: "the ordered system which is a meal represents all the ordered systems associated with it. Hence, the strong arousal power of a threat to weaken or confuse that category." For Douglas then, meat is the centerpiece of the main meal, which is heavily imbued with the significance of social relations. In this way meat eating can be seen as part of the "habitus" – its permissibility is unquestioned by most people.

But what makes meat so symbolically powerful? Twigg argues that cultural paradigms can be discerned from the patterning of our individual actions and food choices. In the case of meat, there are a specific set of deeper meanings because meat originates in animals. In her view, it is blood that places it in such a high position because it bears the special essence of the person or the animal, and is associated with virility, strength, aggression, and sexuality. At the same time, it is a dangerous and potentially polluting substance. The consumption of red meats is seen as the ingestion of the very nature of the animal itself, including its strength and its aggression. However, in Western culture, there is an element of ambivalence. The ingestion of too much of this power is dangerous. Thus, there is a boundary in the food hierarchy and above that boundary are items which are generally defined as too potent for humans to eat regularly. These include other humans, raw meat (excluding sushi), uncastrated animals, and carnivorous animals, all of which are precluded from the transformations that remove them from the realm of nature and enter them into the realm of culture. Indeed, the cultural significance of cooking or heating marks a transformation whereby purely natural foods move into the realm of human culture. This is not to say that humans are not natural beings. Rather, humans are both products of nature and culture. The need to eat is one way we are constantly faced with this paradox, and cooking is one of the means whereby we attempt to manage it.[13]

Accordingly, the importance of vegetarianism lies in the pursuit of purity, albeit purity that centers on a perception of nature as good and peaceful. Vegetarians often claim their diet is less violent and that eating vegetables and grains means eating closer to nature. Yet Symons argues this signals a denial of nature's "nature." He maintains the rejection of meat, even among those who do so for environmental or health reasons, is underscored by a universal experience: revulsion. What vegetarians are rejecting is nature. This is because they distort nature in such a way that their diets reflect a move away from it and toward "civilization." Moreover, they do not identify with animals because "cuisine 'disguises' food; eyes remind us of animals and our own bestiality."[14] Thus, he claims, the vegetarian is alienated. Even Twigg understands vegetarianism, in all its forms, to be at variance with nature:

> Vegetarians choose to eat far away from the ambivalent animal power. But there is a deeper ambiguity present. Vegetarians do not eat meat because it makes you one in substance and action with animal nature, it stokes the fires of an abhorrent animality. But vegetarians also reject meat because we are one with nature and thus to do so is cannibalistic and horrible. Vegetarians have an ambiguous attitude to nature: they both fear it and desire to be one with it.

Rather than eating outside the realm of dominant culture, the vegetarian diet presumes a connection to food categories and the place of food in the nature–culture divide. Vegetarians eat nearer to the bottom of the list, purportedly closer to nature. Moreover, they do so in a fairly typical way. Vegetarians progressively work down the hierarchy, progressively giving up higher foods – first red meat, then poultry, fish, and so on. Vegetarianism is therefore a reaction that can be seen in the process of eliminating meats.

This is not surprising for Adams, who reads meat in terms of the dominant culture's patriarchal attitudes. Nor is the fact that women have always consumed less meat than men on average and are likelier to become vegetarian.[15] Her interpretation differs significantly in that she believes the consumption of meat to be indicative of acculturation specifically within patriarchy. This is because meat eating is the domain of men. For her, ingesting the bodies and blood of animals as a means to symbolic strength, virility, and so forth, is closely associated with preoccupations surrounding masculinity. Consequently, meat represents a sexualized politics where both animals and women exist as objects to be dominated and consumed. This is achieved by means of fragmenting and denying their wholeness – by appropriating their bodies, including their reproductive capacities. For her, vegetarians recognize *the animal* in meat whereas those who consume their flesh turn them into "absent referents." In meat, she asserts, animals are made absent in name and body. The dead body replaces the live animal, and animals are absent from the act of meat eating by virtue of their transformation into "food." To Adams, women may eat less meat because it is denied to them. But likelier, and especially when they choose to do so, women may eat less or no meat because they identify with and experience oppression similar to animals or because of body-image issues associated with idealized standards of femininity. In this sense, the vegetarian diet seems to be linked to larger ideologies surrounding gender, as well as race and class. Consequently, choosing vegetarianism is something more than an action that stems from private reasoned choice or intuitive response. Instead, it is reflective of a particular form of social and material inculcation and enculturation toward eating and food choice.

Conclusion

This essay has addressed the question of whether vegetarian dieting should be regarded as a matter of personal taste. I have argued that the larger framework of vegetarianism can help explain why individuals reject meat; that their food choices are related to meanings surrounding the tenuous place of animals in modern culture. I have also argued that our preferences surrounding food reflect both independent choice and the power of larger social forces surrounding gender and class. Undeniably, the shift to a meatless diet involves personal choice. Often it subjects its adherents to scrutiny, mockery, and even pressure to eat meat. But it would be erroneous to ignore the social contexts in which such decisions are made. Moreover, we would be mistaken to ignore a somewhat coherent demographic among vegetarians, as well as a near universal experience of becoming so. Rather, this suggests vegetarians make food choices within a larger culinary structure. To this end they unavoidably engage vegetarianism by rejecting meat.

Notes

1   Bourdieu, Pierre. *Distinction: A Social Critique of the Judgement of Taste*. Trans. Richard Nice. Cambridge, MA: Harvard University Press, 1984.

2   Ibid.: 170.

3   Wicks, Deidre. "Humans, Food and Other Animals: The Vegetarian Option." *A Sociology of Food and Nutrition: A Social Appetite*. Ed. J. Germov and L. Williams. South Melbourne: Oxford University Press, 1999: 111–12.

4   What I have described as two categories of vegan is really more of a continuum. There are vegans who do not eat meat, eggs, dairy, and honey, yet who may not actively avoid some foods containing animal derivatives (particularly the obscure ones). There are vegans who are equally concerned with eating products that do not support genetic modification or environmental irresponsibility. There are even vegans who refuse to eat, wear, or use, not just animal products, but anything resembling animal merchandise – no pleather, no veggie hotdogs or burgers, etc. In sum, there is a range of possibilities for people who identify as vegan as well as a range of products, services, and resources available to vegetarian and vegan consumers. Additionally, there are some ambiguous food products, such as desserts, many cheeses, or Caesar dressing, which necessitate the death (and not just the exploitation) of animals from whom they are derived. Because they are not marginal foods, usually most vegans and vegetarians would exclude these from their diets. These foodstuffs are gelatin (from animals' skin and

connective tissue), rennet (from mammals' stomach lining), or anchovy paste (from fishes' bodies), in that order.

5 George, Kathryn Paxton. "Should Feminists Be Vegetarians?" *Signs* 19.2 (1994): 405, n. 2.

6 Adams, Carol. *The Sexual Politics of Meat: A Feminist-Vegetarian Critical Theory*. New York: Continuum, 1990.

7 When making this assertion she does not refer to other animal-derived foods such as gelatin, or honey, although she does discuss bees' production of honey within the context of vegan dieting and the feminized exploitation of animals (p. 91). It thus seems that Adams' definition of 'vegetarian' diet would more commonly be referred to as an 'ethical vegan' diet.

8 Beardsworth, Alan and Teresa Keil. *Sociology on the Menu: An Invitation to the Study of Food and Society*. New York: Routledge, 1997.

9 United States Department of Agriculture. *Agriculture Fact Book* 102. Washington, DC: USDA, 2002.

10 Twigg, Julia. "Vegetarianism and the Meanings of Meat." *The Sociology of Food and Eating: Essays on the Sociological Significance of Food*. Ed. Anne Murcott. Aldershot: Gower, 1983: 29.

11 Twigg, Julia. "Food for Thought: Purity and Vegetarianism." *Religion* 9 (1979): 13–35.

12 Douglas, Mary. "Deciphering a Meal." *Implicit Meanings: Selected Essays in Anthropology*, 2nd edn. Ed. Mary Douglas, London: Routledge, 1999: 250.

13 Wood, Roy. *The Sociology of the Meal*. Edinburgh: University of Edinburgh Press, 1995.

14 Symons, Michael. *Eating into Thinking: Explorations in the Sociology of Cuisine*. Dissertation, Flinders University of South Australia, 1991: 247.

15 Socio-demographic research shows vegetarians are most likely to be younger women working in middle-class professions. One conspicuous absence in the socio-demographic research concerns race/ethnic background. Maurer mentions ethnicity and indicates that vegetarians are predominantly white. For further, albeit intuitive, discussion of why this might be the case, see Maurer, Donna. *Vegetarianism: Movement or Moment*. Philadelphia: Temple University Press, 2002: 9–10. Certainly, attention to the racial/ethnic dimensions of vegetarian dieting is long overdue.

4

Sublime Hunger: A Consideration of Eating Disorders Beyond Beauty

Sheila Lintott

Imagine this: You wake up at 5 a.m., dizzy, with an empty feeling in the pit of your gut. Your first thoughts are of food, but not in any simple sense. Instead of thinking about some delicious meal that might satisfy your hunger, you think quite the opposite. You think that today you will not eat until 5 p.m., or 6 p.m., or, best of all possibilities, not at all. You deliberate, figuring when you will have to eat, and how you will be able to avoid eating until then, without detection. Today, you affirm, as you do every day, that you will eat less than yesterday. Before falling asleep last night, while doing your sit-ups in bed, you already made a plan to run five extra miles this morning to make up for the potato you ate yesterday. You are guiltily aware that you were not supposed to eat that potato; you know you should have eaten only some celery. You know that if you eat, you may lose control and devour more food than most people eat in a week. But you find comfort in your confidence that if this happens, you can deal with it; you can vomit it up. You know the tricks – how to make yourself vomit, silently and quickly if need be. As soon as you pull yourself out of bed, you rush to the bathroom because the box of laxatives you ate last night is winding its way through your lower intestines, searching in vain for some morsel of food to push through your system. You weigh yourself before you let go of the laxatives, and then again after. For both weigh-ins, the two-digit number you see is still too high; yet you compliment your-self for your efforts – you have lost a pound since yesterday. You put on several layers of clothes – for warmth and to hide your body. You have some coffee, perhaps a couple of cigarettes, whatever might help you as you begin another day on your mission of self-starvation. You have a full-fledged eating disorder: anorexia nervosa with bulimic tendencies (or vice versa). The really shocking thing is that you have never felt so alive and invigorated, have never before lived so purposively. Today brings the cherished opportunity to revel in the sublime hunger to which others succumb. You feel this way, despite the fact that it is only a matter of time until your disordered eating makes an invalid, or a corpse, of you.

The Cult of Thinness

Many women are preoccupied, if not obsessed, with thinness. They are aware of the quest for it every time they see the bathroom scale, survey their image in the mirror, are embraced by their lovers, or search through their closets for something to wear. The wish for thinness is present when stricken by envy at the sight of a thin woman who appears incredibly free in her skin, when swallowing hunger with salad greens covered in fat-free dressing, and in bed with hopes of a thinner tomorrow.

The dominant ideal of female beauty perpetuated *ad nauseam* in visual culture is a woman of unnatural, unhealthy, and in many cases impossible thinness. This ideal provides a radically incomplete explanation of the phenomenon. After all, what is beautiful about a 5′ 7″ woman weighing far less than a hundred pounds? Where is the beauty in a woman's body that exposes every rib through scaly, dull, fat-free skin? What is beautiful about a woman who is losing her hair, falling down, passing out, and throwing up? The answer, of course, is nothing. The person suffering from a full-fledged eating disorder is decidedly not beautiful. Her quest might begin as an attempt to embody the ever-elusive ideal of female perfection, but at some point in the progression of the disorder, that external goal becomes a side issue and eventually a non-issue. Might aesthetic ideals other than beauty have a role in motivating eating disorders?

Sheila Lintott

Sublimity, Respect, and Admiration

Immanuel Kant discusses the notion of the sublime in his *Observations on the Feeling of the Beautiful and the Sublime* and in his *Critique of Judgment*. Like beauty, the sublime affords us pleasure. However, it is a truly unique sort of pleasure, for it "is produced by the feeling of a momentary inhibition of the vital forces followed immediately by an outpouring of them that is all the stronger."[1] The moment of inhibition inherent in the sublime is an element of frustration or fear. The pleasure that follows the moment of frustration or fear is a "negative pleasure." So, the experience of the sublime is simultaneously one of attraction and repulsion. Moreover, the true object of admiration and respect is not the object that occasions the experience of the sublime. Rather, it is that portion of us able to reflect on and respond positively to frustrating or frightening stimuli. Thus, the sublime makes salient our depth and power, and an awareness of our capacity for the sublime is intimately connected to self-admiration and respect.

On Kant's view, there are two ways we find objects to be sublime: mathematically and dynamically. The mathematically sublime is that which is "absolutely large"; it is that which "in comparison with which everything else is small."[2] Imagine looking at the clouds above you and contemplating the size of the sky. In its formlessness, the presentation of the sky is suggestive of infinity, but we cannot perceive infinity. Nor can we perceive the sky in its entirety, for much of it eludes our perception. Apprehending such an object, an object that is so large we cannot form a clear idea of it, is frustrating. Our minds race, we look harder and farther, trying to bring the object in its entirety into our minds. But we cannot; at every apparent ending, we find that the sky continues. We know that the sky continues, even though we cannot perceive that it continues. This moment of frustration is the moment within which the sublime is born: for we realize that although we cannot perceive the absolutely large, we can conceive of it. This recognition is the sublime: "sublime is what even to be able to think proves that the mind has a power surpassing any standard of sense."[3] Thus, the mathematically sublimes offers us the cherished verification that our mental capacities transcend the sensory stimuli that surround us.

Whereas the mathematically sublime concerns objects that are massive in size, the dynamically sublime concerns objects with an abundance of power. Among examples of the dynamically sublime are violent storms, erupting volcanoes, and the rough tides of the ocean. When we apprehend such objects, we are aware that we could not withstand their fury, that the power exhibited there could easily destroy our physical selves. We know our physical strength pales in comparison. We find this disturbing, and such realizations evoke in us strong feelings of fear and discomfort.

The element of fear is a necessary aspect of the experience of the dynamically sublime. However, the fear need not be great enough to get us out of the situation; in fact, it should not be. Instead, the sublime occurs when it is possible to "consider an object fearful without being afraid of it . . . we judge it in such a way that we merely think of the case where we might possibly want to put up resistance against it, and that any resistance would in that case be utterly futile."[4] Although such an experience makes us unmistakably aware of our impotence in the physical world, it has the potential to occasion a positive experience. The consideration of fearsome natural forces may cause us to recognize our strength – not our physical strength, but rather, our strength of spirit. If we are in a safe place, the object is fearful, but not sufficiently so that it warrants retreat. If so, we may revel in the moment, taking pleasure in our ability to do so. The realization that we can contemplate and savor the fearsome allows us to see that there is something in us that transcends the dominion of nature. The sublime can "raise the soul's fortitude above its usual middle range and allow us to discover in ourselves an ability to resist which is of a quite different kind, and which gives us the courage [to believe] that we could be a match for nature's seeming omnipotence"; we realize that as physical beings we are no match for the force of the dynamically sublime, that "our ability to resist becomes an insignificant trifle."[5] We also notice that there is some aspect of ourselves not threatened by this great force of nature. We can acknowledge, therefore, that a part of ourselves is superior to nature and its laws.

To fully experience the sublime, the predominant feeling we have when confronted by the threatening force must not be one of fear, for ultimately the sublime experience is one of strength. The sublime gives us the opportunity to gain some perspective on life, for we see that in comparison to the current threat, we must "regard as small the [objects] of our [natural] concerns: property, health, and life."[6] The process is one of gaining self-knowledge; we realize not that the object in nature is sublime, but rather that the sublime resides in our own selves. The hurricane and tornado are not, strictly speaking, sublime, but they help us become aware of our own sublimity. What we glean from the experience of the dynamically sublime, therefore, is of great existential and moral value.

The experience of the sublime shows us that we can transcend our natural inclinations, and if need be, resist them entirely. We learn that a part of us is strong and free, and thus worthy of respect. We gain confidence in ourselves when we are afforded the opportunity to "regard nature's might . . . as yet not having such dominance over us, as persons, that we should have to bow to it if our highest principles were at stake and we had to choose between upholding or abandoning them."[7] In the sublime, according to Kant, the superiority of the human above nature is made manifest.

In summary, then, sublime experiences are those that begin with a moment of serious frustration or threat. Yet, rather than leaving us befuddled or running for safety, they allow us the opportunity to verify that there is something within ourselves that can deal with the frustration or stand up to the threat. This realization of the extent of our own conceptual depth and mental fortitude is the sublime. Furthermore, our capacity for the sublime – entailing as it does intelligence and strength – is grounds for respect and admiration, including, most saliently, self-respect and self-admiration.

Eating Disorders and the Sublime

In *Wasted: A Memoir of Anorexia and Bulimia*, Marya Hornbacher distinguishes eating disorders from attempts to lose weight. Eating disorders, she explains, are not about losing weight, nor about being thin, nor about meeting cultural standards. Drawing on her own experience as an anorectic and bulimic, she explains that at some point, "an eating disorder ceases to be 'about' any one thing. It stops being about your family, or your culture. . . . [I]t becomes a crusade. . . . It is a shortcut to something many women without an eating disorder have gotten: respect and power."[8]

Hornbacher's insightful remarks suggest that the concept of the sublime might provide answers to questions such as: What compels an eating-disordered individual to torture herself, to deny herself food, and to harm herself through deprivation and purging? What is her quest for, if not for beauty, thinness, acceptance, or approval? What is her crusade, and how is it a means to respect and power? Utilizing a Kantian conception of the sublime provides us with novel answers to these questions that are far from romantic or mysterious.

How, then, does the Kantian notion of the sublime inform our understanding of individuals suffering with eating disorders? We can cast the motivation of the eating-disordered individual in reference to Kant's presentation of the experience of great power in nature: "Might is an ability that is superior to great obstacles. It is called dominance if it is superior even to the resistance of something that itself possesses might. When in an aesthetic judgment we consider nature as a might that has no dominance over us, then it is dynamically sublime."[9] We can begin to understand the eating-disordered individual as motivated by the sublime in the following way. Human beings have certain animalistic needs, desires, and wants. One basic need is the need for nourishment. We must eat to survive. Moreover, we are drawn to food for pleasure and comfort. In order to lose weight, one must curtail this natural hunger and attempt to distinguish between the desire for food based on need and the desire for food for pleasure or comfort. It would take an abundance of strength to overcome the desire for food to the extent that one avoids not only unnecessary calories but virtually all calories. This is what the eating-disordered individual attempts to accomplish. The anorectic does so by refusing to eat. The bulimic devises a plan by which she can enjoy the pleasure without satisfying the actual physical need related to eating.

However, if the sublime is a motivating factor in the experience of the eating-disordered individual, the satisfaction she feels must arise from her internal achievement and not primarily from the fact that the world around her is pleased with her weight loss. Hunger is a strong force that controls by compelling us to satisfy it several times a day; denying it for extensive periods of time only stokes it. When confronted by a desire for food, the eating-disordered individual rejects the dominance of nature over her physical self by refusing to eat or refusing to take nutrients from the food. This domination of self over nature is the crusade of the anorectic and bulimic.

Immediately we notice that the eating-disordered individual has a dualistic view of herself. In "Anorexia Nervosa: Psychopathology as the Crystalization of Culture," Susan Bordo articulates the dualism between body and self found throughout the history of Western culture that we have clearly inherited. She isolates the central features of this dualism as follows:

[T]he body is experienced as alien, as the not-self, the not-me. . . . [T]he body is the brute material envelope for the inner and essential self, the thinking thing. . . . [T]he body is experienced as confinement and limitation . . . from which the soul, will, or mind struggles to escape. . . . [T]he body is the enemy. . . . And, finally, whether as an impediment to reason or as the home of the 'slimy desires of the flesh' (as Augustine calls them), the body is the locus of all that threatens our attempts at control. . . . This situation, for the dualist, becomes an incitement to battle the unruly forces of the body, to show it who is boss.[10]

Following in this tradition, the eating-disordered individual believes she is a being with a body, but she cannot entirely identify herself with her body. Eating disorders involve the view of one's body as 'other,' as something that can be dominated. In order to view the body and its needs as a natural force that can be overcome, there must be something responsible for the overcoming. In other words, as Kim Chernin laments, an eating disorder is "above all, an illness of self-division and can only be understood through the tragic splitting of body from mind."[11] The eating-disordered individual locates her self in that part of her that is able to contemplate objects immense in size and to resist forces that threaten to destroy her: her hunger and desire for food.

Recall that the mathematically sublime, according to Kant, is an object of such immense size that one cannot grasp it by sensory means alone. Instead, one contemplates it and realizes that the depth of her reason far exceeds any sensible aspect of the world. Stoked as it is by starvation and deprivation, the hunger of the eating-disordered individual is as immense and formless as the sky above. The lingering awareness of this hunger offers a momentary glimpse into one's own depth. The bulimic goes one step further, playing with the hunger, pretending to satiate it, only to abruptly and completely renege by way of purging. Ira Sacker and Mark Zimmer convey to us the potential intensity of the bulimic's purge, and allow recovering bulimic Erin Palmer's description of her first purge to stand as evidence of such: "The whole purge process was cleansing. It was a combination of every type of spiritual, sexual, and emotional relief I had ever felt in my life."[12]

Notice that she is the non-eater. Unlike Kant in a thunderstorm, the eating-disordered individual does not fear physical destruction but the destruction of her spirit – of the part of her that is more than flesh. Succumbing to hunger threatens to destroy her identity as someone who can withstand hunger at any price. She cannot let down her guard for even one bite; a recovering anorectic makes the following confession: "I can see that I am thin. But I also know that there is a fat woman inside me, dying to get out. And if she gets out, I'm still afraid that she'll kill me."[13]

Moreover, she needs food, for her identity is that which denies food. It is typical for the anorectic or bulimic to prepare elaborate meals for friends and family and not indulge at all. She is entirely preoccupied with food and surrounds herself with it, as if to tempt and test her will.

The sublime is not meant to be a way of life, but eating disorders most definitely are. Kant tells us that "Those in whom both feelings join will find that the emotion of the sublime is stronger than that of the beautiful, but that unless the latter alternates with or accompanies it, it tires and cannot be so long enjoyed."[14] The sublime is a valuable experience, but it must be tempered with controlled experiences of beauty and perhaps even boredom. The situation is even worse for individuals suffering with eating disorders, because the eating-disordered person uses herself as the catalyst toward the feeling of the sublime. Whereas, in typical cases, the object that provokes the feeling is external – a storm or immense vista – here it is the home of the feeling as well. Janice Baker, a recovering bulimic, describes the moment she came to realize the self-defeating nature of her eating disorder:

I remember feeling so angry, I was shaking. . . . I mean, I was furious. My body was the one thing I could really manage precisely, and now it was managing me. It was making me make choices, and that made me feel like I was living inside a foreign territory where the environment was really hostile.... At that moment, I felt completely defeated, and I remember saying to my doctor, "I just can't win for losing," and he said to me, "You finally understand. You can't really win if all you want to do is lose." That one comment got us talking for an hour.... Through that hour, and over the months to come, I kept one thing in the front of my mind: If I get caught up fighting with my body, I will lose no matter what. Because my body will fight for a while, and that will be hard to control. And when my body finally stops fighting the war, I'll lose again. Because I'll be the only casualty.[15]

Sublimity Through Excessive Dieting

The extreme behaviors of anorectics and bulimics do not arise in a vacuum. The eating-disordered individual's choice to pursue respect via self-deprivation is not arbitrary. It arises in the context of a dieting culture. An ability to follow a diet is an achievement in itself. To overcome cravings for 'empty calorie' foods and emotional desires for food requires willpower. Exercising this willpower is something that is respected in society, and anyone who is able to do so seems to earn the right to be extremely proud. Moreover, our culture is one that respects successful weight loss and in fact demands it of women. In most cases, respect for the dieter and the disdain for the non-dieter are present, regardless of the means utilized or the actual health need for weight loss. As Bordo explains:

> Our culture is one in which Oprah Winfrey, a dazzling role model for female success, has said that the most "significant achievement in her life" was losing sixty-seven pounds on a liquid diet. (She gained it all back within a year.) ... It is a culture in which my "non-eating-disordered" female students write in their journals of being embarrassed to go to the ice cream counter for fear of being laughed at by the boys in the cafeteria; a culture in which Sylvester Stallone has said that he likes his woman "anorexic" (his then girlfriend, Cornelia Guest, immediately lost twenty-four pounds); a culture in which personal ads consistently list "slim," "lean," or "trim," as required of prospective dates.[16]

Is it at all surprising, therefore, that one might be tempted to excessive dieting in this context? Recalling the early stages of her eating disorder, Karen Anderson reports: "I really started to shed pounds, and everyone around me told me how impressed they were with my willpower. The more I lost . . . the more overwhelming the praise."[17]

In his *Observations on the Feeling of the Beautiful and the Sublime*, Kant discusses the notions of the beautiful and sublime in gender-charged terminology. He suggests that the sublime is the domain of men, while beauty is that of women:

> [A] woman is embarrassed little that she does not possess certain high insights, that she is timid, and not fit for serious employment, and so forth; she is beautiful and captivates, and that is enough. On the other hand, she demands all these qualities in a man, and the sublimity of her soul shows itself only in that she knows to treasure these noble qualities so far as they are found in him.[18]

For Kant, not only is women's domain primarily that of beauty, but women are allegedly content with this. However, contra Kant, women also crave the "noble qualities" of courage and strength – not simply to possess them in a mate, a brother, or a father, but to feel them for herself – in herself. She wants and will demand to be recognized for more than her beauty, to do more than captivate.

The dieter is different both in degree and kind from the anorectic or bulimic. The dieter might truly wish her appetite to vanish, whereas the anorectic or bulimic depends on her hunger for her identity. The eating-disordered individual identifies deeply with the part of herself that the world tells her she has no right to possess. Whereas the dieter, by equating thinness with worth, believes she must physically conform to externally prescribed ideals, the eating-disordered individual blatantly rejects these ideals by far surpassing them in her excessively thin body. The eating-disordered individual's self-starvation is therefore a twofold protest. First, she lays claim to that supersensible portion of humanity that Kant (and others) reserved primarily for men. Her protest is motivated by her refusal to embrace and enhance the physical aspects of herself to please others. By judging her primarily in terms of her physical appearance, the world around her is undervaluing, if not outright denying, that there is anything to her other than that appearance.

Second, her eating disorder, the logical conclusion of the impossible and contradictory messages society sends her, provides her with the voice of protest against the ideals dictated to her. Her very existence – in all its boniness and weakness – testifies to the absurdity of the ideals championed by the world around her. She will not allow them to define her, especially in reference to her looks. The sublime can offer a new perspective on life, for it highlights a threat in comparison to which we must "regard as small the [objects] of our [natural] concerns: property, health, and life."[19] To this list we might certainly add the relatively trivial concern to be considered beautiful.

Conclusion

In looking at the role of aesthetics in eating disorders, I have argued that aesthetic tastes and factors play an important role. In exploring the aesthetic dimension of disorders such as anorexia and bulimia, I have drawn on the distinction between two aesthetic ideals, that of beauty and that of the sublime. It is the first, beauty, which may start many women on the path to developing an eating disorder. However, if the analysis offered above is correct, it is the second, the aesthetic ideal of the sublime, that keeps many on that path, sometimes to their very death.

I have sought to explain the mysterious and dogged determination with which some women seek to control their own bodies. It is my argument that this exercise of control may be usefully understood as providing women with intense and "socially acceptable" experiences of the sublime. As I have illustrated above, an experience of the sublime offers a unique source of valuable information. Via the sublime a woman is assured that her value as a person transcends her value as an imperfect and limited physical being; her confidence that she is free and worthy of respect is stoked.

Understanding the motivations of those who suffer from eating disorders in terms of the sublime gives us the basis for a more complete understanding of them. That is, eating disorders are incorrectly understood as attempts to pursue cultural stereotypes of thinness and beauty. Moreover, it allows us to see eating disorders as the extreme end of a continuum of "normal" human behavior. To some extent, human beings are naturally attracted to the sublime. For instance, rock climbing is accepted as a legitimate enterprise; yet some rock climbing is deemed unsafe, and thus too extreme. Likewise, controlling one's body through diet and exercise is seen as a legitimate enterprise; nonetheless, some body control, such as that practiced by eating-disordered individuals, is deemed unsafe and thus too extreme. The analysis I have offered explains the intensity of eating disorders, their appeal to those suffering from them, the resistance to treatment, and the fact that the disorders frequently appear to have little to do with beauty ideals.

In closing, let me insist that my purpose here has in no way been to glorify the disorders of which I speak. At the same time, I hope to have shed some light on the motivations behind such apparently bizarre behavior by suggesting that those suffering from eating disorders are motivated by neither shallow nor trivial concerns. Eating disorders, as I have argued, are not employed merely as an attempt to fit the beauty ideal *du jour*. Rather, the disorders arise in response to a world that conceives of a woman's worth in terms of her physical appearance and culminates in a quest to prove there is more to her than meets the eye. The eating-disordered individual is engaged in a struggle, albeit a tragically misguided one, to demonstrate her strength and freedom and to win respect, especially from herself. Of course, strength and freedom cannot be sustained in a body too frail to hold itself up. Eventually, whatever strength and freedom appear to have been achieved will be forfeited by the ailing body she herself has created.

Notes

This essay was originally published, in modified form, as "Sublime Hunger: A Consideration of Eating Disorders Beyond Beauty." *Hypatia*, vol. 18, no. 4, Fall/Winter 2003, pp. 65–86. Reprinted with permission.

1 Kant, Immanuel. *Critique of Judgment*. Trans. Werner Pluhar. Indianapolis: Hackett Publishing, 1987: 245.
2 Ibid.: 248, 250.

3   Ibid.: 250.

4   Ibid.: 260.

5   Ibid.: 261.

6   Ibid.: 262.

7   Ibid.: 262.

8   Hornbacher, Marya. *Wasted: A Memoir of Anorexia and Bulimia*. New York: Harper Collins, 1998: 64.

9   Kant, *Critique of Judgment*, p. 260.

10 Bordo, Susan. *Unbearable Weight: Feminism, Western Culture, and the Body*. Berkeley: University of California Press, 1993: 144–5.

11 Chernin, Kim. *The Obsession: Reflections on the Tyranny of Slenderness*. New York: Harper and Row, 1982: 47.

12 Sacker, Ira M. and Mark A. Zimmer. *Dying to Be Thin: Understanding and Defeating Anorexia Nervosa and Bulimia – A Practical, Lifesaving Guide*. New York: Warner Books, 1987: 28.

13 Ibid.: 57.

14 Kant, Immanuel. *Observations on the Feeling of the Beautiful and the Sublime*. Trans. John T. Goldthwait. Berkeley: University of California Press, 1960: 51.

15 Sacker and Zimmer, *Dying to Be Thin*, pp. 44–5.

16 Bordo, *Unbearable Weight*, p. 60.

17 Sacker and Zimmer, *Dying to Be Thin*, p. 54.

18 Kant, *Observations*, pp. 93–4.

19 Kant, *Critique of Judgment*, p. 262.

First Course

Taste & Food Criticism

De gustibus non disputandum est. (There is no disputing about tastes.)
Latin saying

5

Taste, Gastronomic Expertise, and Objectivity

Michael Shaffer

The pleasures of the table are for every man, of every land, and no matter of what place in history or society; that can be a part of all his other pleasures, and they last the longest, to console him when he has outlived the rest.

Jean-Anthelme Brillat-Savarin,
The Physiology of Taste, *1825*

The Riddle of Taste

There is a long historical tradition of gastronomy that dates back at least to early antiquity and in accordance with this fact it has often been thought that there are those among us with the special distinction of being *bona fide* gastronomes. Gastronomes are thought to possess some ability that others lack with respect to taste in much the same way that experts of all stripes possess special abilities. In virtue of this special ability we often appear to unhesitatingly accept that gastronomes are expert authorities when it comes to certain matters of taste. If, for example, an alleged gastronomic expert claims that morel mushrooms taste of loam or that Kumamoto oysters taste fruity, then if we take him or her to be a real expert we must apparently accept that such pronouncements are true, even when we are perceptually incapable of noticing such things ourselves.

However, as famously defended by David Hume, there is also a general and widely recognized understanding that matters of taste are wholly subjective. In "Of the Standard of Taste" Hume notoriously tells us that,

> a thousand different sentiments, excited by the same object, are all right: Because no sentiment represents what is really in the object, It only marks a certain conformity or relation between the object and the organs or faculties of the mind; and if that conformity did not really exist, the sentiment could never possibly have being. Beauty is no quality in things themselves; It exists merely in the mind which contemplates them; and each mind perceives a different beauty. One person may even perceive deformity, where another is sensible of beauty; and every individual ought to acquiesce in his own sentiment, without pretending to regulate those of others. To seek real beauty, or real deformity, is as fruitless an enquiry, as to pretend to ascertain the real sweet or real bitter. According to the disposition of the organs, the same object may be both sweet and bitter; and the proverb has justly determined it to be fruitless to dispute concerning tastes.[1]

According to this widely held view, disputes about taste can no more be settled objectively than can disputes about our judgments of beauty or personal preference. There simply is, according to the Humean view, no objective component in taste experience on the basis of which such a dispute could be settled. Given these two views it should be apparent that our attitudes about taste and gastronomic expertise are curious to say the least, if not simply inconsistent. It would appear that something has to give if we are to maintain a coherent stance on this matter.

In light of this situation one might be tempted to think that philosophers would have expended considerable intellectual effort in examination of the nature of the faculty of taste and its relation to expertise about taste, especially in its most basic manifestation – the literal sensory capacity of tasting. At least to date, however, the sense of taste has never enjoyed the spotlight in philosophical discussions. This includes general philosophical discussions of the nature of perception, specific discussion of perceptual objectivity in the theory of knowledge and even in the gastronomic corner of aesthetics. Historically, Jean-Anthelme Brillat-Savarin's *The Physiology of Taste* and Hume's "Of the Standard of Taste" are perhaps the only really significant exceptions to this rule. In retrospect Brillat-Savarin's work is particularly exceptional in that it treats taste at length and from the philosophical, aesthetic, and scientific perspectives, although not of course in light of our contemporary physiological understanding of perception. In any case, Carolyn Korsmeyer's *Making Sense of Taste* is similarly the only extended contemporary investigation into the philosophical nature of taste perception and so there is little or no intellectual tradition to draw on here to help resolve the incoherence in our attitudes towards gastronomic experts and the nature of taste.

That taste has been so consistently ignored is an interesting historical and conceptual lacuna because taste is one of the most primitive and direct senses. As such, the philosophical analysis of taste is uncluttered by some of the complexities that have made, for example, discussion of vision exceptionally difficult. What will be addressed and discussed here are two issues that will hopefully help to resolve this matter. First, we will examine the conditions that must be satisfied in order for an attribution of a taste property to be regarded as objective given our modern scientific understanding of how taste perception works.[2] Addressing this issue will require introducing some of the details of our current understanding of the physiology of taste perception and some thorny issues in the philosophy of perception. Second, we will investigate the nature of gastronomic expertise given this scientific account of taste perception. The perhaps surprising conclusion that will be defended here is that, at least as things stand in our understanding of taste perception, there is very little reason to believe that gastronomic expertise is anything more than an ability to more eloquently describe fundamental taste experiences. So, in effect, there is nothing especially deep and more accurate about most of the pronouncements of gastronomical experts.

Direct and Reflective Tasting

Before proceeding any further into the complex and somewhat messy philosophical and physiological details, we must distinguish between the direct and the reflective senses of taste.[3] This distinction can be illustrated more clearly through the consideration of an example. In *The Cheese Companion* Judy Ridgway offers the following description of the taste of Ossau-Iraty-Brebis Pyrénées:

It has a distinctive, sour, wine-like aroma with a touch of the farmyard and a really tangy, spicy taste. Lemons and leaf mold remain in
the lingering flavor which is sweet, salty and mellow.[4]

The concept of a direct taste experience is then to be understood
as the experience of a taste property at the most basic level, where
it has yet to be interpreted in terms of our more elaborate system of
taste concepts.[5] So, if we examine Judy Ridgway's report concerning
the taste of Ossau-Iraty-Brebis Pyrénées we might note that she
reports that the cheese elicits certain objective taste experiences in us
and which are not described in terms of our more conceptualized or
metaphorical language. In this case we might see that sweetness, sourness, and saltiness are properties being ascribed to the cheese in this
way and they are ascribed in virtue of the nature of the cheese and
the nature of our sensory apparatus. But note that this is done independent of our more reflective interpretations of these qualities.

Reflective taste experiences are then direct taste experiences that
have been interpreted in terms of some concepts via processing
in the parts of the brain that allow for higher level cognitive functioning and thus allow for more sophisticated description. In our
example concerning Ossau-Iraty-Brebis Pyrénées, the attributions of
lemon and leaf mold flavors appear to be good examples of these
sorts of reflective taste attributions. They do not refer directly to basic
objective qualities that our sensory apparatus are tuned to detect and
they are far more metaphorical and descriptive. Presumably, then,
the concepts that we use to interpret perceptual inputs like taste
experiences are imposed on direct experiences at some higher level
of cognitive functioning, so that we can reflectively think about such
experiences in a richer manner that allows such experiences to be
integrated into out broader perspective on the world. This is crucial
because even casual familiarity with the pronouncements of gastronomic experts suggests that the bulk of gastronomic pronouncements
seem to concern reflective tasting. This may well be because it is
typically quite uninteresting to simply describe complex tastes in terms
of simple attributions of the basic qualities that our taste faculties
are tuned to detect: sweetness, sourness, saltiness, bitterness, and savoriness. So, it is the more florid and rich kinds of description of tastes
that appear to be the real meat and potatoes of supposed gastronomic
expertise.

The main thesis of this essay will be based on the observation that since there is little reason to believe that so-called gastronomic experts possess different physiological, non-cognitive, taste faculties, there are no good reasons to believe that such expertise involves non-reflective differences in tasting. To be sure, we are aware of physiological variations in the population that do account for variation in some types of direct taste experiences and we will look at a particular case of this sort a bit later, but there is no general reason to believe that there is such physical variation between gastronomic experts and non-experts or among various gastronomic experts. As a result, if there are disputes about taste properties in these cases, they can only really be disagreements about how the direct taste experience is to be conceptually interpreted or described and not about the objective experience itself. This has the interesting consequence that there are no good reasons to accept much of the testimony of such gastronomic experts as being true.

Disagreements About Properties in Tasting and the Science of Taste Perception

In considering gastronomic expertise as a special sensory acuity or ability a particular and difficult problem arises, especially where there is significant perceptual variation between individuals. The seemingly obvious suggestion is that in such cases appealing to intersubjective community agreement could circumvent these sorts of difficulties. We could simply say that when such disagreement occurs we should accept the judgment of the majority. Of course, this unfairly biases the issue in favor of such a majority and ignores the possibility that the common perceptions of the majority of perceivers are those that are inaccurate.

In any case, given a scientific take on the issue of taste and even passing familiarity with the science of gastronomy, we have good reason to believe that if we work to develop it we are capable of possessing a reliable, and rather ordinary, way of coming to know about how things really taste, even when those taste properties are complex and subtle. The substantive point is that if there were an adequate explanatory theory of the perceptual mechanism sensitive to such properties, then we could ignore the issue of depending on intersubjective agreement when dealing with appeals to special perceptual faculties. In the case of gastronomic expertise, this sort of explanation would have to account for the reliability of that faculty and thus for the acquisition of taste information. It would also have to permit us to distinguish the perception of "expert" perceptions from the perceptions of non-experts. In effect, we would not have to worry about, for example, how many people agree that Crottin de Chavignol (a famous French cheese from the Loire valley) tastes flinty or not if we could settle the matter by finding out whether or not those who say it is flinty actually possess some physiological ability to detect flinty tastes.

The Strange Case of the Phenol Tasters and the Physiology of Tasting

In order to illustrate this important line of thought consider the analogous case of taste sensitivity with respect to the substance phenol and other related substances. The general population happens, as a matter of fact, to be partitioned into two groups with regard to tasting phenol. One group, the minority, reports that phenol tastes bitter. The other group, the majority, reports that it is tasteless. The natural question to ask is then whether or not phenol is really bitter. Can we simply assume in this case that the majority is correct, and that phenol is not bitter? Surely we cannot respond in this naïve manner. We do not, and should not, automatically impugn the claims of those who appear to be sensitive to phenol simply because the majority of us are not sensitive to this apparent property. Problems can and often do arise, however, both when we try to account for such differences in perceptual abilities and when we attempt to ascertain the significance of such perceptual states. Most crucially, it is remarkably difficult in such circumstances to determine whether phenol really is bitter or not. But before we address this crucial issue we first need to look carefully at what science tells us about the faculty of taste.

According to our best physiological theories of taste we, and other mammals, can experience five basic tastes or taste qualities. These taste qualities are sweetness, saltiness, sourness, bitterness, and umami, or savoriness. The ability to experience these tastes is due to the presence of receptors on the tongue and in the mouth and throat, where they can then interact with substances we ingest. Tasting occurs because we have such taste receptor cells that are found on a certain kind of epithelial cell in the mouth. These specialized cells act like neurons and exhibit many of the functions that neural cells exhibit. Taste buds are collections of these taste cells and are located on papillae found in various parts of the mouth, throat, and tongue. Taste buds themselves come in three varieties: fungiform, foliate, and circumvallate, depending on their shape. Nerves then connect the receptors to the brain. In the case of the tongue, the chordia tympani carries messages from the outer third of the tongue. The glossopharyngeal nerve carries messages from the outer third of the tongue and a nerve in the superficial petrosal branch carries messages from receptors located in the larynx and epiglottis. These nerve fibers actually respond to more than one taste, but each one responds most strongly to just one direct taste quality. So what are known, for example, as "sourbest" nerve fibers are those that respond most strongly to sourness.

The nucleus of the solitary tract, the parabranchial nucleus, and the thalamic gustatory areas are where these signals are processed in the lower brain and presumably are where reflective tasting begins to occur. However, there are in fact two current paradigms concerning how taste information is processed in the brain. The labeled-line theory suggests that signals from taste receptor cells are carried to the brain without being modified, so the signal is directly recognized as being of one of the particular taste qualities. The pattern hypothesis, on the other hand, suggests that the brain also takes into account the particular details of the pattern of neural firing. Whichever happens to be correct, it is clear that tasting is localized both on the tongue, etc. and in the brain. Moreover, whichever theory is correct it is clear both that tasting capacities vary significantly from person to person and that prior experiences and beliefs influence taste perception. The point concerning variation in taste sensitivity is especially important here. People differ both in terms of the number of receptors that they have and in terms of the sensitivity of taste receptors. To a great extent this is explained as being the result both of broadly environmental factors like smoking, age, etc. and of genetic factors.[6]

So in the phenol example we might reasonably believe that phenol is bitter because phenol activates bitter receptors and that there is some physiological difference in the sensory apparatus of the phenol tasters and the phenol non-tasters. As it turns out, despite the fact that the majority may not possess the ability to detect such properties, there are many cases of minorities that possess special sensory acuities that we take to be accurate precisely because we have detailed understanding of the physiological basis of those special sensitivities. So, while it may or may not be the case that the individuals in the different groups actually have different perceptions because they have different sensory abilities, one lesson is clear: the size of the group claiming to have a particular taste experience tells us nothing about which group is having sensations that are objectively correct.

The real worries that might arise in the case of the phenol tasters are twofold. First, there may be no objective property being identified in this case. In other words, perhaps the bitter taste experience is just a subjective quirk of these peculiar tasters that does not correspond to any capacity of the substance to produce bitter taste experiences. Second, the taste experience that is reported by this group may not be the objective property of tasting bitter that is being detected by the phenol tasters. In other words, perhaps they are misidentifying some other taste property, saltiness or sweetness for example, as being bitter. So absent sufficient independent reasons to believe that the phenol tasters are really accurately detecting some objective feature of how phenol interacts with our sensory apparatus, it is surely possible that this is just the result of some subjective quirk in the phenol tasters' physiology, that they are merely detecting some pedestrian property of phenol and not its actual bitterness, or that they are merely interpreting the taste of those substances as being bitter even though they are not so.

In point of fact, in the case of phenol and some other compounds, 6-n-propylthiouracil, phenylthiocarbamide, etc., the difference in the ability to taste the bitterness of such chemicals is genetically determined.[7] So persons in one genetic group are tasters and those in the other are non-tasters due to a known genetic variation that affects our ability to detect bitter tastes. In fact, due to this genetic difference phenol tasters have larger numbers of papillae that hold our taste buds and determine taste sensitivity to bitterness in the manner described above. Interestingly, there is also a subgroup of tasters who are what are known as supertasters of these substances, those who report not only that they taste bitter but also that they are over-whelmingly bitter. Predictably, supertasters have the largest number of papillae.[8] As a result of our knowing how and why differences arise in the perceived taste of phenol, those of us who are non-tasters (whether we constitute a majority or not) and those of us who are tasters and supertasters are all justified in believing that the tasters and supertasters of these substances have objective experiences of those substances in question. The justification, however, is provided only in virtue of our possessing an adequate scientific explanation of the variation in perceptual apparatus between phenol tasters and phenol non-tasters that accounts for the special acuity attributed to tasters and supertasters.

Consequently, those who want to hold that gastronomic expertise is a reliable sensory capacity must, given our scientific theories of taste perception, specify some neuropsychological difference between such experts and non-experts. This difference must supply reason to believe that our perceptual organs are detectors of the kinds of properties involved in such alleged expertise, and be sufficient to distinguish such special perceptual states from ordinary perceptual states using those same detectors. Absent any differences of this sort, we would have no good reason to believe the claim that there is some objective taste and that it is being detected by those with such a special sensory acuity merely based on their testimony. The same point would arise even if the partition sizes were reversed. The lesson is that if we are to scientifically ground belief in the existence of objective properties of some type on the basis of this special sort of perception, there must be a fully adequate physiological account of the difference between those who perceive that property and those who do not. The reason why we must have such an account is that we must be able to distinguish such perceptual states. That this is required of us is especially important in cases where there is perceived to be significant variation in perceptual ability and, for example, where there is serious disagreement about the properties perceived. In the case of the kind of gastronomic experience attributed to gastronomic experts it seems reasonable to hold that these conditions are met, and so those who defend the objectivity and authority of gastronomic experience are obligated to provide an adequate account of the special sensory acuity that is the basis of that alleged expertise.

Skepticism and the Nature of
Disputes About Tastes

Let us look at the kinds of disagreements in taste property ascription that have been alluded to above, and let us consider a particular case in which we have disagreement about taste properties involving gastronomic experts. To begin, let us consider a typical review offered by a putative expert, in this case by again referring to *The Cheese Companion*. The book offers not only a stimulating history of cheese and some insight into some of the technical details of cheese making, but as we have seen it also includes some fairly detailed descriptions of the taste properties of various famous cheeses. For example, Judy Ridgway offers the following account of the taste of Langres, a cheese from the Champagne region of France:

> The rind is the typically bright orange color of washed rind cheese and this gives it its pungent farmyard-like aroma.
>   The paste is very creamy with a pretty pale yellow color and a sweet aroma of lemons and a touch of bacon. The flavor is strong but creamy. There is a definite suggestion of old socks but this balanced by a lovely lemony tang.[9]

What are we to make of such descriptions? Notice first that there is no reference to direct taste qualities here and that the taste property ascriptions being made are of the reflective sort.

Clearly, a number of very specific taste properties are being attributed to this particular cheese, specifically lemon and old sock flavors, as well as some other properties that are not clearly taste properties: bacon and farmyard odors and creaminess. Presumably the author believes that Langres has these taste properties, and this is suggested insofar as nowhere does the author contend that these are merely personal, subjective, reactions to Langres. Her claims are presented as *bona fide* claims about the taste of Langres. Suppose however that a different (purely hypothetical) expert, Skip Tickle, disputed Ridgway's particular property ascriptions to Langres and gave the following alternative account of the experience:

> The rind is the typically bright orange color of washed rind cheese and this gives it its pungent farmyard-like aroma.

> The paste is very creamy with a pretty pale yellow color and a sweet aroma of oats and a touch of crayon. The flavor is strong but creamy. There is a definite suggestion of bicycle tire but this is balanced by a lovely monkey flavor.

Moreover, suppose that there is no significant difference in the expert reputation possessed by Judy and Skip, that neither of them is physiologically unusual in any respect and that we cannot directly taste the cheese ourselves at this time.

In this hypothetical case we are faced with two equally good appeals to expert authority and so the issue of what to believe in such a case cannot be settled by appeal to differences in reputation, but neither can it be settled by appeal to the general population, or, in this case, by appeal to direct tasting. The only thing that would reasonably suffice to settle the dispute would thus be to establish that there is some physiological difference between Judy's and Skip's reliability, as in the case of phenol tasting. However, this does not seem to be plausible, as Judy and Skip might well still differ on the taste ascriptions even though there is no relevant physiological difference between them. Moreover, presumably Judy Ridgway is really not physiologically different than you or I in terms of her taste apparatus, or at least we have no good reason to suppose that she is unusual in this respect.

In effect what we are really then left with are two competing explanations of such disagreements. The first explanation regards the two competing accounts of the taste of Langres as objective and posits some unknown physiological difference between Skip and Judy that would account for their differing property ascriptions. Provided they are not both deceived, one of them is then correct. The second explanation is simply that such taste ascriptions are not direct, but rather are reflective, and that this accounts for their differing descriptions of the taste of Langres. They simply use different concepts or terms to describe one and the same taste experience and so the reports are subjective in nature. However, they are then both right.

When we then turn our attention to answering the obvious question about which of these explanations is better, certain difficult problems arise. If, on the one hand, we opt for accepting the first "explanation" as best, then we are saddled with making sense of an explanation that appears to be utterly *ad hoc*, at least as things stand. Without data that verify relevant physiological differences between Judy and Skip, this simply is not an explanation at all. It would be no more than a possible account of why there *might* be a difference in the taste descriptions. Also, there do not appear to be any good reasons to believe in general that there really are significant physiological differences between various experts. *Ipso facto* this approach cannot then be the best explanation of the situation, and so we have no rational reason to accept either Judy's or Skip's descriptions as correct. If, on the other hand, we accept the second explanation as best, then we must concede that the experts are not reporting *bona fide* taste properties of the cheese in the direct sense. The best we could say is that what expertise they have consists in selecting certain concepts or terminology to apply to the direct experiences that they share in reflective taste. But this is to render their expertise totally impotent, as it provides for no connection between their reports and the objective taste properties of the cheese.

The problem is more radical still. Suppose that we subsequently find out that Skip is no expert at all, but that, nevertheless, Skip is still not significantly different from Judy in terms of the relevant physiological features. Notice that this changes almost nothing. There is still no reason to accept that Judy's description of the cheese is any more accurate in the direct sense than that of Skip unless we have some way to account physiologically for the "unknown" differences in the sensory abilities of Skip and Judy. In this case, given an explanation like the second one offered above, all we could say is that based on reputation Judy's reflective taste reports about the cheese are preferable. But in what way are they preferable? It certainly cannot be a compelling reason on any scientific theory of perception, and so the best one could say is that Judy's reflective descriptions are to be preferred because, in some non-rational sense, we like the concepts she selects to describe taste properties. That Judy has more past experience in applying concepts to describe tastes makes no rational difference, as it merely underwrites the claim that Judy is perhaps more eloquent than Skip. But on this reading it has nothing to do with Judy's being more reliable in identifying objective taste properties in the direct sense.

Conclusion: Taste Skepticism and Everyman's Gastronomic Authority

So the qualified conclusion established here is that if we accept our best scientific theory of taste perception and want to say that gastronomic expertise is genuine, then we must be able to specify the nature of that ability. However, disputes about taste ascriptions cannot be settled by appeal to numbers, and we do not have a theory of taste that meets the physiological conditions above as it applies to grounding typical cases of gastronomic testimony. As such, gastronomic expertise is not a sort of rational expertise because it involves nothing more than the perceived ability to apply concepts to direct tastes reflectively, and thus is essentially subjective in nature. Note however, that our current physiological understanding of taste perception indicates that there is some objective component to taste experience, so we need not concede that Hume is entirely right about the subjectivity of taste. Specifically, we have very good scientific reasons to believe that any properly functioning human can detect real, objective, tastes such as saltiness, sourness, bitterness, and so on. However, there are no good reasons to suppose that there are real differences in capacities when it comes to reflective taste, and such are the meat and potatoes of gastronomic expertise. So Brillat-Savarin, a paradigmatic gastronomic expert, was ironically correct in making his aphoristic claim that "[t]he pleasures of the table are for every man, of every land, and no matter of what place in history or society."[10] That such pleasures are truly for every man is simply a consequence of the fact that the alleged gastronomic experts do not generally possess any special sensory abilities absent in most any Tom, Dick, or Harry.

Notes

This essay is dedicated to John and Diane Shaffer. Thanks to both for the introduction to gastronomy. Also, the author would like to thank the St. John restaurant in London for an inspirational meal.

1   Hume, David. "On the Standard of Taste." *David Hume: Essays Moral, Political and Literary*. Ed. Eugene Miller. Indianapolis: Liberty Classics, 1985: 230.

2   It is important to note that I am not treating tastes here as properties in the objects tasted, but rather as capacities in those objects to cause effects in our sensory apparatus. So the main issue raised here should not be confused with the issue of whether tastes correspond to real properties of food objects. Rather, the main issue is that of the objectivity of those complex interactions between those food objects and our taste apparatus. To be sure, such experiences do carry information about the nature of foodstuffs and, for example, it has long been conjectured that the ability to taste bitter tastes is the result of the intertwined evolutionary need for animals to avoid ingesting alkaloids, many of which are poisonous, and for plants to avoid being eaten (see, for example, Levin, D. A., "Plant Phenolics," *American Naturalist* 105 (1971): 157–81; Whitaker, R. H. and R. G. Feeny, "Allelochemics: Chemical Interaction Between Species," *Science* 171 (1971): 757–70). In this general understanding of the nature of the objectivity of perceptual states I am in broad agreement with Harold Brown and other defenders of versions of the causal theory of perception. See Brown, Harold, *Observation and Objectivity*. New York: Oxford University Press, 1987.

3   See Jean-Anthelme Brillat-Savarin, *The Physiology of Taste*. Trans. M. F. K. Fisher. New York: Counterpoint, 1949: 40–1.

4   Ridgway, Judy and Sara Hill, *The Cheese Companion*, 2nd edn. Philadelphia: Running Press, 2004: 126.

5   For discussion of perceptual modularity, see Fodor, Jerry, *A Theory of Content and Other Essays*. Cambridge, MA: MIT Press, 1990; Fodor, Jerry, *The Modularity of Mind*. Cambridge, MA: MIT Press, 1983; Fodor, Jerry, "Observation Reconsidered," *Philosophy of Science* 51 (1984): 23–43; and Churchland, P. M., *A Neurocomputational Perspective*. Cambridge, MA: MIT Press, 1989.

6   The account of the physiology of taste perception offered throughout this essay is based on Reed, D. R., T. Tanaka, and A. H. McDaniel, "Diverse Tastes: Genetics of Sweet and Bitter Perception," *Physiology and Behavior* 88 (2006): 215–26; Bartoshuk, L. M., "Comparing Sensory Experiences Across Individuals: Recent Psychophysical Advances Illuminate Genetic Variation in Taste Perception," *Chemical Senses* 25 (2000): 447–60; Duffy, V. B. and L. M. Bartoshuk, "Food Acceptance and Genetic Variation in Taste," *Journal of the American Dietetic Association* 100 (2000): 647–55; Mojet, J., E. Christ-Hazelhof, and J. Heidema, "Taste Perception with Age: Pleasantness

and Its Relationships with Threshold Sensitivity and Supra-threshold Intensity of Five Taste Qualities," *Food Quality and Preference* 16 (): 413–23.

7 See Bartoshuk, "Comparing Sensory Experiences"; Bartoshuk, L. M., V. B. Duffy, D. Reed, and A. Williams, "Supertasting, Earaches and Head Injury: Genetics and Pathology Alter Our Taste Worlds," *Neuroscience and Behavioral Reviews* 20 (1996): 79–87; and Duffy and Bartoshuk, "Food Acceptance and Genetic Variation in Taste."

8 Duffy and Bartoshuk, "Food Acceptance and Genetic Variation in Taste." Interestingly, Brillat-Savarin noted that differences in taste sensitivity correlated with differences in density of papillae: see *The Physiology of Taste*, pp. 35–7.

9 Ridgway and Hill, *The Cheese Companion*, p. 113.

10 Brillat-Savarin, *The Physiology of Taste*, p. 3.

6

Who Needs a Critic?
The Standard of Taste and
the Power of Branding

Jeremy Iggers

Burger King and the Branded Life

In an article that appeared a few years ago in *The Nation*, Lehigh University professor David Hawkes describes visiting his campus cafeteria. During this visit, he discovered that what had been a "well-loved food counter offering homemade fare" had been replaced by a Burger King. "Questioned about this innovation, the head of 'food services' insisted that it had been implemented in response to consumer demand. An exhaustive series of polls, surveys and questionnaires had revealed, apparently, that students and faculty were strongly in favor of a more 'branded feel' to their dining environment."[1]

Hawkes goes on to explore the significance of this "quantified approach to human nature,"[2] but I am interested in a different set of questions: Why would anyone prefer to dine in a branded environment? What does the Burger King brand add to the Burger King burger? And does the consumer of a Burger King burger have a different aesthetic experience when he bites into a Whopper than I have when I eat an unbranded burger?

I have a philosophical interest in this question, but I also have a personal and professional interest. I make my living as a restaurant critic for a major metropolitan newspaper (the *Star Tribune* of Minneapolis-St. Paul), and I am discovering that over the years, more and more of my readers prefer to dine in branded environments. Actually, increasing numbers of them not only choose to dine in branded environments, but they also choose to live in branded communities, shop in branded environments, wear brand-labeled clothing, and in short, live a branded way of life.[3]

Branded restaurants seem to be the wave of the future. Increasingly, food services in public schools are being operated by fast food chains. Most population and restaurant growth – at least in the Minneapolis-St. Paul metropolitan area where I live and work – is in the outer tier of new suburbs; in those suburbs, and especially in suburban malls, new restaurants are almost exclusively branded restaurants, whether franchised or corporate-owned. Independents, which lack the resources to sign mall leases, are a vanishing breed. And it is not only the restaurants that carry brand labels; rather, they are part of a suburban culture in which nearly every element of the environment carries a logo – from Blockbuster Video store to the Whole Foods natural foods market to the Crate and Barrel store.

In recent years, I have occasionally invited readers of my restaurant reviews to call in with feedback on restaurants that I am about to critique. As space permits, I then include their comments at the bottom of my review. What I have found is that the restaurants that generate the most reader feedback, by far, are brand-name restaurants such as the Hard Rock Café, Planet Hollywood, and the Rainforest Café. And what I have further found is that readers' responses to these restaurants are overwhelmingly positive, whereas my own reviews of these restaurants are usually quite negative.

For the most part, I find that these restaurants serve generic food, high in salt and fat, low in other flavors, from menus that are virtually interchangeable: nearly every casual dining chain restaurant, regardless of its nominal theme or ethnicity, will offer some variant on deep-fried calamari, Caesar salad (with or without sliced char-grilled chicken strips), fettuccine Alfredo (again, with or without sliced char-grilled chicken strips), and sirloin steak.

When I recite these shortcomings in my reviews, some readers get angry. One not-infrequent response is that I have a prejudice against chain restaurants. I have defended myself against this accusation by noting that prejudice implies prejudgment, and that my judgments are based on actual experience. But that does not satisfy my angry readers. They have had wonderful experiences in these restaurants, and my negative reviews belie the reality of their experience.

There is a noteworthy pattern over time in the way that readers have responded to my reviews. When I first began my career as a restaurant critic, I had few qualifications for the job, and yet my authority as a critic was established as soon as my byline appeared in the newspaper. The power attached to this position is, or at least was, considerable: soon after I started writing for a daily newspaper, I panned a restaurant that had been a popular local institution for decades. Business declined by half nearly overnight and, within six months, it was out of business.

In those early years, few dared challenge my authority as a critic. Readers were usually sufficiently cowed that even when they disagreed with me, they prefaced their remarks by some indicator of my superior epistemic authority, such as "well, I am no expert," or, "I don't know much about food." My status as an authorized knower was not grounded in much real expertise on my part, but was accorded in virtue of my role at the newspaper, as an extension of its own recognized status as a source of truth.

Over time, my credentials as an expert have grown considerably: more than 30 years of experience as a food critic, a stint as principal food writer for a major metropolitan daily (the *Detroit Free Press*), extensive experience living and traveling overseas, numerous cooking classes, and so on. But in that same span, my authority as a critic has actually diminished. In recent years, I have encountered more and more resistance, from readers who find my credentials completely unimpressive, and whose parting shot is, well, anyway, "it's just your opinion." No, I want to shout at them – although it is usually too late – it is *not* just my opinion. Rather, I am right and you are wrong.

I suppose that, on a philosophical level, I could learn to accept the idea that taste is purely subjective, but I also have practical and professional reasons for wanting to cling to the idea that there is a truth to the matter and, furthermore, that I possess it. If it really all is just a matter of taste, how do I justify my claims to epistemic authority? And more importantly, how do I justify my extravagant salary and my expense account?

One answer might be to say that although taste is an entirely subjective matter, my tastes happen to be a good predictor for what the public is likely to enjoy. I think that assertion could plausibly be made without committing ourselves to any extravagant truth claims. The only problem here is that the claim does not seem to be true. What

I have discovered, and with increasing frequency in recent years, is that my aesthetic judgments are not very useful to a significant segment of my readership in helping them to determine whether they are going to enjoy a particular restaurant. As I said above, for example, the branded restaurants that I frequently deride seem to enjoy tremendous popular appeal.

Of course, I should note that disagreement does not completely limit my usefulness to my readers. Very early on in my career, I received a friendly note from an elderly reader who informed me that she found my reviews of Chinese restaurants especially helpful. She knew that if I praised them for the crispness of their vegetables or the spiciness of their Szechwan dishes, then she would find them unpalatable. On the other hand, if I criticized them for mushy overcooked vegetables, then that she would find them precisely to her liking. I suppose that my readers who are fans of the Olive Garden and the Rainforest Café could learn to make similar accommodations. Readers can learn to predict the divergences, but wouldn't it be a lot simpler to find a critic whose tastes are more closely aligned with their own?

Hume on the Standard of Taste

It is at times like this that a restaurant critic wants to turn to the consolations of philosophy, and this does raise philosophical questions that have been wrestled with by such philosophical greats as David Hume and Immanuel Kant, among others. What is the epistemological status of judgments of taste and beauty? Are they purely subjective? Is it true, as the Latin proverb insists, that *De Gustibus Non Disputandum Est* (i.e., "in matters of taste there can be no dispute")?

This is a view that David Hume takes up in his essay, "Of the Standard of Taste":

> There is a species of philosophy, which cuts off all hopes of success in such an attempt, and represents the impossibility of ever attaining any standard of taste. The difference, it is said, is very wide between judgment and sentiment. All sentiment is right; because sentiment has a reference to nothing beyond itself, and is always real, wherever a

man is conscious of it. But all determinations of the understanding are not right; because they have a reference to something beyond themselves, to wit, real matter of fact; and are not always conformable to that standard . . . Beauty is no quality in things themselves: It exists merely in the mind which contemplates them; and each mind perceives a different beauty.[4]

Fortunately for me, Hume rejects this view: this view, he argues, may have achieved the status of common sense, but if you bring a little more common sense to the subject, its falsity becomes obvious:

Whoever would assert an equality of genius and elegance between OGILBY and MILTON, or BUNYAN and ADDISON, would be thought to defend no less an extravagance, than if he had maintained a mole-hill to be as high as TENERIFFE, or a pond as extensive as the ocean.

Hume acknowledges that such persons may exist, but nobody takes such absurd opinions seriously: their sentiments are "absurd and ridiculous".[5]

Ultimately, he winds up trying to have it both ways:

Though it be certain, that beauty and deformity, more than sweet and bitter, are not qualities in objects, but belong entirely to the sentiment, internal or external; it must be allowed, that there are certain qualities in objects, which are fitted by nature to produce those particular feelings.[6]

So, Hume is saying, not all taste is equal: the fact that some writers are better than others is self-evident, at least to people of refined taste. Presumably, the same applies, *mutatis mutandis*, to restaurants and renditions of *osso bucco*.

One way of justifying my status as an authority is to suggest that there is a natural aristocracy of taste. This line would hold, for example, that I happen to have been born with an exceptional aesthetic talent (i.e., my palate), just as some people are born with a great natural physical beauty and others with an exceptional musical or artistic talent. Instead of those virtues, I simply have good taste. This is, in essence, the Humean view:

Where the organs are so fine, as to allow nothing to escape them; and at the same time so exact as to perceive every ingredient in the composition: This we call delicacy of taste, whether we employ these terms in the literal or metaphorical sense.[7]

But Hume allows that, although some of us may be born with a greater talent for discernment than others, practice can refine our sensibilities. As we gain experience, our ability to discriminate becomes more subtle, and our appreciation of beauty becomes more refined. And, though the principles of taste may be universal, the number of people who have really developed their critical sensibilities is small.

So I need not worry about the fact that the majority of my readers do not share my tastes:

Under some or other of these imperfections, the generality of men labour; and hence a true judge in the finer arts is observed, even during the most polished ages, to be so rare a character; Strong sense, united to delicate sentiment, improved by practice, perfected by comparison, and cleared of all prejudice, can alone entitle critics to this valuable character; and the joint verdict of such, wherever they are to be found, is the true standard of taste and beauty.[8]

Hume says, in essence, that there is an objective basis for judgments of taste, and that although it may sometimes be difficult to discern good from great, over time, history will confirm our judgments:

The same HOMER, who pleased at ATHENS and ROME two thousand years ago, is still admired at PARIS and at LONDON. All the changes of climate, government, religion, and language, have not been able to obscure his glory. Authority or prejudice may give a temporary vogue to a bad poet or orator, but his reputation will never be durable or general. . . . On the contrary, a real genius, the longer his works endure, and the more wide they are spread, the more sincere is the admiration which he meets with.[9]

Good taste, in short, is timeless, and accessible to anyone who makes the effort to refine their sensibilities and to cultivate their taste. In the short run, we may be caught up in the fads of the moment, but time will, eventually, separate the wheat from the chaff.

Taste, Class, and Charlie the Tuna

Or so Hume would hope. Alas, history does not vindicate his stance. In fact, with very few exceptions, the changes of climate, government, religion, and language do succeed in obscuring the glory of nearly every writer. Great art has a much shorter shelf life than it had in Hume's day. Whether it is fiction, drama, painting, or sculpture, we come to regard these pieces as period pieces, and to feel that they do not speak to our contemporary condition.

This is not to say that there are not some intrinsic qualities that works of art must have in order to achieve enduring acclaim, but only that those are merely necessary and not sufficient conditions. It may be indisputable that there are qualities to the writing of John Milton and Joseph Addison that John Bunyan or John Grisham lack, but it is not sufficient to simply read their works in order to gain that appreciation. Rather, though our effort may be rewarded, we need a great deal of cultural resources to be able to make head or tail of Addison or Milton. You can stare at Pablo Picasso's *Guernica* or ponder James Joyce's *Ulysses* as long as you like; to appreciate their merits as works of art you need a good deal more than to see the intrinsic properties of the object. Rather, as Pierre Bourdieu has argued, you need certain cultural resources to make sense of them.[10]

I want to suggest that this is the case for gastronomic "good taste" as it is for every other variety of refined aesthetic sensibility: it is the taste of a particular class of people, who have acquired a set of cultural resources. What we call good taste is just the taste of a dominant social class, just as what we call good English is just the dialect of a dominant class. Given the cultural status of this class, it happens that the way this class of people did speak became codified and enshrined as the way everyone who speaks English should speak.

This may be the proper moment to introduce the distinction commonly attributed to the Star-Kist company, between good taste and what tastes good. Charlie the Tuna, as you will recall, was repeatedly rebuffed in his efforts to qualify for elevation to canned status, because he confused having good taste with tasting good. At one point, documented in a Star-Kist commercial, Charlie actually hires a professor of aesthetics to teach him the finer points of self-presentation, but he still fails. Their conversation ran as follows:

Charlie: I need a little tune up in the culture and good taste department.
Professor: Oh, you mean a refresher course in aesthetics?
Charlie: Just belt me with enough good taste to get to Star-Kist.
Professor: But Star-Kist doesn't want tunas with good taste. They want
  tunas that taste good.

The Star-Kist distinction makes for a smart advertising campaign because it acknowledges one of the weaknesses of the product – the low prestige or social cachet of canned tuna – and says, in effect, so what?! Tuna may not have the status of caviar, but it tastes good, and that is what really matters. Star-Kist cleverly plays on a distinction between tasting good and good taste, which is clearly identified as class-based. It gives its prospective customers permission to resist the dictates of the arbiters of good taste.

So am I merely a class enforcer? In the words of Christopher Lasch, "the acquisition of an aesthetic outlook not only advertises upper-class prestige but helps to keep the lower orders in line. In other words, the aesthetic worldview serves as an instrument of domination. It serves the interests not merely of status but of power."[11]

In theory, the world of good taste is open to all, but in practice, how available it is to you is a function of your economic and social resources. Cultivating a taste for fine wines is one of the ways of signaling your membership in an elite class, but it is a costly enterprise, especially since the rules keep changing. Just when you have learned to abandon Chablis or Liebfraumilch for chardonnay, chardonnay is passé. Now it is sauvignon blanc. Or is it albariño or grüener veltliner?

For readers who have the requisite economic or social capital, the newspaper can in fact serve as a manual of instruction for social mobility. Sometimes, it can even serve as a currency exchange, telling you how you can convert one form of currency (e.g., a healthy bank account) into another form (e.g., the social cachet that attaches to a well-stocked wine cellar). What is important to recognize here is that aesthetic judgment is not neutral or innocent: to appreciate the beauty of a Picasso or the pleasure of *uni* (i.e., sea urchin roe), you need a certain kind of preparation whose acquisition is a matter of class.

But can we acknowledge that differences in taste have a class component, and still maintain that judgments of taste have some validity (i.e., that X really *is* better than Y)? Yes, but only within a particular "regime of truth" which shares certain values and premises, and ways of structuring its experience. The neophyte who learns the vocabulary of wine tasting really will discover a level of subtlety to a first-growth Bordeaux that is lacking in white zinfandel.

It is a mistake to speak of the discourse of gastronomy as if it were a single hegemonic discourse. It has always been a fragmented and stratified conversation. But for a considerable period of time, there was a core of middlebrow taste that expressed the aspirations of the middle-class consumer. The newspaper, and its restaurant critic, have played a central role in shaping that taste. If I said that the pungent flavor of wasabi offers an inspired counterpoint to the sweetness of the peekytoe crab appetizer at Chambers Kitchen, or that Peninsula's Malaysian beef *rendang* has a level of spiciness that is challenging but not excessive, the fact that "Iggers said" is duly noted at dinner parties, and becomes part of the diner's experience when she visits the restaurant. But the circulation of this discourse is literally declining as newspaper readership declines.

What we are witnessing, in slow motion, is the collapse of a regime of truth for which the daily newspaper served as a central instrument, and the ascendancy of a rival discourse, in which advertising, brand, and image are central. The newspaper critic has never held full hegemony over the territory of restaurant judgment, and critics like myself have always owed fealty to the standards of national arbiters. Though there has never been a single pope of good taste, the analogy to a church is inviting, and it is not difficult to identify, on the national level, a college of cardinals.

But the dominion of the church of good taste is under siege. The number of faithful in our pews is declining dramatically, and many of the congregants are becoming increasingly outspoken in their challenges to our authority. Underground churches are emerging, at websites such as Chowbaby, where participants reinforce each other's sense that their sensibilities are more sophisticated and/or adventurous than the middlebrow tastes of the newspaper critics and their audience. The publishing empire of Zagat, which invites all of its readers to rate food, service, and atmosphere on numerical scales, and then publishes their scores, undermines the very premises of the taste hierarchy by treating all of its reviewers as "authorized knowers."

But these are, at worst, schisms within a church, whose faithful embrace many of the same fundamental doctrines and beliefs as the hierarchy. It is very unlikely that any contributor to Chowbaby or Zagat would ever write enthusiastically about a branded restaurant, unless, perhaps, that brand imports the status conferred by the traditional hierarchy – for example, a Wolfgang Puck-branded restaurant in an appropriately upscale venue, such as an art museum. The rupture with the audience that would prefer to dine in a branded environment is much more profound.

Living the Branded Life

So far, we have explained the divergence of tastes between myself and my readers in terms of a code – that I have, by virtue of my class background and training, acquired the code needed to appreciate certain foods, while my readers lack it. But what if the opposite is also true: what if the lovers of the Olive Garden and the Rainforest Café possess a code that I lack?

The answer lies in the brand, and what the brand brings to the consumer of the product. As the anonymous author of *A Short Introduction to Branding* explains:

> While Brand X cola or even Pepsi-Cola may win blind taste tests over Coca Cola, the fact is that more people buy Coke than any other cola and, most importantly, they enjoy the experience of buying and drinking Coca Cola. The fond memories of childhood and refreshment that people have when they drink Coke is often more important than a little bit better cola taste. It is this emotional relationship with brands that make them so powerful.[12]

For the consumer who lives the branded life, the individual brands have come together to create a system of signs, a universe of meanings. The cumulative message of the advertising/entertainment nexus on television is that there is a life that is more dramatic, more exciting – ultimately, more real – than your own life. The people who live this life laugh more, have better teeth and better sex, and your window into this life is interrupted every ten minutes or so with a message telling you how you can cross over from this world to the next. The key is the product, the brand. Consuming the product is the sacrament.

Branded restaurants add two dimensions to the dining experience that are missing from Hawkes' beloved one-of-a-kind lunch counter: a story and an image. Both are conveyed primarily through advertising, on television, in newspapers and magazines, and in the restaurant itself. And both become part of our experience of consuming the product. We enter the restaurant primed by the stories and the images to expect a certain kind of experience, and the story and image become part of that experience. If the erotic is defined as that which creates an intensified feeling of being alive – which is certainly what many brands strive to do – then the images can often be classified as gastroporn.

Gastroporn

By gastroporn, I have in mind the mouthwatering images that can be seen in television commercials, in print advertising, and in the pages of food magazines and coffee-table cookbooks. The term can also apply to text, but in gastroporn – as in traditional pornography – our primary focus is on the image. To refer to these images as pornographic is to suggest a similarity to sexual imagery, and to suggest that there is something perverse or deviant about such images and the way they are used.

The historical context of the emergence of gastroporn includes the rise of the advertising industry, and the rise of the image itself. I would like to suggest that this rise of the image has transformed the role of pornography, in such a way that whereas what was once erotic about the erotic image was its resemblance to the human body, today we gauge the body by its resemblance to the image. In sum, the relationship between sign and object is reversed: the sign is now more real than the object. And that is what is so attractive about dining in a branded environment: it feels more real. The message that consuming offers a bridge between this world and the world of the image, of the celebrity, is most explicit in restaurants like Planet Hollywood, where the fantasy is that if you do not run into Bruce

Willis or Arnold Schwarzenegger, you can at least sit at the same table where they once sat.

In 2005, Burger King spent nearly half a billion dollars on advertising its burgers, with the largest share going to television advertising. That is less than a third of the $1.66 billion spent by industry leader McDonald's.[13] Like my readers, I am also exposed to these signs and images, but because I almost never watch television, and live in an urban environment where brands are a much less prominent part of the landscape, my level of exposure to these images is much lower than many of my readers.

Branding makes food taste better. A number of studies have confirmed this claim, including a study which found that a popular peanut butter scored much higher when identified by brand than it did in a blind tasting, and a wine tasting in France where wine experts heaped scorn on supermarket wines and lavished praise on wines from prestigious wineries, until they learned that the contents of the bottles had been switched.

A classic study of 96 beer drinkers and 8 brands of beer published in 1964 found that in blind tastings, the beer drinkers could not tell the brands apart, and changed their evaluations of the beers once the brands were identified: "Brand B was considered a light-tasting beer until its brand name became known. Then it was classed as overwhelmingly heavy-tasting."[14]

The product, as one advertising executive recently observed, is merely an artifact around which consumers have experiences. There are then at least two ways whereby the manufacturer can alter the behavior of the consumer: by altering the product, or else by altering the consumer's perception of the product (i.e., its brand image). A company can enhance the perceived value of its t-shirts, or its hamburgers, by sewing spangles onto its t-shirts or upgrading the quality of its beef, or it can sew those spangles onto the brand by developing an advertisement campaign that creates positive associations in the mind of the consumer.

All things considered, it is much more cost-effective to produce the product as cheaply as possible and to spend money on the brand rather than on the product. Indeed, the most successful products are ones that are themselves utterly generic products: think of the sweet brown carbonated water that is Coca Cola, the round generic patty of ground beef that is a McDonald's or Burger King or Wendy's, or the cheap blend of paper tobacco and cellulose that is a Marlboro cigarette. After this reflection, think about all the trappings of brand image: the packaging, the advertising, the marketing promotions, and the product placements. It may even be that the fewer qualities that the actual product has, the more free the image is to impose its own fantasies.

The brand message is not so much about the product as it is about the consumer. Brands, taken in their totality, become a vocabulary through which the consumer can articulate an identity; it is a shared language. I know what it means when I order an Absolut martini with a twist, and so do you, at least in rough outline.

What I want to suggest is that not only our tastes but our identity are shaped by our culture, and that as our culture evolves so do both our tastes and our means of articulating our identity. Within a given regime of truth it is possible to establish standards of taste, because they are common to people with a shared way of life. But there come times when a radical rupture takes place in what people value and how they construct their sense of identity. In an important sense, the people who prefer branded food really do live in a different world.

Notes

1   Hawkes, David. "Artistic Economics." *The Nation*, January 21, 2002: 28; at www.thenation.com/doc/20020121/hawkes.
2   Ibid.: 28.
3   See, for example, Twitchell, James B., *Branded Nation*. New York: Simon and Schuster, 2004.
4   Hume, David. *Selected Essays*. Ed. Stephen Copley. Oxford: Oxford University Press, 1998: 136.
5   Ibid.: 137.
6   Ibid.: 141.
7   Ibid.: 141.
8   Ibid.: 147.
9   Ibid.: 139.
10 Bourdieu, Pierre. *Distinction, A Social Critique of the Standards of Taste*. Trans. Richard Nice. Cambridge, MA: Harvard University Press, 1984.
11 Lasch, Christopher. Review of Pierre Bourdieu's *Distinction*. *Vogue* November 1984: 279–80.

12 *A Short Introduction to Branding*, copyright 2003, from the website of BrandSolutions, Inc.; at www.brand.com/intro.htm.

13 "The Top 200 Megabrands." *Advertising Age* June 26, 2005; at www.adage.com/images/random/lna2006.pdf.

14 Allison, Ralph and Kenneth P. Uhl. "Influence of Beer Brand Identification on Taste Perception." *Journal of Marketing Research* August 1964: 36–9.

7

Hungry Engrams: Food and Non-Representational Memory

Fabio Parasecoli

The Neurologist and the Chef

"Let me introduce myself: I have been a neurologist and a neuro-physiologist for twenty years, and a chef for six." This is the matter-of-fact statement that opens *La Cocina de los Sentidos*, the first book by Miguel Sánchez Romera, chef and owner of the renowned restaurant L'Esguard in S. Andreu de Llavaneres on the coast of Catalonia, Spain.[1] Now in his fifties, Sánchez Romera has worked for many years in hospitals and scientific institutions, focusing particularly on epilepsy. He was always passionate about cooking and food, but the turning point in his career was his fortieth birthday dinner, when he cooked for fifty people together with his friend, the famous Catalan chef Ferran Adrià.[2] The dinner turned out to be such a success that the gatherings at the Sánchez Romeras became a tradition. It was only in 1996 that the neurologist decided to open a restaurant, namely, L'Esguard, receiving a good deal of attention throughout Europe, and recently, the world.

In his book, Sánchez Romera's diverse interests meet in the most intriguing and stimulating fashion on theories regarding the senses, the mind, and memory. Being both a successful chef and a respected scientist, he is in a privileged position to analyze the connections between cognition and recollection in the realm of food and flavors. His whole argument, which also influences his cooking style, hinges on the concept that memory and other mental functions, at least in the case of food, are closely connected with emotions, through the senses, the body and its most basic needs, hunger and thirst.

When we eat and drink, we find ourselves at the juncture between biological necessity, the world of drives and instincts, the inputs from the outside world, and the tremendous landslide of thoughts, feelings, and emotions resulting from uninterrupted brain activity. In a similar way Sánchez Romera, as a chef, is located at the crossroads between the material world of edible products and culinary arts as a creative experience that connects human physiology to culture. His work enhances the notion that food is at the frontier between the biological and the cultural. No other organ in the human being embodies the complexity of this frontier better than the brain itself, where electric and chemical signals become the texture of perception, memory, thought, creativity, and emotions. The fact that Sánchez Romera focuses on food and its appreciation – that is to say, pleasure – is particularly relevant since taste and smell have been the less studied senses, whose importance and impact on mental processes and especially on memory have been often neglected. This connection between food and memory appears to be almost a fixation for the Sánchez Romera family. The chef relates that his sister Carmen, a specialist in the science of education, is doing research to demonstrate the connection between smell, emotion, memory, and the learning process in primary school and preschool children. For instance, she mentions various smells (e.g., a chewed on and wet pencil, an eraser, some ink) as constitutive olfactory elements in a developmental phase that is paramount to learning. Carmen Sánchez Romera actually argues that certain smells evoke affective states that can draw near or reject children from learning in a school environment.[3] In *La Cocina de los Sentidos*, an unconventional cookbook where ingredients and quantities for the dishes are not given in the usual, detailed manner, Sánchez Romera delves into the most recent findings of neuroscience research about sensations, emotions, memory, and rational processes, which we will discuss later. While highlighting the connections between food and memory, he states:

Remembering is first of all a dynamic process, and not only a trunk of memories or a library of experiences lived once that can be later evoked according to the circumstances. It is something as lively and nimble as our own self, since . . . individuals create memories in connection to many personal necessities.[4]

In Sánchez Romera's work, food becomes a preferential access to an appreciation and an analysis of memory that clashes with traditional conceptions of memory as representation, which consider the senses and the mind as faculties that limit themselves to mirroring nature. According to these theories, their contents are constituted by more or less precise reflections from an external reality. On the other hand, for the Spanish chef, recollections are rather the result of ongoing interactions between the different properties of the brain and the stimuli deriving from the senses. In this context, memory is not fixed once and for all, ready to be accessed when needed, but rather a creative and dynamic faculty that allows human beings to relive the past each time in different ways.

Furthermore, memory depends heavily on the body, not only because most of the material on which the mind elaborates is derived from the senses, but also because the body and the emotions connected with it (e.g., pleasure, pain, fear) influence the way memories are stored and eventually retrieved. The necessary conclusion is that rational processes, hinging heavily on memories, cannot be totally isolated from what is traditionally considered irrational, physical, and instinctual. Many activities, such as eating, cooking, having sex, dancing, singing, and exercising, place themselves beyond the mind/body split that has informed much of Western thought. In certain quarters, these activities are still not considered theoretically relevant because they intrinsically erase the separation between inquirer and inquired, the subject and its object, and because they are not concerned with truth, with the eternal and the immutable, but rather with "the transitory, the perishable, the changeable."[5]

Cognitive Science and the Fallacies of Memory

The concept of non-representational memory, heavily indebted to the most recent research in neuroscience, is radically different from current theories embraced by cognitive sciences. These theories interpret memory as a storage device where pieces of knowledge, actions, and even emotions are kept in neat equivalents of computer bytes, ready to be retrieved and, if necessary, mechanically substituted by electronically originated elements. Mnemonic materials are considered discrete, composed of recognizable, circumscribed, interchangeable, reproducible components that can also be disposed of.

For these reasons, contemporary culture often references computers to create metaphors for our brain. Many important scientists seemed to share a similar take on mind and memory, developing a new branch of research (viz., cognitive psychology) during the second half of the twentieth century. As Ulrich Neisser stated in 1966, "the term cognition refers to all processes by which the sensory input is transformed, reduced, elaborated, stored, recovered, and used."[6] Cognitive psychologists are not primarily interested in analyzing the mind at the physiological or neural level, understanding its structure and function starting from the cellular level up. Rather, the goal is to assess the brain's unconscious processes in functional terms. One of the main tenets of these theories is that information works according to patterns and rules constituting a formal logic that is totally independent from the actual medium that carries it out.[7]

The medium can be indifferently a brain or a machine. As a matter of fact, terms that are widely used in information studies, such as 'code,' 'signal,' 'processing,' 'transformation,' 'module,' and 'processor,' are employed in fields connected with the human mind, such as neuroscience, semiotics, and psychology. To a certain extent, humans and computers can be theorized as different manifestations of the same phenomenon: they constitute thinking engines, based on systems organized in ways similar to computers, which function using signs.[8] Many neuroscientists have been opposing this approach. In his seminal work *The Emotional Brain*, Joseph LeDoux noted that it is not possible to separate the rational from the emotional elements. Furthermore, LeDoux argues, the hardware, the actual physical structure of the brain, is non-secondary in understanding the mind, especially when it comes to emotions.[9]

One of the most influential voices in this field is Gerald Edelman, who received a Nobel Prize for medicine in 1972. In his book *A Universe of Consciousness*, written with Giulio Tononi, he underlines the features of the brain that point to fundamental differences with computers. Since no two brains are identical, the overall pattern of connections in a brain can be defined in general terms, but the microscopic variability of these connections in different individuals are enormous because of their developmental history and their past experiences. For instance, when it comes to eating, although children of the same family are exposed to the same food and might be genetically similar, they all have their individual likes and dislikes, different tastes, sometimes even diverging memories concerning the same events. Synaptic connections change, die, are created every day, and vary in each individual, affecting the way things and events are remembered.[10]

Nevertheless, the inputs from the external world to the brain are not an unambiguous series of signals, as in the case of computers. The brain has developed functions aimed at filtering and organizing perceptions into categories; these categories are instrumental to our interaction with the world. Furthermore, our perceptions and the categories we use to give them order are not impartial and dispassionate. In fact, the brain has developed several mechanisms, called value systems, which evaluate all the incoming sensory inputs to assess their relevance, that is to say their importance for the brain and the body. As we will see below, these systems employ certain parts of the brain not involved in rational thinking, as well as substances (e.g., neurotransmitters, hormones, and peptides) which respond to emotional stimulation and travel all over our body through all kinds of fluids, including blood. All these elements influence the strength of synapses (i.e., the contact points between neurons) and have a great impact on learning, categorizing abilities, and adaptive behaviors. Because of these factors, the human memory differs from a computer's in that it is selective. Not every item is retained in the same way, or always retrieved in the same way.

Applying the computer model to food and food memories proves particularly misleading. The French scientist Hervé This, who specializes on the physics and chemistry related to food and cooking, claims that in the case of taste also, the brain forms its overall perceptions by synthesis of signals, or sensory stimuli, derived from different kinds of receptors on the tongue, in the nose, and at the ends of the nervous tissues in the mouth area. He also points out that there is no "taste central" in the brain.[11] Furthermore, biologists at the University of Miami proved that different kinds of receptors on the taste buds react to different kinds of "bitter" tastes, to describe tastes for which we don't have words yet.[12]

Taste and flavor cannot be analyzed in terms of discrete units; the traditional classification into a few basic flavors – whether four, five, or six of them – requires further scientific scrutiny. Taste cannot be determined by any kind of algorithm, no matter how complex it might be. No set of combinatory rules is able to create the infinite palette of food flavors just by mixing basic elements in different proportions. Furthermore, the interaction with emotional factors such as disgust and desire, and physical elements such as hunger, render the computer model unable to explain the complexity of the phenomenon. In other words, it does not consider faculties such as creativity, imagination, intuition, and, in the case of food and taste, the capacity for aesthetic or sensory evaluation and appreciation.[13]

Flavors and Memories

The theme of the connection between body and mind is also recurrent in numerous works of literature, often expressed through the power of food on memory. The most famous examples are probably Marcel Proust's omnipresent and unavoidable *madeleines*. After describing his sudden insight, he comments:

> It is the same for our past. We would exert ourselves to no result if we tried to evoke it, all the efforts of our intelligence are of no use. The past is hidden outside its realm and its range, in some material objects (in the sensation this object would give us) of which we do not suspect.[14]

And after experiencing a deep sense of joy after tasting a bite of tea-soaked *madeleine*, at first he tries to find the origin of that emotion in the cake itself, but then he realizes that the secret is hidden in his soul:

> It is deep uncertainty every time the spirit feels to be defeated by itself; when the searching spirit is at the same time the obscure land that has to be searched, where its luggage will have no use. Searching? Not

only: creating. The spirit faces something that does not exist yet and
that only the spirit itself can make real and then make it enter its light.[15]

Proust clearly affirms that remembering is not only searching, but
also creating. It is not only a question of retrieving pre-made pieces
of past connected to some present sensation or condition, but of
recreating the memory every time.

The same elements emerge in *Absalom, Absalom!*, a novel where
William Faulkner deals with the power of memory. The whole nar-
ration is an unnerving and seemingly endless recovery of fragments
from a past that needs interpretation and collective emotional work
to make sense, a past that is differently perceived by the different
fictional voices:

> That is the substance of remembering – sense, sight, smell: the
> muscles with what we see and hear and feel – not mind, not thought:
> there is no such thing as memory: the brain recalls just what the
> muscles grope for: no more, no less: and its resultant sum is usually
> incorrect and false and worthy only of the name of dream.[16]

These motifs reappear in different literary traditions all over the
world. They are particularly strong in the so-called "magic realism"
of authors like Gabriel García Marquez (I think in particular of *Love
in the Time of Cholera*) and, above all, Jorge Amado, who has dedicated to smell and taste novels like *Gabriela Cravo e Canela* and
Donha Flor e Sois Dois Maridos. Another example is the work of
Erri De Luca, an Italian author who started writing while in jail for
his connections with a terrorist organization. His books are often
collections of memories where the senses play an important role, like
in the following passage, taken from his novel *Montedidio*:

> From the darkness in the laundry rooms here comes Maria. At thir-
> teen just like me, she looks more of a grown up than I do. She already
> lives inside a mature body. Three inches under her black short hair,
> there is her mouth, quick with words, I see them coming out of the
> side of her thick lips. A smile cuts her face from ear to ear. Maria
> knows the gestures of women. I stay in front of her and I feel my empty
> guts, a hunger for bread, to take a bite out of the same slice of bread
> with butter. She offers it to me, I say no. She has found out that I am
> practicing with a boomerang, she is curious. She hears me going upstairs,

passing by her door. She gets closer, the evening is warm and carries its odors, chocolate, oregano, cinnamon, I sniff it with my nose, it's French cologne, she says, rolling the r sound in her throat.[17]

These authors use taste and smell to evoke memories that get to be actually relived sensually. Nourishment is a fundamental part of our experience; during infancy it constitutes our first relationship to reality. The mother's breast, or any ersatz food giver, becomes the first object of the infant's desire and knowledge. But also from the neural point of view, the connection between memory and food is very strong, as Sánchez Romera emphasizes in his work. Nevertheless, he wonders whether a dish can be pleasurable in itself or if it simply acquires the connotations of the environment that surrounds it when it is consumed: good company, warmth, emotions, the landscape, a specific time in our life, and so on. He writes:

Could a food, by itself and thanks to its organoleptic proprieties (specific flavor and smell), produce pleasure when eaten? Otherwise said: can a food make our brain undergo a pleasurable experience that creates a pleasurable register? And can this register be stored as a specific memory of this flavor or smell?[18]

Hungry Engrams

An answer to these questions can be found in recent research in neuroscience. One of the most respected experts in the study of memory, Daniel Schacter, points to the German scientist Richard Semon as the initiator of a new approach in research on memory. In his monograph *Die Mneme*, published in 1904, where he tried to demonstrate that memory can be preserved through generations by heredity, Semon introduced the concept of an 'engram': the longlasting change in the nervous system that encodes information into memory and that lies dormant until something brings it back to consciousness. Semon argued that the quality of a memory depends both on the engram and the cue that triggers the memory, which he called ecphoric stimulus. Memory thus loses its immutability to become variable and changeable. A few decades later the neuroscientist Karl

Lashley, with his 1950 article entitled *In Search of the Engram*, brought attention to Semon's theory, although he was not able to demonstrate its validity.

The physiological base would be provided later by the Canadian psychologist Donald Hebb, who succeeded in proving that neurons that fire together "wire" together, that is to say that repeated neural activity involving two or more neurons strengthens the connections among them.[19] This phenomenon, known as Hebbian plasticity, determines the structure of memory of each individual, the particular pattern of interconnectivity between neurons: learning is a specific capacity of synapses, the connections between axons (the output channels of neurons) and dendrites (the input channels). Events are recorded by the enhancement of the connections between the neurons that participate in encoding the experience.[20] The human genome determines, more or less precisely, only the structure of the most primitive parts of the brain, in charge of the regulation of basic and innate life processes. Most of the cortical neural connections that are responsible for the mind's higher-order capacities are laid out in a general way, while specific neural connections depend on each individual's history and experiences. Within this framework, the old dichotomy nature/nurture no longer makes much sense, since both nature, the physical layout of the brain, and experience, including education and culture, cooperate to determine the personal and individual synaptic connectivity that makes each individual different.[21]

Not only the strength of the connection between neurons, but also its quality plays an important role in memory. According to the principle of "encoding specificity" developed by Endel Tulving, an event is more likely to be remembered if the retrieval conditions and circumstances, including perceptions, thoughts, and emotions, match the subjective qualities at the moment of its encoding in the brain, or engram. This theory gives another blow to the concept of memory as formed of discrete pieces of information that can be stored without any change and recalled at will, just like we do when we open a file in a computer. What reinforces the connections between neurons in the encoding of an engram or a dispositional representation, and what triggers the subjective states that facilitate access to it? It is at this crucial hinge that the realm of pure thought is invaded by emotions, fear, pleasure, and motivations.

To understand the dynamics that influence the formation and enhancement of neural connections and, as a consequence, the functioning of memory, it is necessary to clarify some basic but paramount neuroscience notions about the structure and modus operandi of the brain.

Edelman and Tonioni propose explaining the brain's arrangement according to three dynamics, involving different anatomical organs. The dynamic that has traditionally drawn more attention is the one taking place in the thalamocortical system, constituted by a three-dimensional dense meshwork of reciprocal connectivity among circuits that are segregated and integrated at the same time. This system, as the definition suggests, involves the brain cortex (the outer layer of gray matter, approximately 2 millimeters thick, covering the entire surface of the cerebral hemispheres) and the thalamus (a collection of nuclei relaying sensory information to the cortex, to which it is closely connected). Their role in mnemonic activities is the closest the brain gets to the traditional concept of representational memory. In fact, each area is connected with a precise aspect of the incoming stimuli. For instance, a visual input is actually composed of various elements such as color, shape, movement, orientation, and so on, each of them elaborated in a specific zone of the cortex. Nevertheless, we cannot speak of a one-to-one correspondence: the same area can carry out various functions.[22]

What happens in the thalamocortical system only partly explains the origin of memories, providing rough material that needs further elaboration. An important role is played by a second system comprising loops formed by several synapses that are arranged in long, parallel, unidirectional paths. Following these loops, the inputs leave the cerebral cortex and go back to it after passing through the basal ganglia – including the putamen and caudate nucleus, the cerebellum, the amygdala, and the hippocampus – which is a particularly important organ in this context because it helps consolidate short-term memory into long-term memory within the cerebral cortex.[23] This second system could constitute the basis for innate elements such as instincts and certain involuntary reaction patterns. For instance, LeDoux demonstrated that external stimuli are relayed to the amygdala, which controls fear reactions, either through the cortex, where conscious memories are able to judge the actual urgency of the stimulus, or directly. In the latter case, the body reacts immediately with little or no interaction with the cortical areas, and the information concerning fears and their original stimuli are stored directly in the amygdala. The second system also operates, together with the thalamocortical system, to acquire new knowledge, which is achieved by continuous modification of neural connections, in the form of "engrams" or "dispositional representations."[24] In the case of food, as we will see, the most important organ in this second system is the hypothalamus.

We can already see how, with the intervention of the second system, emotions become fundamental components of the way we experience reality, and as a consequence of the way we remember it. This emotional aspect of the brain is further amplified by the operation of a third system, a "hairnet" of fibers, resembling a large fan, originating from small nuclei located in the brainstem and in the hypothalamus: the locus coeruleus, the raphé nucleus, the dopaminergic nuclei, the cholinergic nuclei, and the histaminergic nuclei. Each nucleus is formed by a relatively small number of neurons that fire every time something startling, unexpected, or important happens, such as a sudden pain, a violent crash, a bright flash of light, or intense pleasure. When they fire, special kinds of chemicals called neuromodulators, which influence the neural plasticity strengthening the synapses, are released in the brain.[25] These dynamics, reinforcing certain neural connections, have a relevant impact on Hebbian plasticity and hence on memory formation. For instance, engrams or dispositional representations that are created under stress, intense pleasure, or other strong emotional states have a tendency to survive longer. Furthermore, the third system seems to have an important impact on the motivational aspects of our brain activities, pushing the subject into action.

Cognition (representation in the classic sense), emotions, and motivations thus all intervene in the formation of engrams or dispositional representations. It becomes very complicated to sustain the hypothesis that memories are pure images of an external reality mirrored in the mind of a unified, purely spiritual, Cartesian subject. At this point, it must be underlined that there is not a single and unified memory system, and that different mnemonic functions are carried out by different modules.[26] The fact that memory is far from being a monolithic function carried out by a single organ further undermines its status as a representational, purely cognitive faculty.

Food and Non-Representational Memory

It is evident that nothing is simple in memories connected with food, something that most of us actually experience in connection with strong emotional undertones. They are intrinsically multifaceted and variegated, since they are formed by different classes of stimuli deriving from numerous systems:

> To realize how complicated taste is, we can say that, in order for a substance to have a specific taste, there are several factors that influence the final result, such as the chemical stimulus and its concentration, the location and dimension of the area where the stimulus is perceived, previous chemical condition of the mouth, previous dietary conditions, temperature of the chemical substance, age, kind of aroma, texture, color and sound that the substance produces in the nasal and oral cavities (as in the case of carbonated drinks or spices), degree of hunger, ethnic, cultural, environmental, learning factors and genetically inherited predispositions.[27]

Furthermore, food memories are far from being carved in our mind once and for all; rather, they interact uninterruptedly with our emotional, physical, and motivational states. They are not just simple pieces of information that limit themselves to reflect a determined event or sensation as received from the outside stimuli: they are the result of an uninterrupted and complex process of reelaboration. The power of food memories on everyday functionality, even if often unconscious, and their presence since prenatal life, place them in a special position to demonstrate the importance of non-representational memory and its impact on theories that privilege disembodied cognition over a more integrated model, a model that acknowledges the heuristic value of desire, pleasure and pain, emotional states, and motivations.

Notes

1 Sánchez Romera, Miguel. *La Cocina de los Sentidos*. Barcelona: Planeta, 2001.
2 Bolasco, Marco. "Il cuoco dai nervi saldi." *Gambero Rosso* 107 (December 2000): 117–26.

3   Sánchez Romera, *La Cocina de los Sentidos*, p. 99.

4   Ibid.: 220; my translation.

5   See Heldke, Lisa, "Foodmaking as a Thoughtful Practice." In *Cooking, Eating, Thinking*. Bloomington: Indiana University Press, 1992: 203–29; Michel Onfray, "Esthétique de l'éphémère." In *La Raison gourmande*. Paris: Grasset, 1995: 223–58.

6   Neisser, Ulrich. *Cognitive Psychology*. New York: Appleton-Century-Crofts, 1966: 2.

7   LeDoux, Joseph. *The Emotional Brain*. New York: Touchstone, 1998: 27.

8   Haugeland, John. "Semantic Engines: An Introduction to Mind Design." In *Mind Design*. Cambridge, MA: Bradford Books, 1981: 31.

9   LeDoux, *The Emotional Brain*, p. 41.

10 Edelman, Gerald M. and Giulio Tononi. *A Universe of Consciousness*. New York: Basic Books, 2000: 47.

11 This, Hervé. *Casseroles et éprouvettes*. Paris: Belin, 2002: 63–81; my translation.

12 Caicedo, Alejandro and Stephen D. Roper, "Taste Receptor Cells That Discriminate Between Bitter Stimuli." *Science* February 23, 2001: 1557–60.

13 This, Hervé and Pierre Gagnaire. *La Cuisine c'est de l'amour, de l'art, de la technique*. Paris: Odile Jacob, 2006.

14 Proust, Marcel. *Du Côté de chez Swann*. Paris: Gallimard, 1984: 59; my translation.

15 Ibid.; my translation.

16 Faulkner, William. *Absalom, Absalom!* New York: Random House, 1964: 143.

17 De Luca, Erri. *Montedidio*. Milan: Feltrinelli, 2001: 31; my translation.

18 Sánchez Romera, *La Cocina de los Sentidos*, pp. 218–20.

19 LeDoux, *The Emotional Brain*, p. 214.

20 Schacter, Daniel L. *Searching for Memory*. New York: Basic Books, 1996: 59. See also Schacter, Daniel L., *The Seven Sins of Memory*. Boston: Hougton Mifflin, 2001.

21 LeDoux, Joseph. *The Synaptic Self*. New York: Viking Books, 2002: 66.

22 Cytowic, Richard. *The Man Who Tasted Shapes*. Cambridge, MA: MIT Press, 2003: 156–9.

23 Edelman and Tononi, *A Universe of Consciousness*, p. 46.

24 Damasio, Antonio. *Descartes' Error*. New York: Quill, 2000: 105. See also Damasio, Antonio, *The Feeling of What Happens*. New York: Harcourt Brace, 1999.

25 Edelman and Tononi, *A Universe of Consciousness*, p. 46.

26 Carter, Rita. *Mapping the Mind*. Berkeley: University of California Press, 1999: 162; LeDoux, *The Synaptic Self*, pp. 101–33.

27 Sánchez Romera, *La Cocina de los Sentidos*, p. 129.

Second Course

Edible Art & Aesthetics

The preparation of good food is merely another expression of art, one of the joys of civilized living.

Dione Lucas, British chef

8

Can a Soup Be Beautiful?
The Rise of Gastronomy and
the Aesthetics of Food

Kevin W. Sweeney

Can a *potage de Crécy*, a carrot soup, ever be beautiful? Could shrimp Creole, one of the classic dishes of New Orleans cuisine, ever be recognized as profound? Is calling such dishes "beautiful" or "profound" a misuse of these evaluative labels? Because it appeals to our bodily appetite for sustenance, is food not the sort of thing that can be beautiful? Is food too simple a pleasure to be seriously identified with these aesthetic labels? Philosophers have been thinking about these questions for some time, and quite a few of them have argued that food cannot be beautiful.

Plato reserved 'the beautiful' as an appropriate description only for objects of sight and hearing and excluded as laughable any suggestion that food and drink could be beautiful.[1] In the Middle Ages, St. Thomas Aquinas similarly opposed food and drink being candidates for the beautiful, and in the nineteenth century, G. W. F. Hegel continued to insist on this division. He maintained that when they possessed a spiritual quality, objects of sight and hearing could be beautiful; however, objects of our bodily senses of smell, taste, and touch must always remain caught up in the material and be excluded from having any aesthetic character.[2]

If one thinks that this traditional negative view about the aesthetic character of food is mistaken – and many people nowadays do – we ought to be able to come up with a counterargument in favor of a soup or other dishes being recognized as beautiful. One can find the beginnings of such a counterargument to the negative tradition emerging in the early nineteenth century. By then, one starts to see a definite resistance to the view that objects of taste, smell, and touch – particularly, the food and drink we ingest – must be excluded from the beautiful.

An indication that this exclusionary division has come under criticism and that food and drink should be recognized as having a potential aesthetic character is found in the fanciful example of the Mock Turtle's song in Lewis Carroll's *Alice's Adventures in Wonderland* (1865):

> Beautiful soup, so rich and green,
> Waiting in a hot tureen!
> Who for such dainties would not stoop?
> Soup of the evening, beautiful Soup!
> Soup of the evening, beautiful Soup![3]

The Mock Turtle is quite convinced that a soup can be beautiful.[4] Even so, one might object that, in Wonderland, a lot of bizarre and logic-defying events occur. Why should one think that such an example expresses a cogent idea and poses a serious challenge to excluding food from the realm of the aesthetic?

The answer lies in the nature of the soup referred to in the song. The rich green soup in the song is probably mock turtle soup, a soup made out of veal to resemble turtle soup.[5] The importance of mock turtle soup being hailed as a beautiful soup is that such a soup has a mimetic quality (i.e., it *imitates* something, namely turtle soup). The Mock Turtle recognizes food as a medium that can be used mimetically, just like the media that other art forms employ. Crediting a soup with having this mimetic character shows that a soup is the sort of thing that can be beautiful. In the earlier-discussed division between objects of sight and sound and objects of taste and smell, the former could be crafted into mimetic objects whereas the latter, it was thought, could only be examples of themselves. Yet here was an example that challenged that distinction: a food was recognized as being mimetic and, in virtue of that, might be beautiful. Perhaps the distinction could be challenged in other ways as well.

Challenges to the view that food could not be beautiful actually started in the late eighteenth century and, by the middle of the nineteenth century, presented a formidable counter-position. Such challenges developed along two fronts. First, there was a philoso-phical attack that sought to overturn the view that food could not be aesthetic. Second, a social practice developed that introduced changes in the way that food was presented and consumed. This practice encouraged consumers to approach food in a way similar to the way they approached other aesthetic objects. At the time that Carroll wrote in the mid-nineteenth century, the challenge to food's being denied an aesthetic character had been widely debated.[6]

The philosophical attack came in response to a major change in the paradigmatic way we think and talk about our appreciation of works of art and nature. During the eighteenth century, such appre-ciation was held to resemble, *metaphorically*, alimentary experience (i.e., our ingesting of food and drink). Our appreciation of poetry, music, and painting, for instance, was referred to as an exercise of *critical taste*. In his essay "Of the Standard of Taste," David Hume notices the "great resemblance between mental and bodily taste," iden-tifying the former critical capacity as being taste in a "metaphorical sense."[7] Voltaire also holds a metaphorical account of taste. "The external sense of taste," he writes, "with which nature has furnished us, and by which we distinguish and relish the various kinds of nour-ishment that are adapted to health and pleasure, has in all languages given occasion to the metaphorical word *taste*, by which we express our perception of beauty, deformity, or defect, in the several arts."[8]

Thinkers in the eighteenth century noticed several bases for this metaphorical resemblance. First, gustatory experience (i.e., appreciative sensing of what we ingest) was held to be *hedonically judgmental*: we naturally evaluate what we ingest by responding pleasurably or displeasurably, while other sensory modalities seem less pervasively hedonic (i.e., what we see or what we hear does not always provoke a hedonic reaction).[9] Second, gustatory experience was thought to have an *immediacy*: we quickly respond pleasurably or displeasur-ably to what we ingest. (Voltaire claims that critical taste is "a quick discernment, a sudden perception, which, like the sensation of the palate, anticipates reflection.")[10] In seeking your opinion, suppose a chef offers you a spoonful of a *potage de Crécy* which is slowly sim-mering on the stove. If, after tasting it, you were to say that before you give your opinion you would need a little while to think about what you have tasted, such a response would generally be thought to be very peculiar. Rather, we are expected to give an immediate verdict on that spoonful. Third, gustatory judgment, like critical appreciation, must be based on our own sensory experience. Even though a well-respected restaurant critic lavishly praises a restaurant's *potage de Crécy*, we ought to base our judgment of the dish on our own experience of the soup; we ought not to form our critical judgments merely by emulating a judgment based on another's experience. So, the individual's own experience as the basis for judgment, the hedonic character of that experience, and its immediacy were, for many eighteenth-century thinkers, salient comparative qualities for both gustatory taste and critical taste.

Drawing attention to the individual's own experience as the basis for judgment in both alimentation and critical appreciation, Immanuel Kant claimed:

> [T]his is one of the main reasons why this aesthetic power of judging was given that very name: taste. For even if someone lists all the ingredients of a dish, pointing out that I have always found each of them agreeable, and goes on to praise this food – and rightly so – as wholesome, I shall be deaf to all these reasons: I shall try the dish on *my* tongue and palate, and thereby (and not by universal principles) make my judgment.[11]

A corollary to this view is that literal tastes are not established or changed by rational argument. Someone cannot rationally persuade you to change your mind and like gazpacho if you detest it. Nevertheless, one's tastes can be emotionally swayed and culturally influenced. A worrisome consequence of this emphasis on an individual's own validating experience is that critical taste was open to the charge of being idiosyncratic or *subjectively relative*. Critical judgments, on this emphasis, would lack objectivity and reflect only a subjective liking or disliking.

During the nineteenth century, this concept of critical *taste* metaphorically based on gustatory experience is overthrown, and a new paradigm is introduced. The notion of critical taste is replaced by the *aesthetic*, which is a new category referring to a special attitude toward, or critical experience of, nature and of the arts. With the rise of the aesthetic, gustatory taste loses its status as the major paradigm for critical appreciation. Although Alexander Baumgarten is credited with introducing the term *aesthetic*,[12] it is Kant, in the

Critique of Judgment (1790), who popularizes the *aesthetic* as the main category of critical appreciation. By 1794, when Friedrich Schiller publishes *On the Aesthetic Education of Man in a Series of Letters*, the concept is well on its way to being firmly established.[13]

While Kant still preserves the notion of taste as a critical category, he loosens the metaphorical connection between gustatory experience and critical appreciation. As the earlier quotation shows, Kant believes that our aesthetic experience, such as our experience of things beautiful, is like gustatory experience in being based on our own experience; however, in other respects critical appreciation is very different from gustatory experience. Kant suggests that gustatory experience cannot offer a reflective aesthetic encounter. What we eat or drink provokes only an agreeable or disagreeable sensory response. Consequently, no object of gustatory experience can be beautiful.[14] At the risk of reductively simplifying Kant's aesthetic theory, I would like to explore the way in which Kant distinguishes the experience of the beautiful from gustatory-like experiences with respect to the experience of pleasure and the immediacy of the evaluation.

In a prominent example, Kant says about appreciating natural beauty: "for we consider someone's way of thinking to be coarse and ignoble if he has no *feeling* for beautiful nature . . . and sticks to the enjoyments of mere sense that he gets from meals or the bottle."[15] Kant here contrasts "enjoyments of mere sense," associated with food and drink, with our appreciation of things beautiful. Kant distinguishes the "taste of sense," from the more contemplative and imaginative activity of experiencing the beautiful, what he calls the "taste of reflection."[16] The experience of sense, he claims, has only an individual or subjective application, reflecting our individual preferences. I might like *potage de Crécy* or mock turtle soup, and you might not. The *taste of reflection* yields a contemplative enjoyment of the beautiful, one not reflecting individual preferences. He identifies it as a universal form of appreciation which is based on a *common sense* or shared evaluative sensibility. To exercise this common sense, one had to put aside one's personal preferences and approach the object of appreciation *disinterestedly*.[17]

Kant distinguishes the *taste of sense* from the *taste of reflection* in another way. Considering the condition of immediacy, Kant claims that in exercising the taste of sense one experiences a direct, hedonic, stimulated response to an object. Kant says the pleasure comes "first" and, on that basis, one judges the object to be agreeable or not.[18] Exercising the taste of sense, it seems, is a rather passive activity. One confronts the object – one is stimulated by it – and then immediately responds. With the taste of reflection, one could say that the pleasure comes second or follows the contemplative activity that Kant describes as a free play of one's imaginative engagement with the object.[19] Experiences of reflection take some time and constitute a more active form of engagement. One's pleasure follows and reflects the harmonious exercise of one's imaginative and cognitive faculties in free play with the object. Kant refers to this active engagement as imaginative free play because we employ our cognitive faculties without applying a particular (determinate) concept or *purpose* to the object as one would in knowing what the object is. We exercise our imagination so as to experience the object as having what Kant calls a "purposiveness." That is, in imaginative free play with the object, we employ our cognitive faculties but are free from the restrictions of knowing, and we reflectively and imaginatively experience the object as having what Kant calls a "purposiveness without a purpose."[20]

Without going into greater detail about Kant's aesthetic theory, let me summarize the basis for his rejection of an aesthetic appreciation of food. Kant points out that we have individual, and at times quirky, likes and dislikes of particular foods. We sense liking or disliking a soup, for instance, immediately on tasting it, and our appreciative attitude towards food is one of a "taste of sense." However, our attitude towards things beautiful is quite different. To value something as beautiful, Kant thought, demanded a universal assent and should not be based on a personal preference. Appreciation of the beautiful calls for our exhibiting a disinterested attitude. Our enjoyment of things beautiful is not a hedonic reflex. It requires a taste of reflection, a sustained contemplative activity, one which engages our common cognitive faculties, especially our imagination, in an unrestricted way. Our pleasure with such an experience derives from the exercise of this imaginative free play.

Kant's argument for a distinction between the taste of reflection based on a sustained cognitive involvement with an object and the taste of sense consisting of a hedonic reflexive attitude seriously undermined the metaphorical relationship between the critical and the gustatory. Also, the introduction of new critical concepts beyond the traditional concept of the beautiful, such as the *sublime* and the *picturesque*, called for a broader conception of appreciative affective response and hastened the abandonment of metaphorical taste. Sixty years after Kant, John Ruskin disparaged the "baseness" of the concept of taste, noting its inappropriateness for art criticism and referring to it as providing "only a kind of pleasure analogous to that derived from eating by the palate."[21] Nevertheless, although overthrown as the major category of artistic criticism, *taste* at the same time emerged as the basic concern of a new cultural inquiry, as the focus of an investigation into the nature and values of *gastronomy*.

Supposedly, the word 'gastronomy' was coined by the poet Joseph Berchoux (1801), and it quickly became popular, generating a ballooning literary and critical interest in "the art and science of delicate eating."[22] One might wonder whether the surge of interest in gastronomy was unwarranted at this time given the philosophical criticisms of both metaphorical and gustatory taste. The Kantian criticisms of taste seemed to support the charge that alimentary pleasure was idiosyncratic, passive in its penchant for immediate response, and offered little to engage the free play of the imagination. Kant's characterization of the taste of sense suggested that the pleasures of the palate could never offer the imaginative content necessary to support crediting objects of gustatory taste with being beautiful. Kant also accepted the traditional distinction between the higher sensory modalities of sight and hearing and the lower modalities of smell, taste, and touch.[23] As a lower sensory modality, taste was excluded from any experiential connection with the beautiful. The impression left is that for Kant there could never be a *gustatory aesthetic*.[24]

Nevertheless, with the growing interest in gastronomy, several writers challenged the Kantian opposition to an aesthetic response to gustatory experience and in so doing prepared the way for a gustatory aesthetics. I want to explore the views on gustatory taste expressed in Jean-Anthelme Brillat-Savarin's *The Physiology of Taste, or Meditations on Transcendental Gastronomy*, a classic work in early nineteenth-century gastronomy.[25] Brillat-Savarin is not a professional philosopher, yet his attitude toward food and his model for the valuational nature of gustatory experience stand directly opposed to the Kantian perspective.

I understand Brillat-Savarin's use of the expression 'transcendental gastronomy' in the title of his work to be a challenge to the Kantian restrictions on gustatory experience and to set the groundwork for a gustatory aesthetic – a *transcendental gastronomy*. (Use of the term 'transcendental' in an early nineteenth-century work is more than likely a reference to Kant, who popularized it.) While Brillat-Savarin does not specifically refer to Kant in his work – his references are to French thinkers, with Voltaire being his favorite – his characterization of taste challenges both Kant's distinction between the taste of sense and the taste of reflection and Kant's exclusion of gustatory experience, because of its immediacy, from being aesthetic experience. Brillat-Savarin offers a model of gustatory experience that characterizes appreciative alimentation as reflective aesthetic experience. He points out that the physiology of alimentation with its distinctive temporal sequence allows for a reflective experience rather than just an immediate response to a stimulus.

For Brillat-Savarin, tasting food is often a complex experience. We frequently engage with a great variety of gustatory elements, often coming upon new and different elements, in the successive stages of our ingesting experience. We are able to sense this great variety of elements because we engage them with our retro-nasal sense of smell. While Aristotle notes "an analogy between smell and taste," he also noted a major difference: "our sense of taste is more discriminating than our sense of smell, because the former is a modification of touch."[26] Whereas Aristotle distinguishes smell from taste – smell is the lesser sense and taste the greater – Brillat-Savarin does not. "I am not only convinced," Brillat-Savarin insists, "that there is no full act of tasting without the participation of the sense of smell, but I am also tempted to believe that smell and taste form a single sense."[27] This allows him to posit that the "number of tastes is infinite."[28]

Instead of taste being a rather limited sense in keeping with the traditional view of its being a kind of touch, Brillat-Savarin thinks of the amalgam of taste and smell as a complex sensory faculty. Contemporary scientific research supports his view of the integral nature of taste and smell: much of what we claim to taste we in fact smell. The synaesthetic experience of taste and smell is now commonly referred to as one of *flavor*. True, there are simple tastes one senses without benefit of olfactory engagement: sweet, sour, bitter, salt, and most recently, umami (generally associated with tasting protein). However, there are "tastes" (e.g., vanilla) which are sensed exclusively by smell. Brillat-Savarin identifies several simple tastes: sweet, sour, and bitter, but, mirroring Kant's view that the taste of sense only registers what is agreeable or disagreeable, he refers to such simple tastes as also only being *"agreeable* or *disagreeable."*[29] The majority of our gustatory experiences, he believes, involve a much broader range of intricate flavors, ample resources for a complex aesthetic encounter.

In order to show that gustatory experience can allow for a reflective encounter, Brillat-Savarin divides the temporal sequence of ingestion into three main stages; each, he claims, features its own set of sensory qualities. He refers to them respectively as *direct, complete*, and *reflective* sensations. Let me quote his description of the tripartite process of appreciative ingesting which he illustrates with the example of eating a peach:

> The *direct* sensation is the first one felt, produced from the immediate operations of the organs of the mouth, while the body under consideration is still on the forepart of the tongue.
>
> The *complete* sensation is the one made up of this first perception plus the impression which arises when the food leaves its original position, passes to the back of the mouth, and attacks the whole organ with its taste and its aroma.
>
> Finally, the *reflective* sensation is the opinion which one's spirit forms from the impressions which have been transmitted to it by the mouth.
>
> Let us put this theory into action, by seeing what happens to a man who is eating or drinking. He who eats a peach, for instance, is first of all agreeably struck by the perfume which it exhales; he puts a piece of it into his mouth, and enjoys a sensation of tart freshness which invites him to continue; but it is not until the instant of swallowing, when the mouthful passes under his nasal channel, that the full aroma is revealed to him; and this completes the sensation which the peach can cause. Finally, it is not until it has been swallowed that the man, considering what he has just experienced, will say to himself, "Now there is something really delicious!"[30]

One should note that this process of successive ingesting is developmental, leading to an overall impression of the structure of what one tastes. After experiencing the aroma, one initially encounters what one is tasting on the forefront of the palate; one then proceeds into a middle range of flavors produced when what one has ingested affects the olfactory receptors in the retro-nasal passages. Finally, one swallows and enters the last third of the experience, the reflective phase, where a set of aftertastes provides both a final tonal development and the opportunity for a reflective assessment of the structure and character of the whole experience.

Yet there might still be some doubts about whether such an experience is imaginative, as opposed to merely registering the sum of the sensations or conceptually fitting them into a particular determinate form (e.g., the taste of a peach). When we taste, how *actively* and *imaginatively* engaged are we? For Brillat-Savarin, such a successive experience is not merely a compounding of *direct* sensory details. The initial tastes, Brillat-Savarin's *direct* sensations – say of sweet, sour, and bitter – might produce only an immediate effect, but the full experience, in its successive developmental unfolding, encourages an extended period of consideration. It is an occasion for reflection, requiring one to compare the beginning, middle, and end of one's experience. One might even have to retaste what one has ingested to evaluate it more fully or to check one's earlier evaluation. Such a sensitive tasting calls for a contemplative attitude.

In our extended reflective experience with what we ingest, we do not simply experience a sum of sensed qualities. Instead, in the temporal sequence of our gustatory experience, we imaginatively shape the character and overall structure of what we taste: we recall and imaginatively compare the flavors that we encounter at different stages of the process, note complementary and contrasting qualities, and come to realize how these qualities form unities and other regional structures. There are also stylistic and expressive features that we come to experience. Suppose a New Orleans chef prepares shrimp Creole for us. Its complex aromas assault us. We taste the shrimp in the dark *roux* that combines onion, garlic, tomato, and peppers. We note the way the spicy heat lingers, how that heat integrates with spices such as thyme, clove, allspice, and perhaps a touch of sassafras. There is a lot to taste and think about in such a dish. Together these flavors express some of the distinctive features of southern Louisianan cuisine. The dish not only speaks to us of its regional origins but its culinary history with French, Spanish, African, and Native American contributions. We are sensitive to the way the chef expressively crafts the dish, perhaps emphasizing qualities of the particular ingredients, their seasonal character or association with the time of the harvest. All of these expressive and stylistic features are not simply identified; they imaginatively infuse the whole tasting experience. Savoring such a dish with its complex tastes and expressive character, we might very well think of it as profound.

Thus, I believe that Brillat-Savarin is proposing something like a Kantian reflective aesthetic in his account of appreciative tasting. Of course, he does not employ the full Kantian psychology, though he does advocate a shared sensibility or *common sense*. As human beings, we share a "physiology" of alimentation. Yet tasting, over and above direct stimulation, is not a reflexive act. We have to pay attention to what we are consuming, to cultivate an interest in what we ingest. The ordered sequence of gustatory experience supports such a view, but requires our imaginative attention. Of course, a skeptical critic of gustatory aesthetics might object that a shared physiology and developed structure of imaginative experience will not overcome the problem of the idiosyncrasies of preference. However, the quirkiness of preference is not a characteristic unique to taste. We like or dislike particular colors, and, for some, bagpipe music is excruciating. We exhibit individual preferences towards objects of all sensory modalities. Yet, Brillat-Savarin has done a great deal to counter the view that objects of taste provoke a simple hedonic response. His account of taste demands that we think of gustatory experience as affording a complex evolving gustatory encounter worthy of reflective enjoyment.

While Brillat-Savarin and others wrote to change the way their contemporaries thought about food,[31] there were changes afoot in the presentation and consumption of food. Individuals were given the space and opportunity to encounter food in an appreciative way, a way that was similar to the way they approached other aesthetic objects. The end of the eighteenth century and the beginning of the nineteenth century saw a culinary revolution in Paris and other European cities.[32] No longer the exclusive concern of aristocratic households, fine dining and culinary appreciation developed a bourgeois following and witnessed the rise of different culinary and gustatory paradigms associated with the works of famous chef-authors such as Antonin Carême, Félix Urbain Dubois, and, most popularly, Auguste Escoffier. These chefs wrote influential cookbooks which spread their ideas to a growing interested public and to other chefs in the huge number of restaurants that opened in the first decades of the nineteenth century. Culinary invention available in these restaurants became just as important as creative change in the arts.

The rise of the restaurant, as Rebecca Sprang has meticulously shown, contributed to the development of an aesthetic interest in food in several important ways.[33] First of all, restaurants were open not just to the aristocracy or the extremely wealthy but to all who could pay for their meal. Cuisine became not just the isolated hobby of the rich or aristocratic but served to develop an interest in gustatory pleasure in a growing middle class. Just as the opening of public art museums such as the Louvre in the early nineteenth century introduced the world of the visual arts to the bourgeoisie, so restaurants introduced food as an aesthetic experience to middle-class palates.

Second, food was presented to the consumer in a different way in restaurants than in earlier establishments where one could sit down to eat prepared food. Since antiquity, prepared food had been available to the public in inns. However, it was served in a style now referred to as a *table d'hôte*: there was a large table around which people sat; all the food, restricted to a few dishes, was placed on large platters in the center of the table, and people helped themselves. There was no choice of dishes, just what the establishment was serving that day.[34] In restaurants, the form of service was as it is today. Patrons sat at their own table and chose particular dishes from a menu. Those dishes were served in courses, one at a time, usually starting off with an appetizer or soup and proceeding through various courses to a dessert. This form of presenting the food in individual servings in a sequence of courses was called *service à la russe*. It replaced an earlier form of food presentation, called *service à la française*. The latter form of presenting a meal consisted of presenting all the food, in a buffet style, from soup to dessert, all at once on a central table. People just helped themselves to whatever they wanted. In seventeenth-century France, this was the way food was served in aristocratic houses or at the royal court.[35]

By the late eighteenth and early nineteenth century, people's ideas about the nature of food and their experience of food had undergone a change. There were new ideas promulgated by innovative thinkers, but there were also new opportunities to taste food worthy of an aesthetic interest. The birth of the restaurant and the changes in the presentation of food brought about by adopting *service à la russe* encouraged people to approach a meal differently. Middle-class people began to savor what they tasted and to notice the distinctive aesthetic characters of the different dishes that they consumed. Because of these changes in the way a meal was presented, people had the opportunity to contemplate the food they consumed. Food was more likely to be approached in an aesthetic way.

In conclusion, we can answer the question "Can a soup be beautiful?" in the affirmative because a soup can be the object of a complex aesthetic experience that warrants an evaluative label like 'beautiful.' Unlike those who hold that food offers only an immediate simple pleasure, we – as beneficiaries of Brillat-Savarin – now recognize that food offers us a contemplative experience, because of the alimentary sequence by which it is consumed and the sensory modalities of taste and smell with which it is engaged. The sensory experience of eating presents us with a rich and varied aesthetic sequence of gustatory qualities that we must register and imaginatively order into different structures. This response to food is not an immediate reaction but an imaginative activity. In addition, new practices for the presentation of food, such as *service à la russe*, developed at the time of the rise of the restaurant, have further encouraged our aesthetic engagement with food. Thus, with these innovations, both theoretical and practical, if there are beautiful soups to be tasted, people are prepared to encounter and savor them.

Notes

I would like to thank Donald W. Crawford, Elizabeth Winston, and my editor, Fritz Allhoff, for helpful advice with this essay.

1   Plato. *Hippias Major*. 297e–298a. For a discussion of Plato on taste, see Summers, David, *The Judgment of Sense: Renaissance Naturalism and the Rise of Aesthetics*. New York: Cambridge University Press, 1987: 54–5; and Korsmeyer, Carolyn, *Making Sense of Taste: Food and Philosophy*. Ithaca, NY: Cornell University Press, 1999: 12–18.

2   St. Thomas Aquinas. *Summa Theologiae* (1265–73). Ia 2ae 27, 1; Hegel, Georg W. F. *Hegel's Introduction to Aesthetics* (1820). Trans. T. M. Knox, with an interpretative essay by Charles Karelis. New York: Oxford University Press, 1977: 38–9.

3   Carroll, Lewis. *Alice in Wonderland: Authoritative Texts of Alice's Adventures in Wonderland, Through the Looking-Glass, The Hunting*

of the Snark. Ed. Donald J. Gray, Norton Critical Edition. New York: Norton, 1971: 84.

4   When Alice says that she does not know what a Mock Turtle is, she is told: "It's the thing Mock Turtle Soup is made from." In Sir John Tenniel's illustrations of the Mock Turtle which accompany Carroll's text, the creature has the head, rear hooves, and tail of a calf, but the shell and front flippers of a turtle.

5   In the mid-eighteenth century, turtle soup was considered an elaborate and expensive dish found only at the tables of England's wealthy and aristocratic families. The green turtles used to make the soup had to be brought back to England all the way from the West Indies. In a desire to emulate the ways of the rich, nineteenth-century middle-class English families were fond of serving mock turtle soup, which resembled turtle soup but substituted a veal head for the turtle. It was, of course, considerably less expensive. A recipe for mock turtle soup first appeared in the sixth edition of Hannah Glasse's popular cook book, *The Art of Cookery Made Plain and Easy* (1758). See Wilson, C. Anne, *Food and Drink in Britain from the Stone Age to Recent Times*. London: Constable, 1991: 225.

6   The debate has by no means ended. In the twentieth century there were still advocates of the position that objects of taste could not be credited will a full aesthetic character. See Prall, D. W., *Aesthetic Judgment*. New York: Thomas Y. Crowell C., 1929: 57–75; Beardsley, Monroe, *Aesthetics: Problems in the Philosophy of Criticism*, 2nd edn. Indianapolis: Hackett, 1987: 98, 99, 111; and two works by Roger Scruton: *The Aesthetics of Architecture*. Princeton: Princeton University Press, 1979: 104–34; and *Art and Imagination: A Study in the Philosophy of Mind*. London: Routledge, 1982.

7   Hume, David. "Of the Standard of Taste" (1757). In *Essays, Moral, Political, and Literary*. Ed. Eugene F. Miller. Indianapolis: Liberty Classics, 1987: 235.

8   Voltaire, "An Essay on Taste," translated from Voltaire's article on taste in Diderot and D'Alembert's *Encyclopédie* (1757) in Gerard, Alexander. *An Essay on Taste*, 2nd edn. (1764). New York: Garland, 1970: 209.

9   For a fuller account of the nature of critical taste and its conceptual history, see the chapter "Taste" in Townsend, Dabney, *Hume's Aesthetic Theory*. London: Routledge, 2001: 47–85.

10 Voltaire, "An Essay on Taste," p. 209.

11 Kant, Immanuel. *Critique of Judgment*. Trans. Werner S. Pluhar. Indianapolis: Hackett, 1987: Book II, sects. 33, p. 148.

12 Shiner, Larry. *The Invention of Art: A Cultural History*. Chicago: University of Chicago Press, 2001: 131–2.

13 See Schiller, Friedrich, *On the Aesthetic Education of Man in a Series of Letters* (1794). Trans. Reginald Snell. New York: Frederick Ungar, 1965: 3.

14 I say that Kant suggests this because in the *Critique of Judgment* he never flatly makes that claim. Nevertheless, he does use a series of prominent gustatory examples that suggest such a position.

15 Kant, *Critique of Judgment*, pp. 169–70.

16 Ibid., pp. 55–64.

17 To illustrate the distinction between an *interested* versus a *disinterested* appreciation, Kant gives the example of some seventeenth-century Iroquois *sachem* who came to Paris and were not impressed with the appearances of the palaces but greatly admired the Parisian rotisseries. The *sachem*'s admiration for the rotisseries was not a disinterested appreciation but reflected their interest in the food, the roast meats. Our enjoyment of food was not a disinterested pleasure, Kant thought, since it reflected the interest of satisfying our appetite (p. 45).

18 Ibid., p. 61.

19 Ibid., p. 62.

20 Ibid., p. 65.

21 *Modern Painters*, vol. 3 (1856), reprinted in *The Art Criticism of John Ruskin*. Ed. Robert L. Herbert. New York: Da Capo Press, 1987: 167.

22 Mennell, Stephen. *All Manners of Food: Eating and Taste in England and France from the Middle Ages to the Present*, 2nd edn. Urbana: University of Illinois Press, 1996: 266. For an English translation of part of Berchoux's poem "Gastronomy, or the Bon-Vivant's Guide," see *Gusto: Essential Readings in Nineteenth-Century Gastronomy*. Ed. Denise Gigante. New York: Routledge, 2005: 275–81.

23 Kant, Immanuel. *Anthropology from a Pragmatic Point of View* (1798). Ed. and trans. Robert B. Louden, introduction by Manfred Kuehn. New York: Cambridge University Press, 2006: 46–9.

24 For further discussion of Kant's opposition to a gustatory aesthetic, see Korsmeyer, *Making Sense of Taste*, pp. 54–63.

25 Brillat-Savarin, Jean-Anthelme, *The Physiology of Taste, or Meditations on Transcendental Gastronomy* (1825). Trans. M. F. K. Fisher. New York: Harcourt Brace Jovanovich, 1978.

26 Aristotle. *De Anima*. II, 9, 421a; as quoted in Townsend, *Hume's Aesthetic Theory*, p. 49.

27 Brillat-Savarin, *The Physiology of Taste*, p. 39.

28 Ibid., p. 38.

29 Ibid., p. 38.

30 Ibid., p. 40.

31 Notable among these writers was Grimod de La Reynière, who in his yearly publication *Almanach des Gourmands* (1803–12) was at the forefront of this culinary revolution. See MacDonogh, Giles, *A Palate in Revolution: Grimod de La Reynière and the Almanach des Gourmands*. London: Robin Clark, 1987. For an English translation of some of the *Almanach* and the writings of other writers in this movement, see Gigante, *Gusto*.

32 Mennell, in *All Manners of Food*, cautions: "The story of how the great Parisian restaurants arose after the Revolution is a little more complicated than how it is sometimes told. It was not simply that the cooks formerly employed in the kitchens of aristocrats who had fled abroad or perished in the Terror, finding themselves without work, were obliged to open fine restaurants. Noble emigration and the guillotine certainly did play their part in making available an increased supply of skilled manpower. Yet the first of a new form of eating-place open to the public – that which came to be known as the restaurant – made its appearance in Paris during the two decades before the Revolution. All the same, though it may seem paradoxical in the light of Paris's later reputation for its great restaurants, 'eating out' seems to have been more a part of the way of life of respectable gentlemen in eighteenth-century London than in Paris" (pp. 135–6). Kenneth James, however, resolutely holds that the restaurant and the culinary revolution are Parisian phenomena; see *Escoffier: The King of Chiefs*. New York: Hambledon and London, 2002: 25–7.

33 For a full account of the development of the Parisian restaurant, see Sprang, Rebecca L., *The Invention of the Restaurant: Paris and Modern Gastronomic Culture*. Cambridge, MA: Harvard University Press, 2000. For a fine overview of this culinary revolution, see Gigante's "Introduction," pp. xvii–xliii.

34 Sprang, *The Invention of the Restaurant*, pp. 7–8.

35 For an overview of the transition to *service à la russe* and the role that the great French chef and culinary author, Antonin Carême, played in the transition, see Kelly, Ian, *Cooking for Kings: The Life of Antonin Carême, the First Celebrity Chef*. London: Short Books, 2003.

9

Can Food Be Art? The Problem of Consumption

Dave Monroe

Suppose that, one warm June evening, you and I are dining in Rome's Piazza Navona after having taken in a performance of *Il Barbiere di Siviglia* at Il Teatro Costanzi. The restaurant at which we dine affords us a lovely view of Bernini's famous fountain, as well as the wondrous sculpture and architecture of the church of Sant'Agnese in Agone. The main course of our dinner is a delightfully tender, seared veal chop served with rosemary-scented demi-glace and wild mushrooms. Over dinner, our pleasant conversation naturally turns to the subject of art, as we have spent much of our day in the presence of some masterpieces. We recount our experiences with these artworks, discuss their merits and place in art history, and struggle to figure out what sensual qualities make such objects so magnificent. In the course of this discussion, we turn our attention to the dinner in front of us. The flavor of the veal harmoniously blends with the sauce and the mushrooms, creating a subtle, earthy flavor evident with each tantalizing bite. It delights our senses in a unique and delicious way, and we are tempted to call this, too, a work of art. But are we permitted to make that claim? Is food a genuine artistic medium?

Interestingly, some philosophers think that it is not and that claims about the artistic value of food are misguided. They would tell us that all but one of our putative "artistic" experiences during our Roman day is of art; all, that is, but our dinner. One reason historically cited is what I call the "problem of consumption": food is often dismissed as a genuine artistic medium on the grounds that the object of culinary art is consumed as it is enjoyed. A perfectly prepared veal chop, unlike Bernini's masterpiece, exists only as long as it takes a diner to eat it. The objects of higher art forms, like painting and sculpture, do not suffer from this defect and, so the thinking goes, are proper art objects, while food is not.

In this essay, I will argue that the act of consumption is insufficient to rule out food as a proper art object. To this end, I will begin by developing the contrary position. My subsequent rejection of this position will be based on revealing an overly narrow understanding of art objects upon which such a position depends. I will further argue that culinary art objects share structural similarities with already accepted members of the art family – such as music, dance, and theater – and, given this, argue that logic requires the inclusion of culinary objects. I will attempt to defend this maneuver against a second problem introduced by food's consumption, namely the fact that it seems to limit the possibility of unbiased judgments of quality.

Setting the Table

Like a well-prepared meal, a philosophical argument proceeds in fairly formalized stages, or courses, if you like. The first step in analyzing our matter at hand is getting a clear picture of the problem and arguments in question. We are setting the table, as it were.

I first became aware of the consumption problem while reading Carolyn Korsmeyer's book *Making Sense of Taste: Food and Philosophy*.[1] She cites the famous (or infamous, depending upon your philosophical loyalties) nineteenth-century German philosopher G. W. F. Hegel as a chief proponent of what I shall call the Consumption Exclusion Thesis (CET).[2] This thesis basically holds that the consumption of food eliminates for it the possibility of being a "proper" art object. Behind this thesis is, I think, an assumption that genuine art is timeless in some sense: experiences of true artworks offer a glimpse into an eternal, unchanging reality which transcends the changing, temporal world of everyday life.[3] Furthermore, I suspect that many endorse the CET regarding food because there is a metaphysical issue of identity lurking in the background.[4] In the case of "higher" art objects like paintings, sculptures, and architecture, a particular object is created. A given particular art object persists beyond its creation and thus enjoys the possibility of iterated, but widespread, objective enjoyment; consider Bernini's fountain. It is the *same* fountain – the one created by Bernini in Piazza Navona, identical to itself – regardless of who experiences it and when. You and I, as we dine, can both see the fountain from where we sit in the piazza, and we can presumably come back the following day to yet again gaze upon it. Moreover, the particular object is not changed, destroyed, or consumed by our enjoyment of it. According to the CET, then, this persistence is a necessary condition for genuine art objects.

And, of course, this condition is not satisfied by our dinner. Our very act of dining destroys and alters by consumption the particular object of our gustatory delight. That object, then, is far from timeless in any sense, and should we return tomorrow to order the *very same dish*, our desires would be necessarily thwarted. The particular veal chop we ordered tonight is gone forever; surely, we can order one like it, but it is not, and cannot be, *one and the same dish*. Consequently, the possibility of objective knowledge and experience of that dish is lost in the past. Since, by food's own nature, it cannot satisfy the persistence requirement for art worthiness, culinary art thus fails CET and is not a proper art object.

Thankfully for those of us who do view food as an artistic medium and cooking as an art form, the above argument is flawed, so we need not endorse CET. I will challenge this argument by offering up three courses of challenge. For starters, I will argue that CET depends upon a dubious conception of artistic objects; I will offer an alternative understanding of art objects according to which culinary art may qualify. This move allows me to show that culinary art can, and does, persist in a limited sense beyond its consumption. The most important course in my objection will be to show that unless CET concedes my moves, it will, by a nifty principle of logic, be forced to draw a rather unsavory conclusion. We will not, as a result of this criticism, be forced to endorse CET. I turn now to my first offering.

First Course of Objections

For starters, the above argument depends upon a very narrow construal of 'object.' The general tone of the argument suggests that art objects are primarily material objects. Furthermore, we are meant to believe that culinary objects (e.g., our delicious veal chop) consist entirely of their material constituents – that is, the foodstuff out of which they are made. There is nothing over and above a dish's ingredients, in other words, that could account for its persistence after it is consumed. Our food, once eaten, is wholly consumed. And if this understanding of what constitutes a culinary object is correct, then the CET might be true.

But we need not accept this conception of food. I start by posing the following question: Are all legitimate works of art primarily materially composed? Can we find examples of artistic "objects" which depend as much upon immaterial conditions for their existence as they do their material components? If we can supply examples of art that are of this sort, then we are well on our way to refuting this understanding of art objects. Fortunately, examples of this type are ready to hand.

Consider music, theater, and dance. The object here is a performance, rather than some stable, concrete item objectively situated in the world like Bernini's sculpture. Performance arts such as these seem to very much depend upon how they are structured or arranged, maybe more so than they do upon the material conditions (e.g., musicians and instruments, actors, dancers, etc.) which constitute them. Music, for example, might be understood as a collection of performed notes arranged in a very specific way. Dance performances are choreographed; the dancers in a ballet are directed to move in a certain way in relation to a musical score. In theater, as we all know, actors are directed according to a script which determines their appropriate locations, movements, and spoken utterances. Musical scores, choreography, and scripts are more than just important to these performance objects; rather, they are necessary conditions for those performances being what they *are*. To see this, consider the following hypothetical scenario regarding Beethoven's *Moonlight Sonata*.

Imagine that we took the set of all notes used in *Moonlight Sonata*, and included the correct number of repetitions for each. Next, we provide this set of notes to a pianist and ask her to perform it. However, instead of playing it according to the customary arrangement, we insist that she play this set of notes at random. The resulting cacophonous performance, though it contains precisely the same notes as *Moonlight Sonata*, will sound *nothing like* Beethoven's masterpiece. In fact, it will not *be* a performance of *Moonlight Sonata*; it is something entirely and probably dreadfully distinct.

The necessity of this structure to music applies equally to the other performance arts and their respective objects. Furthermore, this imposed structure is distinct from the material components in which, or by which, it manifests. We philosophers sometimes refer to these manifestations as 'instances'; *Moonlight Sonata* can be performed by different pianists on a range of qualitatively divergent pianos, at various times, and in diverse places, with or without an audience. Despite these wildly fluctuating conditions, each is a recognizable performance (i.e., instance) of *Moonlight Sonata*, and not some other work of Beethoven's or our hypothetical auditory jumble. This shows that the structure itself, the crucial condition, is distinct from *any particular material instance*. An implicitly embedded point here is that given the fluctuation of material conditions, it is by recognizing the formal structure of these objects that we are able to identify them.

Certainly none of this shows that distinct instances can be *numerically identical* (i.e., one and the same), which is what raised our initial problem. And, in fact, they are not: for two things to be the same, they would have to share all their properties. If *Moonlight Sonata* is played in different places, different times, or different whatever, the different instances cannot be the same since they would differ in at least one of their properties. Thus, a contemporary third grader's performance of *Moonlight Sonata* is patently *not* one and the same "object" as the original performance since the two performances differ temporally, spatially, and constitutionally. Bernini's fountain, on the other hand, is one and the same object that was created by Bernini, is in the Piazza Navona gracing us with its presence, and so on. But how does this help?

For one, it shows that a persistence condition founded on numerical identity for particular art objects is too strong. If we apply that condition to performance art, we land at the conclusion that only the first instance of a particular performance object can qualify as being *that art object*. Because such performances are temporally limited (i.e., no one can play *Moonlight Sonata* forever), they seem to lack the kind of objectivity espoused by CET. Even if an original performance could count as an art object, any subsequent rendition would not qualify as *that* object, since the latter would be a different thing. But this conclusion runs against our deeply held gut feelings, or intuitions, about performance art and their objects. Intuitively, we (including CET proponents) recognize the art worthiness of performance arts; we do not typically denounce contemporary renditions of *Moonlight Sonata* on the grounds that they are not numerically identical with the original performance. We happily embrace them as art, and as being the same object, so long as the performance is up to snuff. If CET leads us to disregard these as performances of genuine art objects, then the principle is too strong.

What of food, then? Our discussion only concerns music and other performance arts insofar as it sheds light on our issue. Is there something helpful here that will get food off of CET's hook? Indeed there is, and it is not much of a strain to see similarities between culinary creations and musical performances. Culinary objects, dishes, entrees, or whatever you like to call them, share a kind of *formal structuring* that parallels that found in performance art but, instead of calling it a score, choreography, or script, though, we call it a *recipe*. Like a script, a recipe structures the way in which the food elements are combined, thus effecting an overall object of our appreciation. As with our thought experiment involving the musical notes, we could easily show the crucial role recipes play in making a dish precisely the dish that it is, that the structure is distinct from the ingredients in which it manifests, and so on. In short, all of what has been said concerning performance art can be adapted to culinary art.

So, I might define a dish, or culinary art object, as the *unique combination of a set of material ingredients with a formalized method of preparation*. The formalized method of preparation is the recipe which structures the ingredients such that they compose the given dish. When eaten, then, the entire object is not consumed. There is something over and above the ingredients which can account for its persistence. One does not, literally, eat the way in which a dish was made.

However, there is a question of how the recipe "exists" beyond the eating of an instance of it. The answer is fairly obvious: the way in which a dish is made must be recorded or symbolized in some way, such that it can be again used to create subsequent renditions. This recording may not even need to be written, though this is the most common means of capturing a dish's particular structure. It could be that the recipe is safely kept by the memory of whoever originally created a dish, and any given recipe can be passed on orally or through writing. Importantly, though, for the culinary art object to persist, the recipe must have some way of being recorded and kept, even if only as a datum in a particular person's memory. If this condition obtains, then there is no difference between the ways in which *Hamlet* or *Moonlight Sonata* persist and the way in which my crème anglaise does.

A Palate-Cleansing Positive Argument

The last course of our argument was negative, in that it exploited a weakness in CET. This is an important step, to be sure. However, we also want to offer a positive argument in favor of the view that culinary art objects should be considered art worthy. It is important to offer reasons for one's own position, for this builds a stronger case than one constructed merely by elimination. So, in this course, I will fold in an ingredient crucial for our case.

There is a logical principle which requires us to treat like cases alike; this rule is sometimes called the principle of universalization. For example, suppose a doctor has two generally healthy male patients under his care, both of whom display identical symptoms – let us say they have salmonella. For the first patient, the doctor prescribes an antibiotic to help his immune system overcome the bacteria. Happily for this patient, the antibiotic works and, within days, his salmonella is gone. Now, if the second patient's case is relevantly similar to the first's, should not the doctor prescribe the same antibiotic for him? The answer seems clearly to be yes, unless the doctor has countervailing reason to do otherwise – namely, a relevant difference between the two cases.

We can apply this same principle to our investigation. In the preceding section, I pointed out similarities between certain performance art objects and culinary art objects, and I showed that the existence of both depends on formal considerations distinct from each instance. Furthermore, I argued that both sorts of objects have limited life spans insofar as performances end, and food is consumed. Now we can apply the principle of universalization: given the important similarity between these objects and the fact that performance art objects count as proper art objects, we can tentatively classify culinary objects as proper objects of art.

Why is our classification only tentative at this point? Why hesitate to assert the classification and be done with it? The answer is that we have not ruled out possible CET objections to the use of this principle; there are two ways in which an opponent could argue against this conclusion. First, one could note that the principle only requires that we treat relevantly similar things alike. Other than this, it tells us nothing about how the matter should be decided. So, one way to block the conclusion for culinary art's legitimacy is to deny that performance arts enjoy the status of having proper art objects. If one makes this move, then the principle of universalization entails that food is not a proper object either. Fortunately, we do not have to worry much about this move because it is wildly counter-intuitive; no one would deny the artistic status of music, dance, and theater.

Another, more plausible, line of advance for an opponent would be to point out disqualifying dissimilarities between culinary objects and those of performance arts. The principle requires that we treat like cases alike, but if the cases are dissimilar, then the principle does not hold. Pro-CET folks have recourse here, for there seem to be dissimilarities between food and plays, symphonies, and so on. In fact, the biggest difference stems from the problem that generates this essay's topic: food is eaten (consumed), while performance arts are not. Furthermore, food is eaten for more than just enjoyment of its flavor; it is digested and absorbed into the body, thus sustaining the life and vitality of the person who eats it. In short, it has nutritive value over and above its flavorful aesthetic properties. This gives food a pragmatic dimension that appears to be missing in the other cases.

Is consumption a relevant dissimilarity, though? It seems as though it may be, for this useful aspect of food runs against another widely held, but disputed, intuition about art; namely, that genuine art objects must have only intrinsic value. Art objects ought not to be useful *for* anything over and above artistic appreciation, in other words. This understanding of art funds a traditional distinction between genuine arts and crafts. The objects and activities of the latter seem artistic, but the artifacts of crafts are created more for what you can do with them than for generating aesthetic experiences.

It is uncontestable that food is the sort of thing that is *for* something over and above its flavor. Good food is nutritious and contributes to a human's well-being, health, and sustenance. So it clearly has instrumental value. Thus, one could argue that a relevant difference has been introduced which threatens to disqualify food as art while simultaneously preserving performance art. If this line of argumentation is correct, then it could ground a disanalogy between food and art.

This is a substantial challenge, for it takes us into some heady issues in the philosophy of art. Whether or not art has, or can have, instrumental purposes beyond the aesthetic is a matter of considerable historical and contemporary dispute. In fact, the issues are so complex that I cannot hope to resolve them all here. Clearly, I favor a certain resolution of this debate while my would-be opponent endorses the other. If art objects can have instrumental value, then my argument for the art worthiness of food goes through. If they cannot, then there is a relevant difference between food and art. In the space that remains, let me offer some preliminary comments in favor of my preferred position.

The first thing to note is that from the fact that an artwork has intrinsic value it does not follow that it cannot have instrumental value. These concepts are logically distinct, and thus there is nothing contradictory about asserting them of the same thing. Insights from the moral realm help to make this clear; one could maintain that acts of charity are intrinsically good, and thus ought to be performed. However, one might also claim that helping others helps to promote an orderly society within which one is safer to pursue one's own goals and projects. According to the former claim, charity is intrinsically valuable, while the latter casts charity in instrumental terms. Nothing prevents us, however, from accepting that both claims are true of charity – it is both valuable for its own sake, and valuable for what we gain by it. Furthermore, the fact that there is instrumental value to charity does not impugn its intrinsic value. So why should we think that conjoining these conceptions of value is to be avoided in the case of art objects?

It seems to me that what motivates the opposition is a desire for objective judgments about the merits or demerits of art objects. One avenue to objectivity is to posit certain characteristics of objects and our experiences of them (e.g., intrinsic value) or else requiring of our aesthetic judge a certain frame of mind (e.g., disinterested contemplation).[5] If the object has qualities valuable for their own sake and not for the sake of anything else, it seems to allow one to consider its quality on those grounds alone, free from instrumental temptations. Parochial, subjective considerations are thus removed. But does our ability to form unbiased qualitative judgments ultimately depend on a purely intrinsic understanding of artistic value? It is not clear to me that it does.

As far as I can tell, an object's having only intrinsic value is not a necessary condition for our ability to form disinterested judgments about it. What seems ultimately to matter is how a person engages with an object, and that could be an object with both intrinsic and instrumental aesthetic qualities, as well as other instrumental values. We are able to narrow our attentive focus to specific aspects of objects and interact accordingly, in other words. I can, and most would, I think, eat my veal chop for the sake of its *flavor* rather than its caloric content. The delicious qualities of the veal are the reason I eat it; the fact that the meat contributes to my vitality, despite being an independent reason that could explain my eating the veal chop, need not at all factor into my decision to consume it. Importantly, the fact that I eat the veal for reasons of its tastiness reveals that I am already in an aesthetic frame of mind. This is not to say that we will have this focus in every instance of eating. No doubt there are many times I eat simply because I am hungry. But cases like the veal chop example show that we are able to approach eating from an already aesthetically minded standpoint and that we are able to single out qualities of also-functional objects for purely qualitative appreciation.

Thus, there does not seem to be reason to think it is impossible that we could not have disinterested experiences of the aesthetic qualities of objects which do have extrinsic, as well as intrinsic, value. The only way to show it is impossible is to show that *only* purely artistic, intrinsically valuable objects are capable of generating such experiences, and our previous discussion has thrown doubt on that claim. So, it seems that it is possible to have such experiences, even when the object of that experience has instrumental value over and above its intrinsic aesthetic qualities.

Granted, there remains a worry about whether or not we can *know* whether our experience is pure and disinterested. Can we be *sure* that we are eating our veal chop for reasons of its flavor alone? Couldn't it be that we are subconsciously motivated to eat the chop not because of its flavor, but rather for its contribution to our well-being? Admittedly, this possibility is not ruled out. But I do not see a reason that this should really trouble us; we do not seem to have too much introspective trouble in distinguishing times at which we eat simply from hunger, or simply for taste, or a mix of these with various other reasons. What are the grounds for doubting our introspection here? Sure, we can sometimes be wrong about our experiences and what motivates us, but the possibility of error is insufficient to rule out general accuracy in most cases. Surety with respect to our aesthetic experiences and subsequent judgments about them is too stringent a requirement. Furthermore, the epistemic worries are beside the point of my metaphysical investigation.

If I am right about this, then the requirement that genuine art objects have only intrinsic value seems pointlessly exclusionary. It seems at least possible to have disinterested experiences of objects that have additional uses, and food cases nicely highlight this fact. Thus, I am fairly confident that one can rule against the relevance of the functional difference based on consumption. If that is true, then we are reasonably safe classifying culinary art as art in just the same way we do performance arts.

Conclusion

So, taking stock, I have argued that the fact that we consume food does not disqualify it as a proper art object; the alternative thesis fails because it depends on an overly stringent notion of 'art object.' Subsequently, I argued that some art objects, like performance arts, share structural similarities with edible art objects. Given these similarities, I argued the edict to treat like cases alike requires that we extend art worthy status to food. I then attempted to defend that move against the objection that consumption reveals a relevant dissimilarity between performance arts and culinary arts. I take it that I have established my aim in this essay, which was to show that the fact of consumption is insufficient to rule out food as a proper art object.[6] Insofar as I have been successful, we are reasonably safe in counting our veal chops among the art objects that we have encountered on our delightful day in Rome.

Dave Monroe

Notes

I would like to thank Joseph Ellin, John F. Miller III, James Knight, Rhonda Steele, and especially Fritz Allhoff for their patient readings, insights, and helpful comments.

1 Korsmeyer, Carolyn. *Making Sense of Taste: Food and Philosophy*. Ithaca, NY: Cornell University Press, 1999.
2 Ibid., p. 62.
3 Also lurking in the background is a philosophical prejudice which ranks the senses according to their epistemic import. The distal senses (vision and hearing) are traditionally held to deliver more "objective" knowledge to a subject because their objects are observable at a distance. Proximal senses, like taste and touch, are considered too subjective to deliver genuinely objective knowledge. I will pass on discussion of this prejudice, as it is central to Korsmeyer's book. Her treatment of this matter is comprehensive, illuminating, and clear.
4 For those unfamiliar with this lingo, metaphysics is the study of the nature of reality, and especially the things which constitute it (i.e., ontology). One traditional issue in metaphysics is how to account for the way in which things persist through time (so-called diachronic identity); that is, how they maintain their identity throughout widespread and often dramatic change.
5 By "disinterested contemplation" I mean consideration of the merits and aesthetic qualities of an art object which involve no reference to non-aesthetic subjective merits the object might have.
6 One should note that developing a full account of culinary art would require far more than what I have argued for in this essay. It is necessary to follow Korsmeyer in a discussion of the senses, and argue against the prejudicial ranking mentioned in note 3, above. Furthermore, we would have to specify further conditions on when and how a given dish counts as art; surely, not just any food could, or should, count. But I leave these matters for another time.

10

Delightful, Delicious, Disgusting

Carolyn Korsmeyer

Encountering an artichoke, one might wonder how the first person to eat that vegetable ever got past the exterior spines and the interior core of throat-raking needles to discover the sweet heart hidden within. Many foodstuffs present similar mysteries, such as rhubarb, whose poisonous parts surround succulent stems, or vegetables and meats whose toxins require hours of careful flushing before they relinquish edible substances. The vast family of peppers can burn the tissues of the mouth, eyes, and nose so painfully that they are sometimes used as punishment, yet they also have become immensely popular in the diet of many peoples. None of these examples represents bounties of the earth immediately inviting to the palate, and given the sheer difficulty of finding the nutriments to be had from fierce, dangerous, or toxic substances, we might well wonder that human beings ever learned to eat anything beyond the first fruits of the garden of Eden – one of which proved to be the most dangerous of all! The ultimate origin of our diets is lost in the shadows of prehistory and evolution, though one suspects that sheer necessity often prompted discovery of food from forbidding sources. The remarkable thing is not just that we managed to eat, but that we managed and continue to manage to take considerable *pleasure* in foods that present us with challenges to both our senses and our sensibilities. It is the perplexing and elusive nature of this pleasure that will occupy me here, especially the difficult pleasures to be had from what I call "terrible eating."

Discussing pleasure in eating is a surprisingly delicate theoretical undertaking. Food and the sense of taste are not standard topics for philosophical discussion for reasons that have to do with the nature of this sense and the kind of pleasures it affords. Since classical antiquity, our philosophical tradition has ranked two senses above the others, elevating sight in particular to the top of the list because of its role in the development of knowledge. Sight is the chief sensory means by which we make discoveries about the world, assess practical decisions, and achieve aesthetic insights. Vision and its companion hearing are philosophically, scientifically, and in common parlance considered the "higher" senses, while touch, taste, and smell are "bodily" senses, and by the long tradition that ranks mind over body, they are also considered "lower" senses. While sight and hearing operate at a distance from their objects, food and drink are taken into the body, providing it life-sustaining nutrition. Indeed, the chief purpose of food is to nourish, and this heavily functional role is another factor that commonly excludes eating from the intellectual interest of the philosopher. Food is *merely* functional, keeping the body healthy so that more important mental business may proceed. Socrates probably speaks for the majority when he declares that a philosopher should care neither for food and drink nor sex (*Phaedo* 64d).

All of the senses can give us pleasure, but again we find a crucial distinction drawn between the "intellectual" pleasures of sight and hearing and the "bodily" pleasures of touch, smell, and taste. Enjoyment of objects of the eyes and ears – beautiful scenes, sounds, works of art – directs attention outward to the world around. The "objective" intentional direction of vision and hearing aids our knowledge of the world and gives us *aesthetic* pleasure. (Indeed, in modern philosophy beauty is actually identified as this particular brand of pleasure.) By contrast, the pleasures of touch, smell, and taste supposedly direct our attention inward to the state of our own bodies.[1] These senses are considered cognitively dull, and what is more, pursuit of their pleasures leads to self-indulgence, laziness, gluttony, and overall moral degeneration.

The complicated philosophical history of pleasure has posed some obdurate difficulties for those few theorists who have attempted to argue on behalf of the aesthetic dimension of taste and for the comparability of food with works of art. Fine cuisine certainly is to be admired for, among other qualities, the subtle pleasures it delivers. And this has been the chief grounds for defense of the artistry of food and the delicacies of taste invoked by such writers as the

146

gastronome Brillat-Savarin and philosophers David Prall, Kevin Sweeney, and Elizabeth Telfer.[2] They argue – correctly in fact – that a discriminating palate is a result of sophisticated learning and experience, and that the artistry of the great chef or vintner yields subtle qualities in their products that are fully as difficult to discern as are the aesthetic properties of music or painting. While at first this approach seems to put art and food on common ground, it inadvertently subverts and truncates the comparison because gustatory pleasures appear insignificant compared with aesthetic pleasures. The crux of the matter is that the meanings that works of art convey and the insight and understanding they deliver are hardly captured at all in the way we conceive of bodily, sensuous pleasure. Therefore, no matter how refined and subtle is the experience afforded through eating and drinking, it invariably falls short of the more profound aesthetic dimensions of works of art. This view is acknowledged even by those who argue on behalf of food, such as Elizabeth Telfer, who must grant that food is a minor art, if it is art at all.

Yet food and works of art share significant features that are often overlooked if one focuses only on sensuous taste pleasure. The more important similarities lie in the meanings that they capture and convey to the mind as well as the senses. This approach to food does not simply ignore pleasure, however. (Where would be the fun in that?) Rather, I want to argue, *our pleasure responses to tastes are themselves complex cognitive responses that involve highly compressed symbolic recognition.* The concept of pleasure itself will undergo reassessment in the course of this argument, including that type of pleasure that is often taken to be relatively simple: sense pleasure.

No full and complete sensation is free from an awareness of its object. That is, there is no coherent sensation without cognition – i.e., without taking the object of sensation to be something or other. Different interpretations of the object of taste or smell yield different sense experiences. This is not the claim that one has a sensation that is then interpreted and categorized, but rather, that without a category the sensation itself is inchoate and indistinct, even though very strong smells and tastes may provoke powerful physical responses. (Bear in mind that full flavor necessitates the use of more than one sense, requiring both taste and smell and probably also touch.) For example, certain blue cheeses have a sharp smell that is often

Carolyn Korsmeyer

described approvingly as "piquant." This quality when added to salad or fruit enlivens a dish and increases its tastiness. Yet the odor of blue cheese is rather similar to the smell of bile or vomit, and unless one is prepared to encounter cheese, the wafting vapors alone will not register as pleasant at all. Once identified, the sensation comes into focus and takes on its aesthetic properties. In short, the first argument that food has meaning that always enters into its aesthetic properties simply inserts the content or object of sensation into taste experience. A full understanding of taste pleasures and their significance, however, must venture much further than this.

Foods and their tastes may represent and express significance in a distinctively "aesthetic" fashion, and one can elaborate the meanings that foods embody with all manner of examples from the whimsical to the profound by considering Easter eggs, candy canes, birthday cakes, ceremonial meals, and religious rituals.[3] Ceremonies and rituals make use of the most obvious food references (such as the so-called sacred trio of oil, wine, and bread; a butter lamb or hot cross buns on the Easter table; or the array of foods on the Passover seder plate), but virtually any food qualifies. Chicken soup not only has a certain taste, but its bland, oily quality signifies comfort and care. (Think of how what are now called "comfort foods" blend childhood, nourishment, and soothing calm into their very tastes.) At this point, however, I would like to travel down a thornier path and focus on eating that challenges both sense and sensibility and yields much more difficult pleasures.

One might think we can distinguish that which *tastes good* by looking for the opposite of that which *disgusts*. This is the implicit assumption of those who follow the quite plausible evolutionary or biological model for basic emotions such as disgust. This emotion is often interpreted as an aversion reaction to that which is foul and toxic, thereby protecting the organism by inducing recoil and revulsion. Conversely, the natural disposition to like sweet substances is considered to have its functional roots in the healthful properties of ripe fruits that nourish the organism. When it comes to cuisine, however, the disgusting and the delicious do not always function as opposites. A good deal of recondite and sophisticated eating actually seems to be built upon (or even to be a variation of) that which disgusts, endangers, or repels. Indeed, much of the haute cuisine of a culture retains an element that some people – *both inside*

148

and outside that culture – find revolting. And the revulsion appears to be deliberately approached and overcome – not as a matter of necessity (as might be understandable in times of scarcity), but apparently as a way to increase the depth and potency of taste experience.

No one can stand outside culture and proclaim a neutral list of disgusting foods, and the following does not pretend to be one. With that caveat, I offer a provisional list of disgusting things to eat.[4] I have six categories that fall into two groups: one that singles out the taste experience itself, and the other that considers the nature of the object being eaten. (1) First, there are objects with initially repellent tastes, such as parsnips or cod liver oil. This includes objects that retain a residue of a substance that is disgusting, such as the decay present in gamy meat. (2) There are also a number of foods that are tasty in small quantities but cloy when one eats too much and reaches surfeit. This phenomenon is especially present with the relatively easy enjoyment of sweet things, such as cheesecake or candy. Objects in these two initial categories disgust because of their taste qualities, but there is a longer list of disgusting foodstuffs that refers to the nature of what is eaten, including two pairs of apparent opposites. (3) Objects that are too alien from ourselves and that we recoil from when we encounter them in nature, such as spiders or snakes. Something repellent to touch is doubly repulsive to touch with the tongue. (4) Or objects that are too close to us, not alien enough. The prime example of this would be another human being. (5) Objects that are insufficiently removed from their natural form – i.e., that appear to be still alive and resisting. Therefore, we prepare our foods, remove meats from their skin, and so on. (6) Objects that have been dead too long and have started to decompose. This category bends back toward the first.

I am sure these initial categories of the disgusting will be controversial, as they should be. Quite apart from the cultural bias that any such list manifests, these are also categories where taste is *deliberately cultivated*. When disgust or revulsion is confronted and overcome, what was at first disgusting can become delicious.

This can come about through a variety of means. The historian of food T. Sarah Peterson recounts how during the sixteenth century, Europeans, desiring to emphasize the continuity of their own culture with that of classical antiquity, diligently altered their customary food habits because of scholarly discoveries about what peoples of ancient Greece and Rome had eaten. This required consuming vast quantities of animal flesh and parts of animals hitherto not commonly eaten and preparing "high" or gamy meat cooked very rare.

> Fashion setters crunched on ears; blood from meat nearly oozed from the mouth; livers silken with fat melted on the tongue; and the taste for pronouncedly high meat, decomposed to the fine point just this side of maggoty . . . was cultivated in France. . . . By at least the eighteenth century the stylish English were more than partial to them too. Although he considered himself to be in the new French fashion, Richard Bradley, the Cambridge botanist, was aghast at the high meat he was now served. "In many places I have sat down to a Dinner which has sent me out of the Room by the very smell of it."[5]

This trend was a deliberate cultivation of taste because of the cultural meanings of the foods consumed, but it became internalized quite literally as people's liking for the new tastes grew. Note the moldability of pleasure out of disgust in these heroic attempts to eat what is initially repulsive (although the case of Bradley demonstrates that not everyone was persuaded to relish the new fashions in taste).

If it is the case that some of the most important types of cuisine and the cultivation of "good taste" arise out of substances that have a disgust quotient, this is not unique among aesthetic phenomena, and indeed it suggests another common ground that links foods and artworks. Philosophies of art and aesthetics are peppered with examples of what can be termed the paradox of aversion: the attraction to an object that both inspires fear or revulsion and is transformed into something profoundly beautiful, an experience that philosophers from ancient times to the present have analyzed as a type of pleasure. There are three standardly recognized categories where aversions can convert into positive aesthetic experiences: The first and most ancient one concerns tragedy. Aristotle discussed the enjoyment to be found in this poetic form, where the evocation of the painful tragic emotions of pity and terror is the foundation for both catharsis and the aesthetic understanding that he interprets as a pleasure in learning. Second, there is the powerful experience of the sublime, which was widely analyzed in modern philosophy in terms of the conversion of fear into thrilling delight. And more recently theories of horror have tried to comprehend how the disturbing spectacles that mark that genre manage to deliver aesthetic pleasure. I am proposing a fourth category: the conversion of the disgusting into the delicious. Certain encounters with what we might consider particularly profound eating transform an initially aversive – terrible or disgusting – experience into something significant and *savorable*. Though I believe there are special parallels between terrible eating and the experience of the sublime, the conversion of the disgusting into the delicious constitutes its own category. Unlike encounters with sublimity, when we eat, the emotion of fear is remote if present at all, though shadows of disgust may linger. In fact, the presence of disgust might prompt one to compare this fourth conversion to horror rather than sublimity. I hesitate to do this because of the debate over whether the appreciative disgust of horror actually converts to pleasure or requires another explanation.[6] But foods that initially disgust can be transformed into the unqualifiedly delicious.

To amplify this claim and establish some terms of comparison with more familiar ideas, let us consider a theory of sublimity that analyzes the conversion of pain into delight in ways that are suggestive for understanding the meaning of terrible eating. In his *Philosophical Enquiry into the Origin of Our Ideas of the Sublime and Beautiful* (1757), Edmund Burke observes that there are three basic feeling states: pleasure, pain, and an in-between state of indifference.[7] Beauty is a particular species of pleasure, but what he calls the "delight" of the sublime is built upon intense emotional pain, namely, terror:

> Whatever is fitted in any sort to excite the ideas of pain, and danger, that is to say, whatever is in any sort terrible, or is conversant about terrible objects, or operates in a manner analogous to terror, is a source of the *sublime*; that is, it is productive of the strongest emotion which the mind is capable of feeling.[8]

Some theorists seeking to resolve the paradoxes of aversion have retreated to the safety of representation to account for the enjoyment in art of subjects, emotions, and situations that in reality are too dreadful to afford any pleasure. (It is the *mimesis* of tragedy that Aristotle believed permits us to enjoy that difficult theatrical form, for example.) But Burke stands out for boldly stating that we need no shield of representation in order to delight in pain, for indeed we are equally fascinated by pains, terrors, and horrors in reality, so long as they do not press too closely. (He offers the shocking speculation that a theater audience would readily forego the pleasures of the best tragedy in order to attend a public execution.) At a sufficient degree of remove that permits safety, human beings are simply fascinated by – and therefore take delight in – all manner of things that terrify, either for their size or might or ferocity or power.

Burke suggests that objects that inspire terror may trigger the ecstatic delight of the sublime because a state of emotional contentment is simply too close to that intermediate state of indifference that lies between pleasure and pain.[9] Just as an unexercised body becomes slack and lethargic, desiring the exertion of its muscles, so the mind can become too relaxed. Encounters with pain, danger, and other fear-provoking situations shake up the mental works in a healthy and enlivening way, even as they cause us to dwell on forces that threaten our safety and raise our mortality to the forefront of awareness. Ironically, the ultimate object of contemplation that is so enlivening is death, and Burke calls the most profound pain an "emissary of this king of terrors."[10]

Burke's own catalog of sublime objects includes a large and disorderly collection of examples from natural events to passages from the Bible. He lists various qualities an object might have that inspire terror, awe, reverence, respect, astonishment – all emotions that can be components of the feeling of the sublime. The qualities of vastness, danger, desolation, infinity, great size, difficulty, and magnificence all have their sublime exemplars, and what they share is a degree of power that puts their might above that of a human being. "I know of nothing sublime which is not some modification of power," Burke remarks.[11] Things over which we exercise control may be physically stronger than we are, but they are not sublime. A beast of burden may be immense, but it does our bidding and inspires neither fear nor awe. "We have continually about us animals of a strength that is considerable, but not pernicious. Amongst these we never look for the sublime: it comes upon us in the gloomy forest, and in the howling wilderness, in the form of the lion, the tiger, the panther, or rhinoceros."[12] Animals that are aversive but not fearsome are merely odious and more likely to arouse disgust than sublimity.[13]

Although I aim to make a case for certain parallels between sublimity and terrible eating, there are additional factors that initially seem to separate eating from anything akin to sublime status: In some way or other, the perceiver must achieve some "distance" from the object of the aversive emotion in order to experience delight. Vision and hearing permit the apprehension of terrifying objects from a distance, affording a physical margin of safety from which dread and terror can be converted into delight. By contrast, distance seems to be what taste will not permit because objects of taste are always literally close to one. Touch and taste are contact senses and require reduction of physical distance; even smell quickly disappears as one begins to move away from an object.

Moreover, the reversed power relations that obtain between the objects one eats and the objects that inspire awe and terror would seem to preclude eating experiences from comparability with the sublime. By the time something has landed on our plate, it is thoroughly subdued; we the eater are in control. Therefore, it would seem there is no possibility that we might encounter qualities that exhibit analogous aesthetic import. But this conclusion relies overmuch on the fact that our dinner poses no immediate danger. Its presence may nonetheless remind us of that king of terrors, as well as other intimations of mortality and loss, evidence that the fourth conversion harbors disturbing and potentially profound aesthetic experience.

This point is bolstered by a brief detour into the role of food and drink in art. Still-life painting, especially the genre known as the gamepiece, has often been used to foreground rot and decay, transience and loss, and ultimate mortality – ideas manifest in forms both frightening and disgusting. These themes appear at their most extreme in the grisly *vanitas* picture, with its grimacing skulls lolling amidst the detritus of human endeavor. Decay and transience is more decoratively present in pretty flower and fruit paintings when they include spotted and browning peaches, spilt drink, and scavenging vermin. The gamepiece with its depiction of bloodstained, disemboweled deer and hare virtually celebrates slaughter, a harvesting of the bounties of nature commemorated in paintings that hang on the walls of tastefully decorated dining rooms.[14] Any worry over an inference from art to practice is assuaged by similar illustrations of dead game and cuts of meat often found in cookbooks, which, while themselves informed by the genres of still-life, provide a segue from paint to plate.

Leon Kass refers to the "great paradox of eating, namely that to preserve their life and form living forms necessarily destroy life and form."[15] As Margaret Visser observes, "Animals are murdered to produce meat; vegetables are torn up, peeled, and chopped; most of what we eat is treated with fire; and chewing is designed remorselessly to finish what killing and cooking began."[16] The addition of chewing to this catalogue implicates us all in the process of destruction. Not all of this violence is apt to disturb, and indeed for some people none of it does. But certain meals deliberately harbor an awareness of the fact that to sustain one's life one takes another. This intuition looms especially close to consciousness when the object of one's dinner fits into the third category listed above: another animal whose form is still recognizable, not having been chopped and shaped into hamburger or pâté. One might describe this as a meal that is still uncomfortably *close* to its living state. Indeed, this kind of eating can appear brutal, and one might surmise it disgusts because of the absence of the kind of distance that separates civilized human from brute.

One means to quell this discomfort is to remove the object one is eating from noticeable signs of its origin. Consider the following passage from the novel *Cold Mountain*, by Charles Frazier. This narrative is set in the waning years of the American Civil War at a time when scarcity and winter take vast tolls on the resources of the defeated. At a point toward the end of the story, four characters find themselves stranded snowbound in the mountains, where they have trapped some squirrels and roasted them for dinner.

> All they had left was a little bit of grits and five squirrels that Ruby had shot and gutted and skinned. She had skewered them on sticks and roasted them with the heads on over chestnut coals, and that evening Ruby and Stobrod and Inman ate theirs like you would an ear of corn. Ada sat a minute and examined her portion. The front teeth were yellow and long. She was not accustomed to eating things with the teeth still in them. Stobrod watched her and said, That head'll twist right off, if it's bothering you.[17]

This passage does not detail an object of *haute cuisine* but a piece of meat desperately needed to avert starvation, and in context it may seem as if the presence of body parts such as teeth is what renders this meal particularly brutal. Twisting off the head removes some of the uglier evidence of the killing required to sustain human life. And in fact, some instances of developed cuisines do go to extraordinary lengths to remove not only meat but also other foods from their original condition, such as by chopping and stewing or molding or hiding in dough casings such as ravioli or won tons. It would be premature, however, to conclude that *fine dining* is distinguished from *brute eating* by the degree of unrecognizability of its objects or their remove from the apparent natural state in which they lived. Indeed, the dramatic opposite is the case. Consider the elaborate dressings of suckling pigs and boar heads, or the displays of meats stuffed back into skins that graced the medieval dining table. Indeed, one can discover within those same categories of foods that initially disgust and repel, both the distancing of the disgusting and repellent qualities to make the food palatable, and the cultivating of the disgust and repulsion into a form of deliberate and purposeful dining.[18] Items that disgust at first may be transformed into foods that we savor – for the very qualities that initially repel.

Consider objects with tastes that offend the senses at first, very hot spices and peppers, which bum, and alcohol, which sickens, All of these substances one can learn to like through practice and maturity (for the tongue and its receptors develop into adulthood), and once these tastes are cultivated, substances without them appear bland. Sometimes such tastes are part of one's home cuisine, other times they are cultivated as gustatory fashions change.

These examples represent foods the very tastes of which must be overcome and then cultivated; but those tastes represent only themselves, as it were. They do not have any additional meaning that may be repugnant. But certain foods both vegetable and animal come packaged with toxins or repellent substances that need to be washed away to make the food edible, and the tastes of these substances mean danger or foulness. At the same time, sophisticated preparation often deliberately retains some of the noxious substances. In his *Grande Dictionnaire de Cuisine*, Alexandre Dumas asserts that kidneys are at their best when they are prepared so that a whiff of urine flavor remains in them.[19] In this case, something one would gag to drink is retained as flavoring – but only for the kidney, not for any other meat. It is a reminder of the origin of the food that stays within its very taste. Similarly, gamy meat harbors a flavor of decay that renders it stronger and more pungent.[20] In both these cases, it is not only that the taste initially disgusts, but that it signals the presence of things that have a repugnant meaning: waste and death.

Yet, the most sophisticated mode of preparation is one that retains rather than expunges the sense qualities that remind the diner of the borderline state of the food.

Perhaps the most notorious example in this category is *fugu*, the puffer fish, so poisonous that in Japan, where it is commonly eaten, only a licensed chef who knows what organs to remove and how to get rid of the toxins is permitted to prepare it. Yet reportedly, the most sophisticated diner is also the one prepared to risk the most to savor the taste of *fugu*, for by request enough of the neurotoxin can be left in the fish that the diners' lips and tongue are slightly numbed, reminding them of the presence of danger and death. (And sometimes overwhelming them, for this is a dangerous meal and every year people die from eating *fugu*.)

Some foods are substances so alien that they seem to represent a category that simply should not be consumed. Insects, which in swarms are commonly featured on lists of disgusting items,[21] are quite nourishing and are eaten in many parts of the world. To others, it is nearly impossible to imagine putting them into one's mouth. These differences in eating habits are usually just noted as varieties of cultural practice, but this overlooks something very interesting: Disgusting foods do not appear only in the diet of the Other. We all have categories such as these that we do eat, foods that we recoil from or treat very cautiously in nature that we learn to consume quite readily. That which is disgusting is not just that which other people eat; it appears on our own tables, transformed into the delicious. (Of course, once this transformation occurs it is hard to recall the initial disgust, which is why we ordinarily consider only unfamiliar foods disgusting.)

Perhaps the most interesting conversion of the repellent or disgusting to the delectable occurs when the presentation of foods mimics them in life, for it is then that the attentive eater can hardly fail to notice his participation in a death-dealing activity. In times past, the heads of animals have been considered delicacies and have been brought to the table prepared for eating, but still in their original containers, perhaps decorated or even bejeweled. This taste has passed in North America, though we still carve whole fowl at the table, which are quite recognizable even without their wattles and claws. Though we now often remove the heads and tails of fish, we can buy fish platters that thoughtfully trace heads and tail fins in their design so that the succulent middle can be placed between. All of these devices remind us of the original state of what we eat. Although this reminder often goes unnoticed, at times our realization is enhanced to a point that achieves a parallel with sublime experience, and sometimes it lapses into horror. Here are two examples.

Richard Gordon Smith was an Englishman who lived in Japan in the early years of the twentieth century. He recounts a meal he requested in a remote part of that country, where he asked the cook at an inn to prepare a carp in the traditional way reserved for the nobility. Delighted at the request, the cook prepared a live fish, still gasping on the plate, surrounded with tasteful symbolic decorations that mimicked the look of the bottom of a sandy ocean. At first it did not occur to Gordon Smith that the fish had already been readied for eating; he writes: "The dish was really pretty in spite of the gasping fish which, however, showed no pain, and there was not a sign of blood or a cut." But the artistry of the chef was only revealed when he dribbled a little soy sauce into the fish's eye:

> The effect was not instantaneous: it took a full two minutes as the cook sat over him, chopsticks in hand. All of a sudden and to my unutterable astonishment, the fish gave a convulsive gasp, flicked its tail and flung the whole of its skin on one side of its body over, exposing the underneath of the stomach parts, skinned; the back was cut into pieces about an inch square and a quarter of an inch thick, ready for pulling out and eating. Never in my life have I seen a more barbarous or cruel thing – not even the scenes at Spanish bull fights. Egawa [Smith's Japanese companion] is a delicate-stomached person and as he could eat none, neither could I. It would be simply like taking bites out of a large live fish. I took the knife from my belt and immediately separated the fish's neck vertebrae, much to the cook's astonishment and perhaps disgust.[22]

I wonder if this meal is markedly more cruel than any other. The startling revelation of the flayed body aside, Gordon Smith's revulsion seems to be chiefly a matter of timing. He was invited to eat a being whose life had not yet expired, but had the fish been killed just minutes earlier, the collision of life and death would not have occurred to him. And yet it would have lingered there in the very fresh taste of the recently killed fish. The freshness of fish, the agedness of gamy meat: both announce themselves *in their very tastes* to the reflective diner. (Perhaps Gordon Smith would have been comforted by Roland Barthes's suggestion that such meals are memorials of sorts: "If Japanese cooking is always performed in front of the eventual diner (a fundamental feature of this cuisine), this is probably because it is important to consecrate by spectacle the death of what is being honored."[23])

My final example also represents the recreation of a meal that is now uncommon and that formerly was prepared only for the elite of a culture. When President François Mitterand knew that he was dying, he resolved to finish his mortal days by eating one final meal that summed up the best that can be presented to the senses. The centerpiece of that meal was ortolan, a small warbler, a migratory wild bird, which is now prohibited by French law from the table. It is said to represent the soul of France, and consuming it is a sin. But Mitterand prevailed in his last wish and served a remarkable meal to more than thirty guests.

The tiny birds are caught in the wild and kept in the dark to fatten. When ready, they are drowned in Armagnac brandy and plucked. They are roasted and served whole, wings and legs tucked in, eyes open. They are brought to the table straight from the fire, and one must consume the entire bird. The diner traditionally eats them with a large linen napkin draped over his head. The napkin traps the aroma of the dish, even as it hides the shame of the feast from the eyes of God.

Mitterand's last meal was re-created and consumed by a curious American writer, Michael Paterniti. Here is his description of eating ortolan:

> Here's what I taste: Yes, quidbits of meat and organs; the succulent, tiny strands of flesh between the ribs and tail. I put inside myself the last flowered bit of air and Armagnac in its lungs, the body of rainwater and berries. In there, too, is the ocean and Africa and the dip and plunge in a high wind. And the heart that bursts between my teeth.
>
> It takes time. I'm forced to chew and chew again and again, for what seems like three days. And what happens after chewing for this long – as the mouth full of taste buds and glands does its work – is that I fall into a trance. I don't taste anything anymore, cease to exist as anything but taste itself.
>
> And that's where I want to stay – but then can't because the sweetness of the bird is turning slightly bitter and the bones have announced themselves. When I think about forcing them down my

throat, a wave of nausea passes through me. And that's when, with great difficulty, I swallow everything.[24]

Both these examples involve meals that virtually force the diner to contemplate the sacrifice of his or her dinner. This suggests that part of the experience of this kind of a meal involves an awareness, however underground, of the presence of death amid the continuance of one's own life. And it seems to me most improbable to account for the development of such cuisine simply in terms of the search for a really good taste pleasure. It is better understood as an aesthetic transformation of an aversion into a pleasure – the disgusting into the delicious. Admittedly, such insights are not always very ready to consciousness. Other habits of mind, including the purely practical demands of eating, form insulating layers over these matters, a factor that reminds us of the intensely functional circumstances that remain to distinguish even the most recherché foods from artworks.

Animals that qualify as sublime, such as the tiger, the panther, and the rhinoceros, are fearsome precisely because they might attack, kill, and eat *us*. The power relation is reversed when we are the eaters, and one of the privileges of being at the top of the food chain is that we rarely must defend ourselves against becoming another creature's meal. Yet we are certainly edible, and we are as mortal as any other living being. Preparation that foregrounds an awareness of the life and death of our meal does not arouse fear for our own safety, but it prompts meditation on the cycles of life and death that we all undergo by forcing reflection on the very moment where we participate in that cycle. The gasping carp puts us in the presence of death. The fragrances that summon up the life of the ortolan are compressed into its taste, a taste that is both nauseously difficult and ecstatically delectable. It would reach neither extreme were it not for one's intense, bodily awareness of this moment when a life and a death are commemorated in a taste.[25]

Notes

This essay is reprinted from the *Journal of Aesthetics and Art Criticism*, 60: 3 (Summer 2002).

1 The alleged subjectivity of taste is examined at length in chapter 3 of my book *Making Sense of Taste: Food and Philosophy* (Cornell University Press, 1999).

2 Jean-Anthelme Brillat-Savarin, *The Physiology of Taste* (1825), trans. M. F. K. Fisher (New York: Hermitage Press, 1949); David Prall, *Aesthetic Judgment* (New York: Crowell, 1929); Kevin Sweeney, "Alice's Discriminating Palate," *Philosophy and Literature* 23 (1999); Elizabeth Telfer, *Food for Thought* (London: Routledge, 1996).

3 In *Making Sense of Taste* I elaborate these roles with the use of Nelson Goodman's symbol systems from *Languages of Art* (Indianapolis: Hackett, 1976).

4 This list fits into the more comprehensive rosters of generally disgusting objects compiled by theorists such as William Ian Miller, *The Anatomy of Disgust* (Harvard University Press, 1997) and Aurel Kolnai, *Disgust* ("Der Ekel," *Jahrbuch für Philosophie und phänomenologische Forschung* 10 (1929)).

5 T. Sarah Peterson, *Acquired Taste: The French Origins of Modern Cooking* (Cornell University Press, 1994), p. 96.

6 Noël Carroll identifies fear and disgust as the two primary emotions of art horror in *The Philosophy of Horror: Or Paradoxes of the Heart* (New York: Routledge, 1990). Unlike some other theorists of horror, Carroll insists that appreciative disgust remains an aversion, which is the price the audience pays for the pleasure of discovery as the plot unfolds.

7 Indifference is important because Burke rejects the idea that pleasure comes about only as the alleviation of a preexisting discomfort, or that pain is the removal of pleasure.

8 Edmund Burke, *A Philosophical Inquiry into the Origin of Our Ideas of the Sublime and Beautiful* (1757), ed. James T. Boulton (University of Notre Dame Press, 1958), p. 39. "Delight" is the term Burke uses to convey the positive magnetism of the sublime despite its pain; Kant calls this phenomenon "negative pleasure," and the oxymoron he chooses sums up the paradox of aversion.

9 Ibid., pp. 134–145. See also Paul Crowther, *Critical Aesthetics and Postmodernism* (Oxford University Press), chap. 6.

10 Burke, *A Philosophical Inquiry into the Origin of Our Ideas of the Sublime and Beautiful*, p. 40.

11 Ibid., p. 64.

12 Ibid., p. 66.

13 Ibid., p. 86.

14 Kenneth Ames, *Death in the Dining Room* (Temple University Press, 1982). See also chap. 5 of *Making Sense of Taste*.

15 Leon Kass, *The Hungry Soul: Eating and the Perfecting of Our Nature* (New York: Free Press, 1994), p. 13.

16 Margaret Visser, *The Rituals of Dinner: The Origins, Evolution, Eccentricities, and Meaning of Table Manners* (New York: Penguin, 1991), pp. 3–4.

17 Charles Frazier, *Cold Mountain* (New York: Atlantic Monthly Press, 1997), p. 347.

18 Items in the second category, tastes that disgust because of surfeit, seem different from the others, all of which permit scope for the fourth conversion. Surfeit indicates an abuse of taste that requires scaling back rather than exploitation. However, as Scott Waltz pointed out to me, phenomena such as pepper or pie eating contests arguably exploit surfeit for its own pleasures.

19 Alexandre Dumas, *Dumas on Food: Selections from Le Grand Dictionnaire de Cuisine*, trans. Alan and Jane Davidson (London: Folio Society, 1978), p. 152.

20 Aurel Kolnai speculates that exaggeration of flavors that results in the "high taste" (*haut goût*) of gamy meat may be a model for the deveopment of an "eroticism of disgust" both literal and aesthetic. See *Disgust*.

21 See Miller, *The Anatomy of Disgust*, chap. 3.

22 Mark Meli drew this account to my attention. Richard Gordon Smith, *Travels in the Land of the Gods: The Japan Diaries of Richard Gordon Smith*, ed. Victoria Manthorpe (New York: Prentice Hall, 1986), p. 205. This part of the diary is from 1906/1907.

23 Roland Barthes, *The Empire of Signs*, trans. Richard Howard (1970) (New York: Hill and Wang, 1982), p. 20.

24 Michael Paterniti, "The Last Meal," *Esquire* 129, no. 5 (May 1998): 117.

25 This paper has benefitted from the comments of several audiences and the careful readings of a number of colleagues. I would like to thank in particular Elizabeth Telfer, Ann Clark, Ann Colley, Rosemary Feal, Regina Grol, Claire Kahane, Barry Smith, and Carol Zemel.

11

Food Fetishes and Sin-Aesthetics: Professor Dewey, Please Save Me From Myself

Glenn Kuehn

Primarily I write about food and philosophy. For 37 years food has kept me alive, and for 15 years the work of philosophers such as John Dewey has helped me figure out (and share with others) the reasons why food is philosophically important. Working off of Dewey's depiction of aesthetic experience, I have argued that food can be seen as affording us a potential aesthetic experience so profound and qualitatively interactive, that it deserves a status of nothing less than the "ultimate art." Yet, I have been wondering, have I taken it too far? Or, more realistically, have I gotten to the point where I have distorted Dewey too much?

I suspect that I have led myself into a corner, personally and perhaps philosophically, regarding aesthetic experience when it comes to food. I believe I have become overly selfish, and have embraced an almost solipsistic aesthetic of isolation and secrecy. I have rejected shared interaction, neglected qualitative growth, and forsaken the community of inquiry. In short, I have sinned against Dewey – and for someone reared in American Philosophy and Pragmatism at SIU-Carbondale, this is problematic.

A Brief History

A few years ago at a Society for the Advancement of American Philosophy conference in Portland, Maine, I responded to a paper by

Professor Lisa Heldke called "The (Extensive) Pleasures of Eating." She argued that in order to eat well, to eat attentively, healthily, and completely, we needed a larger gastronomical worldview. We needed to take seriously the distantly related events, people, and circumstances under which the food we eat is grown, processed, shipped, and prepared for our consumption. This larger attentiveness leads not only to a strong ethical awareness of food, it also heightens (both positively and negatively) our aesthetic relationship with our edible world. While I could not disagree with her, I nonetheless took it upon myself to argue for caution. Too much extensive eating, I stated, was inadvisable because we would have to deal with too much guilt and would end up developing too many hang-ups arising from knowing an excess of information about what we were eating.

I argued for a "reasonable" level of ignorance in eating because it avoided the guilt. I said that the downfalls of knowing too much about the food you eat outweighed the high points – and while pleasure and guilt are often experiential companions, their tenuous relationship is fraught with an endless series of elopements and annulments. I offered four examples from my own history of eating which showed that knowledge could preclude aesthetics: raw liver, grilled dog, fugu, and cow tongue. In the first case, I recognized the liver I once ate as raw liver and that epistemic moment immediately ruled out any possibility of pleasure because it put up a wall in front of my openness to experience. The next two foods were eaten in ignorance, and not being able to identify one as a possible pet and the other as a possible poison, helped me eat pleasurably and without a sense of taboo or fear. The last example, though easily eaten by me as it is a family tradition to eat tongue at Thanksgiving and Christmas, from the perspective of my former partner, was judged inedible because it is a *tongue*, and a tongue, be it a cow's or any other's, is simply not food.

Thus, I counter-argued that knowing the identity ("that is raw liver," "that is a tongue"), the history (that might have been someone's pet), and potential side-effects (this could kill me), seriously detract from aesthetic pleasure and development – they preclude possibility. Precluding possibility is undesirable from a Deweyan perspective. The grand Deweyan ideal (a projected end-in-view) of qualitative growth through inquiry and social development was indeed hindered by knowledge. It was with great incredulity that I proclaimed epistemology to be a deterrent to aesthetic development. So why not argue for ignorance? It is often quoted, "It was a brave man, who first ate an oyster." I for one am most thankful for that bravery – bravery which I suspect was grounded in ignorance.[1]

Heldke admitted in her paper that extensive eating is not easy, and at least for the short term, it can be rather disturbing. So I suggested that we take a step back. Let us lose the desire to know everything there is to know about the conditions under which these veal calves, chickens, tomatoes, and strawberries developed such that I have been able to enjoy them. Superficial eating comes at a price, and it affords a "thin aesthetic," Heldke concluded. I agreed, but added that there is a lot to be said for superficiality and thin aesthetics. As Dolly Parton says, "You'd be surprised how much it costs to look this cheap!"

A comment was made at this session that I was arguing for a sense of the aesthetic that was not intended for communal growth or indicative of inquiry and intelligence. At heart, an aesthetic that misses the mark, falls short, and is separated from the Deweyan project of "artful progress" through aesthetic experience. I was supporting the idea of a sinful, or "sin"-aesthetic. The comment was particularly perceptive, I thought, and immediately realizing its accuracy, I could do nothing other than agree.

My Descent into Sin – Secrecy

The religious folk on TV tell me that I must admit and confess that I am a sinner. So, here it is: I have sinned. But my sin is against the will of a Deweyan god – a god, that is, which is not a transcendent entity sitting on high, waving its finger and chastising me, but rather a god comprised of a unity of ideal ends which supply a guide for our actions and pursuit of a growing community.

My sin lies in food fetishism, or the irrational reverence I seem to have for food in itself, so to speak. I experience food as a fetish in terms of obsession and magical fascination. In secret I have eaten, perhaps unwisely, yet with great pleasure, things I cannot bring myself to share. No, cannibalism has not been part of my eating history. Nor have Rocky Mountain Oysters, monkey brains eaten out of a live monkey with its head poking through a table, or any other extreme eating experience worthy of getting me on a reality show. My culinary indulgences have their provenance in indulgences which would be typically looked upon as excessive, unnecessary, and silly. Yet, for me, they are necessarily secretive. They are pleasures made possibly only in the absence of the Sartrean "gaze." In these moments, aesthetic experience is individual and secret.

Secrecy is imperative for the enjoyment of food fetishism because in order to indulge in this pleasure, one *must* keep it clandestine (perhaps even from oneself in a state of denial); otherwise, where is the secret pleasure? For example, the harsh reality is that I really enjoy fast food and even though I have seen *Supersize Me*, I simply do not want to think about where items such as Big Macs, Filet-o-Fish, Chicken McNuggets, and Taco Bell tacos come from and what conditions make it possible for me to consume them. I do not need to hear about the tortured cows, the hormone-injected lives that they lead, the waste of grains used to make the nutritionally vacuous bun, and how we squander space, time, and the environment by growing so much grain for animals when we could use it for better purposes. I just want to eat the Big Mac, okay? Oh, and yes, I would like that super-sized, thank you!

I have been told that we should beware of people who keep secrets. Holding on to secrets often carries with it the baggage of guilt and shame. I experience guilt and shame for eating these foods in the same way I feel guilt for not sharing a recipe – or only sharing part of it and holding back on a key ingredient. I also feel guilt for what the foods are. That is, I question my sense of aesthetic discernment when I think back and ask myself, "why did I eat that?" And, when the initial revulsion subsides, I give thanks and feel gratitude that no one saw me.

It is clear to me that my sins arise out of two activities. The first involve feelings of shame that arise from the particular food eaten (in secrecy), and the second involve feelings of shame that arise from keeping food information secret. My greater sin is more closely associated with the latter. The following is an attempt to explore, and make amends for, my sins.

Further Descent into Sin – Guilt

Guilt level 1: butter and honey

In *The Garden of Eating*, Jeremy Iggers shows how eating has replaced sex as the primary force of guilt in contemporary America. 'Sin,' he points out, is a word hardly associated with things other than desserts. He states, "Just as sex was once surrounded by mystery, danger, and the promise of passion and fulfillment, food is now the forbidden fruit, the locus of fear and longing."[2] Food carries with it the horror of shame. Forget the "Scarlet 'A'" on your dress; now it is a "Resented 'F'," which stands for Foodie.[3]

Think of those foods that, somehow, constantly and unendingly tempt us with advertisements telling us that we can "indulge" in eating the things we "shouldn't." The cunning and powerful allure of food reaches us covertly.

I have a collection of what I call "local" cookbooks; the ones that are put together by groups such as women's VFW auxiliary organizations, churches, and high school French clubs. Two recipe genres persist in these cookbooks: very creative jell-o salads, and sinful desserts. One in particular typically goes by one of two names: either, "Better than Robert Redford cake" or "Better than sex cake." Now, I will assume that Robert Redford is a nice guy, but cake that is better than sex? Come on. Then I would read the ingredients, which are very consistent: chocolate, caramel, toffee, crumbled Heath bars, more caramel, more chocolate, and topped with whipped cream and more crumbled Heath bars, and then chocolate and/or caramel syrup. Better than sex; maybe they have got something there. More guilt ladled on you than sex, could be. Here is the test question: Would you honestly eat "better than Robert Redford cake" *or* "Better than sex cake" in public view? And further, if you did experience either of these, would you tell anyone about it?

It is blatantly obvious that food is essential for life. It is also obvious that eating can be highly pleasurable. It is arguable that food is art. It is even possible to support the view that food is the greatest of all arts. But it is also true that as much as we might want to share our gastro-aesthetic discoveries with the world, in secret we are food fetishists who eat what we should not when we should not and would simply die if people (or Robert Redford) found out. Secrecy is the sin that makes the pleasure possible. But secrecy leads inevitably to guilt, and when the guilt becomes overbearing, we have to purge.

Whereas often the beginnings of redemption can be found in confession, I will share and confess this with you: I love butter and honey on a spoon. I was a latch-key kid, and I would come home from school alone and typically make dinner for my parents and me two or three times a week. Sometimes, while roasting a chicken or making meatloaf, I would get curious about combining foods and flavors. I would experiment, and it was not until recently that I realized that I have never told anyone about my adolescent culinary pursuits. So, here are a few. I take credit for inventing Oscar Mayer bologna and processed cheese rumaki served with mayo. I found out onion soup mix dip went fairly well on a cheeseburger. I also came to believe that one should mix just about everything with ketchup at least once. Then one day I discovered butter and honey.

It sounds rather obvious that these two items should go together; after all they are longtime companions of toast. But for me, toast with butter and honey was indicative of something more. In themselves, butter and honey must be hiding something because toast by itself was interminably dull. Perhaps the toast was either getting in the way or detracting from something greater that butter and honey possess by themselves. So, I took butter, which I would soften but not heat up, and then marble it with honey in a small rumaki dish. I ate this concoction with a spoon. Well, I did not eat it, *per se*. I licked it as one would lick an ice cream cone; getting just enough to enjoy the flavor and the marbled texture, but not so much so that it was over in one lick. It was more than good. I had discovered a culinary secret: so-called condiments and sides are good in themselves. Yes, I ate butter and honey. My inner voice is screaming, "I cannot believe I just told you that." I imagine that if I ever had indulged in this in front of someone, I am sure they would have scrunched up their face in righteous disapproval – and at the same time long to try it themselves; alone, when nobody was watching. Oh yeah. They would lick it, too.

Guilt level 2: Glenn's cheesecake

Aside from indulging in the stealthy sin of butter and honey, I believe the greater sin involving food secrecy lies in a particular recipe

I have. I used to cater during graduate school, and the one item that was almost always included in a gig was cheesecake. My cheesecakes (although varied in flavor) all come from one master recipe which I did not create. I got it from Ted. Ted was my first chef, and I learned more from him than he knows. One night as I was struggling with a veal piccata, practically counting the number of capers I was going to put in the pan, he approached me with a glass of water and a tin of salt, and instructed me to "season the water." I looked at him, then the water, and very carefully acted like an *artiste* who underwent some sort of mind-meld with the salt as I ran it through my fingers.[4] Ted rolled his eyes, told me (very colorfully) that I was an idiot, shoved his hand into the salt and threw it into the water, looked at me and said: "Never be afraid of the food and if you have to think about it, you won't be able to do it." I felt like I was in the presence of Yoda: "Do or do not . . . there is no try."

Ted was known, though, for his cheesecake. He would make them on Tuesday, and he would do it early in the morning when no one was there. I asked many, many times for the recipe and Ted would only smile. I set a goal of getting that recipe. I begged, I pleaded, and I bribed, but nothing would get it out of him. However, remembering my Kantian training, since I willed the end, I willed the means. One night I took Ted out for drinks, and after I had spent an egregious amount on seemingly countless martinis, I asked him again about the recipe. As his head lay on the bar, he divulged the recipe which I frantically wrote down on bar napkins.

While I am not proud of what I did to his liver, I had nonetheless managed to get Ted's cheesecake recipe.[5] I had acquired gold, or Robert Redford. That recipe has served me well. In my catering experiences, the one common item has always been cheesecake. Though I have been asked many times for the recipe, I have never surrendered it. Sure, one or twice I gave hints, guidelines, and even ingredients, but never the full recipe. I have, as with my other food fetishes, kept it secret. It is mine. My recipe. Me doing it by myself. My cheesecake recipe is sacred! Please, let it be mine alone. And therein lies the real sin.

Some people say that I too easily use being an only child as an excuse for much of my selfish behavior. And perhaps they are correct. All I know is that, for me, sharing has been a very difficult concept to acquire.

Total Sin Revealed: How To Eat Alone In Public

Total secrecy in gastronomic indulgence is possible, even in public. An airport bar is an ideal place for bloody marys, beer, cheeseburgers, jalapeno poppers, and chimichangas. If you have enough layover time, temptation taps you on the shoulder and offers to buy the first round. Sirens lure you to locations where bad food and weak drinks are served at prices you would normally consider to be insane. They call you in, regardless of the time of day. $19.50 later you have had one weak drink and a mediocre-at-best burger. And for some reason, this is pleasing. Why?

"You are never so alone as when you are in a crowd," or so the line goes. And in O'Hare, LAX, LaGuardia, Shipol, Hartsfield, or Osaka International, when you are sitting at an airport bar, you are alone. No one pays attention to what you eat and drink and no one notes with any disapproval the time of day you do it. It is a collective sin of a bizarrely unified individualism because even though you are in public, you are not part of a group. We are engaging in a secret self-indulgence that we would normally deny when our actions could be known.

Self-indulgence is a moment of engaging in that which you know you ought not. You are willfully transgressing and acting in an immediate denial of the guilt you know you will feel later. Wasn't it St. Augustine who said that original sin was possible because of being able to look at God's will and choosing what you want to do instead?

How am I to resolve this issue of reconciling my appreciation for the depths of aesthetic experience along with the innate clandestine nature of enjoying a variety of forbidden foods, coveting my recipes, and eating in secret? I found my answer one year after I responded to Heldke's paper. The answer was simple, and it was Deweyan: eat with others, and talk about it.

Redemption: Deep-Fried Turkey and Sharing

Again, Jeremy Iggers characterizes food-related sins as a replacement of sexual sins. Weight Watchers and Jenny Craig have become institutions of religion which guide our sense of self and self-image. Dieting is not something you *do*; it is a way of life. For him, the difficulties in this context are expressed in the obsession we have with our bodies and the most dreaded of fears: getting fat.

I have come to think that he also indirectly points to a greater guilt. Often, the creation and enjoyment of our "most favorite" foods necessarily relies on the security that they will never be shared. Favorite recipes are often guarded by an indignant passion – just try to ask a Texan for their chili recipe.

Iggers asks, "Why all the guilt?" Why all the fear and irrational psychoses regarding food? I ask, why all the secrecy? Why do we covet food in so many non-communal ways? Why do I eat my favorite stuff in secret? And why am I simply unable to share the recipe for my cheesecake?

If Iggers is correct, and food has replaced sexual practices and desires as the new sin *du jour*, what do we do with the sinners? The issue of redemption must be addressed.

One year after that conference in Maine, I presented a paper at another conference where I shared a session with another fellow food-philosopher, Ray Boisvert. We both talked to and cooked for the audience. Ray made salads, and I made cheesecakes. During the afternoon, while Ray and I were preparing our parts of the meal, the caterer who was handling the rest of the meal was preparing lunch for her staff and invited us to help ourselves to some deep-fried turkey. I had heard of this delicacy before, but never had one. The turkey came into the kitchen looking like ancient Egyptian treasure; it smelled like joy, and we descended upon it.

We did not use plates, forks, or knives, and we made meager use of paper towels as napkins. I had a drumstick with half a thigh still attached. I stood at the table with it in my hand and gnawed on it like a proto-human tasting his first bite of marinated sabre-toothed tiger with a mammoth demi-glace. What really struck me was not simply the flavor and succulence of the bird, but the collective indulgence in something we would normally not share in polite company. We stood there, all of us, devouring this insanely good food, and we did it together. Several of us were specifically focused on the skin of the turkey. Between the spices and the deep-frying, the skin was so crispy, succulent, and flavorful that when I first took a bite I stood back and said, "I am having a moment."

Eating this turkey was a collective indulgence in something so delicious that I could barely stand to think that we were doing it in public. And yet, the openness of it made it even more delicious. Our conversation wafted between talking about the tenderness of the turkey to the decadence of deep-frying. Our musings about flavor combinations were mired in the divine combination of salt and fat. In the end, our insights were blurred by the deliciousness of the moment.

What a community that was formed at that moment. What a sense of understanding. What a moment and transition of personal and communal growth. I was enjoying this most decadent of foods, savoring and wallowing in my own crapulence, and yet realizing that I had been brought to this experience through this new community. I was introduced to a new food through the caterer (a fellow inquirer), and our collective tastes and culinary intelligence had grown.

A thought occurred to me. Food fetishes can be, as Martha Stewart says, a good thing. Perhaps our secret gastronomic desires can be bridges, connections, and catalysts towards community instead of barriers and veils.

In "An Alphabet For Gourmets" M. F. K. Fisher wrote a chapter entitled " 'A' is for 'Dining Alone'." She states, "A is for dining alone, and so I am, if a choice must be made between most people I know and myself. This misanthropic attitude is one I am not proud of, but it is firmly there, based on my increasing conviction that sharing food with another human being is an intimate act that should not be indulged in lightly."[6] I agree completely, but I would like to take that level of gravity concerning breaking bread with another and extend it to our real, favorite foods. If we are going to eat together, we should also eat that which we love most. We should risk sharing our favorite tastes, and be open to the new connections they may nourish.

Several years ago, my good friend Laura (a fellow philosopher and a person whom I call "The Queen of Soups") and I came up with an idea for a restaurant called "Nibbly Bits." It is a restaurant entirely devoted to secret foods that we love to eat but would not sanction in polite company. We went through the obvious choices, but then we got to the "juicy" ideas: hot dogs wrapped in processed cheese, sliced and served with a side of ranch dressing; butter and honey (of course); a microwaved bologna cheese mustard mayo jalapeno sandwich with no bread. I offered the insight that the problem with chicken is with the meat; the best part is the skin. We of course dismissed our plans as dreamy, but unpractical. Yet, what a moment of realization when it came true with deep-fried turkey! What a community these ideas and experiences created – secret foods to be shared!

When attempting to understand basic truths about life and living that take root and guide productivity, Emerson would probably say, go take a walk and figure it out for yourself. Climb a tree or learn to be a beekeeper, and do not worry if other people think you are strange, because, as he said, to be great is to be misunderstood. But I think that Dewey would tell me to do something a little more communal, and I hope that he would say we should start by sitting down and eating together. And when we break bread, let us be honest, open, and willing to talk about what we really think. Only then can the growing community flourish through aesthetic experiences. Only then can the reorientative quality of shared experience take effect, and only then can the connections I have with the social and natural world progress through intelligence and creativity. Oh, and learn to share.

So, here it is. I willingly share with you my cheesecake recipe, and perhaps, even just a little bit, I may be redeemed.

Appendix: Glenn's Cheesecake

Use with caution, and share with many.

Part of the key of this recipe is its initial simplicity. I have more than one cookbook which is devoted exclusively to cheesecakes, and my conclusion is that they generally make it far more difficult than it is – or should be.

I tend to favor graham cracker crusts (and also other crusts made from various types of crackers like ginger snaps, chocolate cookies, and other things that are crumby). I can't say I like pastry crusts for a cheesecake as the message of the dessert seems to get confused. Is it pie, is it cake, or is it a torte? What is it?

So anyway, here's the basic idea:

For a 10-inch spring-form cheesecake, plus a little extra for a small bonus cake, here's what I do.

For a graham cracker/cookie crust, mix the crumbs (I don't have a measurement here as I never measured how much I use) with melted butter. You must use butter. As Anthony Bourdain wrote in *Kitchen Confidential,* "If you don't use butter, there's nothing I can do for you." How much butter? I can't say. The mixture should be like damp sand.

Press it firmly (very firmly) into the spring form and then bake it at 400 degrees until the crust is set.

For the master batter, combine the following ingredients:

3   pounds cream cheese
2–3   cups sugar (amount depends on if you're going to add another flavor)
6–7   eggs
1/3   cup flour
1/4   cup heavy cream
3   tbls vanilla (the real stuff: if you use imitation vanilla extract, again, there's nothing I can do for you)

Now, here's how I mix it.

The cream cheese must be soft.

Combine the cream cheese with the sugar first and make sure it is thoroughly blended so there aren't any lumps. Once the mixture becomes more fluid due to the eggs and milk there is nothing you can do to eliminate lumps.

Add the flour and mix in.

Beat the eggs (very carefully so there are no bubbles) in a separate bowl and then add them slowly.

Add the cream and vanilla.

Mix and you have your basic cheesecake batter. If you want to flavor it, be creative and just dump stuff in: booze, pumpkin filling, cocoa, coffee, whatever. I've tried so many flavors, and the one that most intrigued me was when Ted made a roasted garlic chocolate cheesecake; it was stunningly good.

Put spring form in a larger pan and pour the batter in.

Bathe the cake pan in a water bath; no more than 1/3 inch up the side of the spring form.

Bake at 285 until done. How do you know when it's done? You just do. The middle should be springy and look slightly undone. If it cracks, it's overdone, so take it out immediately. Otherwise, it should finish cooking on its own after it is out. Let it cool, cover and put in fridge.

Now, on to serving. To get the "clean" slices, you must freeze the cheesecake first. Use a very long knife and cut it in half, and then always cut from the edge to the center and always wipe the blade with a cloth after each cut. You will end up with a true gem.

Notes

1 One can imagine the internal conversation in that man's mind: "Hey, look at this slimy, gray thing inside this shell! I know, I'll eat it and find out what it is." This is not indicative of a highly intelligent being.
2 Iggers, Jeremy. *The Garden of Eating: Food, Sex and the Hunger for Meaning.* Basic Books: New York, 1996: 110.
3 Ibid.
4 Picture Indiana Jones in *Raiders of the Lost Ark* when the sand is running through his fingers before he switches the bag for the gold idol. That was me with the salt.
5 While my *Kantian training* was quite thorough, I need to absolve my professors of any peripheral responsibility regarding my obvious blemish in applying Kant's work. It was my decision to ignore the part of the Categorical Imperative pertaining to the whole deal about "never treating others as a means only." But I ask us all to remember the context (and the first thing to recognize about the Categorical Imperative is that it's not contextually malleable). I was after a cheesecake recipe.
6 Fisher, M. F. K. "An Alphabet For Gourmets." In *The Art of Eating.* MacMillan: New York, 1990.

Dessert

Eating & Ethics

The way you cut your meat reflects the way you live.
Confucius, Chinese philosopher

12

Eating Well: Thinking Ethically About Food

Roger J. H. King

I

Some people may find it difficult to take seriously the idea that it matters morally how we eat. Usually we eat what we like, what we are used to, what our families cooked, what's cheap or fast or convenient. In this respect, eating seems like other kinds of consumption. We suppose that producers should be held accountable for how they manufacture products that we use in our daily lives, but we rarely think of our own consumption practices as acts for which we should be accountable. My goal in this essay is to make a case that it matters morally how and what we eat. Consumption, whether of food or other commodities, is an activity about which we can, and should, think ethically. There are better and worse ways to consume – ways that are morally defensible and ways that are morally problematic.

What does it mean to eat well? The question is ambiguous. Eating well can be interpreted as a question about human nutritional needs. To eat well would be to consume sufficient calories, vitamins, minerals, fiber, and whatever else is needed to function well as a human organism. Eating well in this physical sense demands an understanding of how gender, age, physical activity, and general level of health affect the organism's nutritional needs.

Or eating well might be interpreted in aesthetic and cultural terms: people eat well when the food they consume pleases their senses and provides diversity of colors, textures, aromas, and flavors.

Cultural traditions and habits affect what will be pleasing to a particular consumer, so that foods that are eaten with delight in one society may be perceived with disgust in another. Popular writing and films about food often emphasize this sensuous and culturally diverse character of eating well.

Neither of these two senses of eating well addresses moral considerations, strictly speaking. Yet even here we can see how the question of eating well can be pushed in a moral direction. The ability to eat well in either the nutritional or the aesthetic sense depends on how the individual consumer is situated in a broader social network of relationships. Not everyone is able to meet their nutritional needs. Low-income communities in rural and inner-city areas of the United States, for example, have less access to supermarkets and to high quality, affordable food than people living in more affluent areas.[1] Indeed, access to adequate nutrition in all societies depends on many different social factors, including class, gender, and age, that make eating well in this basic sense dependent not just upon individual choice, but also on the moral and political character of the broader social network. And when it comes to the aesthetic sense of eating well, even those who do have access to nutritious food may have lost the cultural knowledge or cooking skills to make eating an interesting, diversified, or culturally authentic aesthetic experience. The causes of these failures may lie in moral and political injustices that deserve moral analysis.

For the purposes of this essay, the particularly moral sense of eating well begins to emerge with the recognition that eating creates relationships. These relationships may be narrow and local or of a much broader scope, but how we eat unavoidably links us to other people, animals, habitats and soils, and to our own sense of personal identity. These relationships, both to others and to our own selves, are potent subjects for moral reflection. Before we can take responsibility for our eating, we must learn to perceive the relational dimension of consumption.

The relationships created by how we eat reach out in many different directions. Close at hand are the relationships created by eating a meal with other people. Meals bring families together, sustain business relations, and create opportunities for romance. People concerned about the breakdown of the family sometimes point to the fact that many families no longer eat meals together as symptomatic of the problem. Eating together has a social significance and meaning that transcends the biological functions of nourishment. It may, therefore, be just as important to think about with whom we are willing to eat, as it is to reflect on what we eat.

How we eat also sustains relationships to ancestors, ethnic groups, or regional location. Despite the fast food industry – and as a rebuke to its homogenizing impact – many regional eating traditions in the United States still exist. Maine cuisine is different from that in Louisiana or New Mexico; New Yorkers eat differently than residents of Dubuque or San Francisco. Many Americans of different ancestries express personal and community identity partly through an allegiance to particular ways of eating. To give up the food of one's people can be not only a symptom of betrayal but also a form of betrayal in itself.

Our habits of eating also create relationships to animals and to the soil. Thousands of wild animals are killed annually in the pursuit of sport hunting. Millions of animals are housed each year in stressful and diseased conditions before being slaughtered to feed those who eat meat. The meat industry is the largest consumer of fresh water in the country and a major consumer of land and grain crops.[2] The conditions in which animals can be housed profitably for mass-market consumption require extensive use of hormones and antibiotics, relating both the meat industry and consumers of meat to the pharmaceutical industry.[3] The concentration of animals in feedlots before they are slaughtered creates vast amounts of waste that can pollute local waters, poison fish, and harm human health.[4]

The relationship to soils created by our use of plants is often equally problematic. Mono-cropping for the economically efficient production of large quantities of grains and vegetables encourages pests who are then dealt with by spraying pesticides.[5] Corporate concentration in the food industry is replacing family farms and the traditions and livelihoods of both small-scale farmers and the communities within which they have flourished. National and international marketing of foods encourages companies both to experiment with genetic engineering and to select seeds that produce foods that can be harvested by machine, stored for longer periods of time, and made visually attractive to consumers. These processes do not necessarily preserve the nutritional or aesthetic qualities of the food we ultimately consume.

Finally, how we eat relates us to citizens in other parts of the world. Much food in our supermarkets is imported from other countries. Our eating, therefore, links us to the people who produce the food, the processes they use to grow and handle it, and the companies that control food production and distribution. Sometimes this connection implicates us not only in what is done but also in what is not done. In some poorer countries, land designated to grow crops for export could have been used to produce food for local consumption. Poor and illiterate farmers are often given agricultural chemicals without adequate training in how to use them safely.[6] To the extent that people are hungry in those countries or exploited by those who employ them in the fields, our choices of how to eat link us inextricably to their plight.

Earlier, I suggested that we often think of eating as a personal act, something that we do as individuals, an act for which we don't consider ourselves morally accountable or responsible. In this section, however, I have implied that how we eat creates multiple relationships to other people, animals, and the land. It links us to corporations; chemicals and drugs; farm laborers; and those who are made ill by fecal wastes, pesticides, herbicides, hormones, or exploited labor. We are implicated in deforestation for pasture, soil erosion from poor plowing or crop rotation practices, and ground water depletion from irrigation that turns fertile soil into desert. Our eating choices, then, might be seen as nodal points in a vast web of interrelations, interactions, and flows of energy. As such, it seems plausible to ask whether we can say something about moral and immoral, better and worse, ways of eating. Consumption begins to look like it has consequences, just as production does.

II

To say that there might be right and wrong ways to eat suggests that there are goals to be attained in eating that go beyond the merely nutritional and aesthetic aims we have already identified. From the nutritional point of view, our goal in eating is to acquire the proper balance and quantity of the nutrients needed to remain healthy. This aim requires significant knowledge of the qualities of various foods, as well as human needs at different stages of development and under different conditions of health or disease. Similarly, from an aesthetic point of view, our goal in eating is to create a particular kind of aesthetic experience: one perhaps that juxtaposes particular colors or matches food qualities with complementary qualities in wine.[7] So what goals might be appropriate to eating well from a moral point of view?

One answer might be that eating well means achieving sustainability. According to one prominent definition, sustainability requires that we meet our human needs in the present without compromising the ability of future generations of people to meet their needs.[8] To the extent that we are not meeting needs in the present and are, at the same time, passing on hardships to the future, we are not eating well, morally speaking. Following this line of thought, morally responsible consumption requires attention to the implications of our eating choices for the wellbeing of contemporary and future generations of human beings. This wellbeing is clearly contingent on the nature of the various relationships to soil, waters, animals, habitats, and farm laborers already described.

This definition of sustainability is perhaps both too narrow and too vague. It is narrow in that it refers only to meeting the needs of contemporary people and future generations. It is vague because the definition does not clearly specify what are to count as needs. The requirements of this definition of sustainability might, in theory, be met while compromising large areas of the planet and harming uncounted numbers of animals. It seems odd to think that we could be acting sustainably while destroying the fertility of agricultural soils, so long as new technological developments allowed following generations to meet their nutritional needs by substituting artificial foods. To use a science fiction example from the popular *Star Trek*, what if everyone could one day have access to the food they need through machines that artificially replicate various molecular combinations? In such a society, we would have met current needs and enabled future generations to meet their needs, although not from "natural" sources, which will have been destroyed. Is this what we want to mean by using sustainability as the measure of eating well?

Economists such as Julian Simon do not find this to be a problematic implication.[9] In Simon's view, environmental resources, such as fertile agricultural soils or crop species, are only valuable because of the economic services they render human beings. If the same services can be provided by alternative materials and technologies, then we have no grounds to lament the loss of any particular resource. Indeed, in Simon's optimistic view, the scarcity of a particular resource encourages the search for and creation of an alternative way of delivering the service that is threatened. If fertile soils, diverse species of domesticated plants and animals, or clean water become scarce resources, then human needs can be adequately met by finding technologically sophisticated ways to substitute artificial means for providing the services these resources give us.

While there are a number of problems with this approach, for our purposes it is sufficient to note that focusing on the economic value of resources does not facilitate an assessment of our moral relationship to them. While soil, animals, and indeed people have economic value in certain circumstances and for certain purposes, and in that context may be seen as economic resources providing economic services, they can at the same time be seen in a moral context as things or beings that can be harmed. While forests and wetlands, for example, function as resources possessing economic value, they are also habitats essential for the survival of non-human species. Domesticated animals, too, provide economic and nutritional services, yet they are frequently made to suffer severely in the process. And the same can be said for the economic vision of human beings in their function as labor. To narrow our vision of sustainability to what affects human economic interests alone obscures the moral dimension of our relationships to animals and the natural world.

If we take these relationships seriously, a more fruitful way of thinking about sustainability might be one that explicitly defines sustainable human actions in terms of our impact on the wellbeing of both the environment and other people. Sustainability would then be neither purely human-centered nor purely Earth-centered. Sustainable eating practices will certainly transform habitats and environments, but they must do so in ways that preserve the evolutionary integrity of the organisms that constitute them. Sustainable eating practices should also be conceived as ones that promote equitable and just relations to producers, laborers, and other consumers as well. Our goal as consumers must be, then, to find out how to eat in ways that do not require the suffering of factory farms, the chemicals of mono-cropping, habitat destruction, or the loss of soil fertility through desertification. Taking seriously the relationships that eating sustains, we may be forced to reevaluate what our food needs really are.

Some may object here that taking this network of relationships created by our eating practices so seriously is both unworkable and ethically excessive. Not only is it impossible for the individual consumer to meaningfully take all impacts into account, but some relationships deserve less ethical attention than others. These concerns are worth some consideration.

It is true that we will never be able to identify all the actual individuals affected by all the choices we make in consumption. In some cases, this failure is a result of the sheer number of people involved, and the magnitude and diversity of the impact on animals and environments. In some cases, the failure results from our very real inability to find the information we would need in order to know all the specific differences that would be entailed by making one choice rather than another. Recognizing these limitations, however, does not absolve us of all responsibility. Some of our ignorance is the result of our own willingness to stay blind to the consequences of our choices. Much information is indeed available about the conditions in which farm laborers work both here and abroad, the conditions in which animals are raised, and the environmental impacts of industrial agriculture. While we may not be able to know everything about the particulars, we can get sufficient information about the generalities to warrant making our eating choices a matter of moral concern.

But having said this, is it not excessive to expect that we take all these relationships equally seriously from a moral point of view? Each of us stands in relationship to many things. Some of those relationships are fairly distant and abstract; others are quite intimate and concrete. Some relationships are entered into intentionally, or by some choice of our own. Some are created by the action of others, or by accidents of association and mere existence. The differences between types of relationship are arguably relevant when it comes to understanding what requires our moral attention. In the context of our discussion of the network of relationships created by our eating practices, it might be argued that the relationships in question are too thin, too abstract to carry much moral weight.

Acknowledging the various kinds of relationship a person may form complicates the moral picture, but does not change it in essential respects. The relationships that eating creates are often hybrid in nature: both near-at-hand and distant, both concrete and general. We may feel the pull of certain elements of the relational network more readily than others, but the more distant links exist nonetheless. The moral urgency of reflecting on how we act, and what eating well means, derives from the fact that eating does in fact connect us to others in ways that are more than just abstractions. While our relationships to poor farmers in other parts of the world are not as intimate and rich as our relationships with family and friends, or with local farmers in our own community, these relationships still demand our attention. We depend upon the services of others – of land, animals, and people. We are being provided with the things we need to live, and to live well, by a network of others, often quite remote from us geographically. Often these things are provided at significant sacrifice to them, in the form of low wages, poor working conditions, environmental degradation, and death. The argument of this essay is that these others make a moral claim that eating well requires us to address.

III

How we eat – and whether we hold ourselves accountable for how we eat – depends to some extent on what we see. Eating either obscures the world or helps to make it visible. Current practice suggests that most of us fail to see what we consume. Nature is simply there as a storehouse of resources to be used to satisfy human preferences, whether for food or other types of consumption. We live toward nature, as Martin Heidegger might say, as a *Bestand* (a standing reserve).[10] The objects of nature are visible only to the extent that they meet a need or desire, or stand in the way of something we wish to accomplish. This mechanical way of looking obscures the internal and autonomous workings and directionality of natural beings and place.

Of course, a parallel problem emerges in our failure to see the human beings who are also integrally enmeshed in the web of relationships created by our eating habits. To the extent that we do not see them, or the conditions in which they work, we act as if they are but instruments to serve our own ends. And this blindness to the subjectivity of these human subjects is precisely the treating of other rational beings as mere means, rather than as ends in themselves, that Kant argued against so persuasively.

A person will not take responsibility for how they consume if their impacts on nature and other human beings are invisible to them. If sustainability requires that human transformation of nature must preserve nature's evolutionary integrity, then such sustainability will be impossible if we do not know how to see this integrity or the ecological processes that support it. And while sustainability requires that we enable present and future generations to meet their needs, it matters greatly whether we allow those others to determine what their needs are, or whether we impose our own concept of basic needs on them. In other words, sustainability, pursued blindly, might only promote a minimal standard of biological need satisfaction, rather than a standard that is culturally appropriate and autonomously chosen by those whose needs are in question.

It does no good here to object that we cannot know what the needs and preferences of future people will be, so our impact on them cannot be a moral concern. In fact, we can know what some future needs and preferences will be, because we share a common humanity and a common biological condition.[11] But more specifically, the needs and preferences of future people are affected in part by what we in this generation do; the future is not entirely independent of the present. Our present choices will affect the magnitude of future generations' needs and the ease with which they can meet them. The present will also determine what resources, institutions, technologies, world-views, ecosystems, and species will be available for future people to use, admire, respect, and desire. Pursuing sustainable consumption, then, requires more attention to the standpoint of others: other people, other generations, other species.

We might talk here about an "ethics of seeing."[12] How we see a person, for example, goes a long way in determining who they are, especially if the person is less powerful than we are. We often obscure the people around us by the categories we use. Race, gender, class, appearance, or educational level can be used to abstract an image of people from the full complexity of their real identity. We relate to them mono-dimensionally, seeing a distorted aspect while remaining blind to the rest. Given that we act on our perception of

185

other people, our actions become equally distorted, even perhaps unjust and exploitative. Holding ourselves responsible for how we act toward other people requires that we learn to see them clearly as they are in themselves, not as mirror images of our own needs and prejudices.

This ethics of seeing is as relevant to the moral problem of how we eat as it is to our moral responsibilities to other human beings. If we see a cow as just meat and leather, wheat simply as flour and bread, or trees only as boards and paper, then we adopt a mono-dimensional, reductive perspective that blinds us to the consequences of these categories. Seeing someone or something as "just an X" may encourage us to act in ways that we would recoil from if we saw X in a different light.

Of course, the process of seeing the other for what they are in themselves, rather than as a reflection of our own prejudices, is a problematic and difficult achievement. Marilyn Frye's distinction between loving and arrogant perception is suggestive.[13] The latter mode of seeing projects our own ideas and agendas on to the other. We see the other – whether human or nature – in relation to our own desires and projects. Loving perception, on the other hand, proceeds with some humility towards its object. The goal is to see the other in its own terms, as having its own life and purposes. But loving perception does not evolve just from the positive desire to see the other clearly. Such perception must emerge from the co-operative and dialectical engagement with the other that allows the other to communicate, to reveal its own limitations as well as potentialities.

The mono-dimensional seeing in arrogant perception takes place when we abstract our eating from the network of relationships to which eating immediately links us. When I only see meat, grains, or vegetables, but not how and where they were produced, I miss something essential in these foods. I miss the chemicals that may have polluted the waterways to make them, or the exploited labor that may have been used to grow them. And this blindness makes choices between local or foreign produce, or between organic and industrial agriculture, appear to be irrelevant or nonexistent. Indeed, this blindness makes the very notion of morally good and bad ways of eating difficult to understand.

IV

There is a constant pull to turn the question of eating well into a question about the consumer's health. This is quite apparent in many discussions of genetically engineered food. The increasing use of genetically engineered foods provides an opportunity to illustrate the thesis of this essay, that eating well has a moral dimension. Should a person who is eating well be eating genetically engineered food products? How should we go about answering this question?

Much of the debate about the ethics of genetically engineered foods centers on whether the new foods are harmful to human health and whether consumers have a right to know if the foods they buy have been genetically modified. Obviously, if genetically engineered foods make people ill, then, from a purely physical point of view, eating well must exclude them. Industry argues that the foods are safe for human consumption and that, therefore, there is no need to label them – doing so will simply worry consumers for no good reason.

Of course, there is some disagreement about this view about the impacts on human health. Since genetically engineered foods contain genes from species of plants or animals that would not normally be found in the natural food product, the risk that consumers will eat foods to which they are allergic increases. Foods that are not normally a risk may become hazardous even though their outward appearance gives no warning of the danger. For this reason, labeling genetically engineered food is a good idea. In addition, there are concerns about the long-term implications of antibiotic markers used during the insertion of the new genetic material. And plans to develop and grow various medicines in genetically modified crops raise questions about how these medicines can be contained and prevented from cross-pollinating with other crops that are grown for food.

However, let us abstract from the parameters of this debate. Suppose that genetically engineered foods did not harm the consumer and provided the nutrients that good foods should, such that these foods would be compatible with eating well from a biological and nutritional point of view. Given these hypothetical suppositions, should we be satisfied that there is no further moral issue here?

This essay argues that the moral dimension of eating well lies in the relationships created or disrupted by particular choices about how we eat. Our relationship to the health of our own bodies is only one of these relationships. The moral status of eating genetically engineered foods depends, therefore, on how eating them affects the entire network of relationships to which our eating lends support and legitimacy. The difficulty many people have in deciding about genetically engineered foods may lie in the fact that it is difficult to trace out the different effects they have on animals, plants, soils, tradition, labor, and other people. Given our tendency to be blind to many of these relationships, the task of sorting out the moral problems with genetically engineered foods becomes even more complicated.

A quick look at the broader implications of eating genetically engineered foods suggests that there is a potentially significant impact on our relationships to the environment and to other people.[14] For example, genetic engineering may affect where a particular crop can be grown, and thus who will profit from growing it. Successful substitution of engineered vanilla for natural vanilla, for example, threatens the livelihood of growers in Madagascar for whom natural vanilla beans are the only source of income.[15]

Moreover, introducing genetically engineered foods in the food system amounts to involuntary experimentation on consumers because the long-term effects of these foods have not been investigated. While engineering pesticides into a food crop may obviate the need to spray pesticides in the environment, the process still produces insect populations that are resistant to the pesticide, while raising questions about the health impacts on humans who consume the pesticide in their food.

Companies who create and invest in genetically modified organisms naturally seek control over their creations. Industrial control over the source of seeds for genetically engineered crops through patents and licensing agreements deepens farmers' dependence on seed manufacturers, siphons profits out of local communities into the coffers of multinational corporations, undermines age-old farming practices that depend on saving seed from year to year in order to promote the local adaptability of particular seed lines, and makes the global food supply more vulnerable by reducing its biodiversity.

When industry inserts genetically engineered foods into the market while blocking efforts to label them, it infringes on the freedom of consumers to make informed food choices based on their own values and preferences. Despite widespread popular belief that producers should provide what consumers want, the manufacturers of genetically engineered food products imply that consumers' desires for information are irrational.

For the purposes of this essay, then, a consumer has not exhausted all morally relevant questions when they determine whether genetically engineered foods will cause harm to their health or to the health of their families. We must expand our moral vision. Genetic engineering transforms the way people relate to the land, to workers in other countries, and to their own rights of self-determination. When widespread, it fundamentally changes the meaning of eating well. Eating is a transaction with the natural environment that has far-reaching ramifications, as we have seen. The development of genetic engineering creates another mediating relationship, another perturbation in the relational network, which threatens the integrity of that transaction. By industrializing eating, whether through factory farms, monocropping, or genetic engineering, we corrupt relationships throughout the vast network our eating creates.

I started this essay with the concern that people might not take seriously the notion that eating well is a moral issue and a task for which we should take responsibility. If my argument has been sound, we should now be able to conclude that how we eat does indeed raise moral issues because of the impact our choices have on relationships with people, animals, and the environment, both near at hand and far afield. Becoming morally accountable for our eating is not just a matter of making sure that we all have enough to eat, nor is it limited to the legitimate outrage at how animals are treated in the industrialized food system. Rather, most broadly, eating well means opening our eyes to the vast network of effects created by our eating practices. We must then use what we see to guide our consumption in ways that protect the health and integrity of the soil, the wellbeing of wild and domesticated animals, the health and rights of those people who work the world's fields and farms, and our own sense of self and community.

Notes

An earlier version of this essay was published in *The Maine Scholar*, vol. 14 (Autumn 2001): 179–86.

1 Cook, Christopher. *Diet for a Dead Planet: How the Food Industry is Killing Us*. New York: New Press, 2004: 20–4.

2 Regan, Tom. "Vegetarianism and Sustainable Agriculture: The Contribution of Moral Philosophy." In *Food for the Future: Conditions and Contradictions of Sustainability*. Ed. Patricia Allen. New York: John Wiley, 1993: 114–16.

3 Mason, Jim. "Brave New Farm?" In *In Defense of Animals*. Ed. Peter Singer. Oxford: Blackwell, 1985: 98–101.

4 Fox, Michael W. "American Agriculture: Ethical Crossroads." In *The Meat Business: Devouring a Hungry Planet*. Ed. Geoff Tansy and Joyce D'Silva. London: Earthscan, 1999: 25–6, 33–4.

5 Holden, Patrick. "The Global Contribution of Organic Farming." In Tansy and D'Silva, *The Meat Business*, pp. 161–2, 165–7; Haynes, Richard P. "Science, Technology, and the Farm Crisis." In *Ethics and Agriculture: An Anthology on Current Issues in World Context*. Ed. Charles V. Blatz. Moscow: University of Idaho Press, 1991: 123.

6 Gudorf, Christin C. and James E. Huchinson. "For Ecological Health or Profit? The POP's Elimination Treaty." In *Boundaries: A Casebook in Environmental Ethics*. Washington, DC: Georgetown University Press, 2003: 44–5.

7 See for example, Maresca, Tom, *The Right Wine: Matching Wine with Food for Every Occasion*. New York: Grove Press, 1990.

8 World Commission on Environment and Development. *Our Common Future*. New York: Oxford University Press, 1987: 43.

9 Simon, Julian. *The Ultimate Resource*. Princeton: Princeton University Press, 1981.

10 Heidegger, Martin. "The Question Concerning Technology." In *The Question Concerning Technology and Other Essays*. Trans. William Lovitt. New York: Harper and Row, 1977: 3–35.

11 Partridge, Ernest. "Future Generations." In *A Companion to Environmental Philosophy*. Ed. Dale Jamieson. Oxford: Blackwell, 2001.

12 "There is great power in being able to see the world as one will and then to have that vision enacted. But if being is seeing for the subject, then being seen is the precise measure of existence for the object." Williams, Patricia. *The Alchemy of Race and Rights: Diary of a Law Professor*. Cambridge, MA: Harvard University Press, 1991: 28.

13   Frye, Marilyn. "In and Out of Harm's Way: Arrogance and Love." In *The Politics of Reality*. (Trumansburg, NY: Crossing Press, 1983: 66–72.

14   Anderson, Luke. *Genetic Engineering, Food, and Our Environment*. White River Junction, VT: Chelsea Green Publishing, 1999.

15   Miller, Alan S. *Gaia Connections: An Introduction to Ecology, Ecoethics, and Economics*. Lanham, MD: Rowman and Littlefield, 1991: 138.

13

Picky Eating is a Moral Failing

Matthew Brown

Appetizer

Common wisdom includes expressions such as "there's no accounting for taste" that express a widely accepted subjectivism about taste. We commonly say things like "I cannot stand anything with onions in it" or "I would never eat sushi," and we accept such from others. It is the position of this essay that much of this language is actually quite unacceptable. Without appealing to complete objectivism about taste, I will argue that there are good reasons to think that tastes are sufficiently malleable and subject to bias that one should be cautious about saying, for example, that one does not like a certain type of food. On many matters of taste, there is reason to believe that your experienced judgments will not necessarily agree with inexperienced and unreflective opinions on the matter.

Radical subjectivism about aesthetic preference can be taken to justify the practice of picky eating (after all, who is better to say what I will enjoy than me?), while the position of this essay is that picky eating is a moral failing. To be a picky eater is to have a significant lack of openness to new experiences and to substantially hamper one's development. It involves an irresponsible level of fallibilism with respect to taste. Never venturing into new aesthetic landscapes leads to a sort of repetitiveness, which in turn leads to a life full of blandness and banality. And, as meals are perhaps the most pervasive of social experience, being a picky eater can violate your duties to others. I argue, not that everyone must attempt or pretend to like what your friends or what expert gourmands like, but that there are significant obligations to openness, self-knowledge, accommodation, and gracefulness that should impact one's food preferences.

Certain cases may provide exceptions or excuses for picky eating. Vegetarianism is one example where moral justification is often given in favor of limiting the types of food one is willing to eat. Physiological, largely genetic conditions make some people more or less sensitive to certain tastes, so-called supertasters and non-tasters. Bitter foods taste far more bitter to supertasters, which may make them averse to these foods. In the former case, I will argue that vegetarianism is only morally correct when it comes out in the balance of reasons, and that the argument of this chapter provides reasons against it that may easily be left out of consideration. In the latter case, I argue that the supertaster has the same duties of openness and accommodation as everyone else, but that they may reasonably be expected to reach somewhat different preferences from normal tasters. These considerations will justify a new, more refined understanding of what picky eating is and why it is morally problematic.

Soup: Common-Sense Subjectivism Critiqued

I like Thai food best, but Andy prefers Mexican. Matt does not like Italian food. Amanda cannot bear to eat onions. Michael will not touch anything that has mustard in it. Joe would never eat sushi or any raw meat. For many people, these are just so many different preferences, of no moral weight or significance. So, you do not like Italian or onions or sushi. So what? Some people like some flavors, and some people hate them. If they think they do not like how something tastes, well, they obviously know best.

While received wisdom is not entirely consistent on this point (your parents say, "Oh, you'll learn to like peas," and we sometimes say, "You've just got to develop a taste for coffee"), taste is often considered to be a harmless matter of personal preference, and picky eating is just having a certain set of such preferences. This commonsense idea is, however, largely mistaken. While a complete objectivism about gustatory values is probably indefensible, it is also not the case that you are always in the best position to know what foods you will like best. Humans are food generalists, having very few innate determinants of food preference.[1] Much of their food preference is left up to culture and experience, which can often even reverse reactions to foods that are initially and innately aversive.

While gustatory pleasures vary somewhat from person to person, there is nonetheless significant overlap in the tastes of cultured palates (people who have experience with a wide variety of foods). A gustatory experience is a complex interaction of factors: there are physiological elements, including the basic tastes,[2] other tongue-sensations like texture, temperature, piquancy (spicy-hotness), minty-coolness, astringency, fattiness, and numbness,[3] as well as associated sensory/physiological elements like smell, hunger/fullness, appearance, effects of caffeine and alcohol, and so on. Previous exposure and experience, as well as learned associations, biases, and social pressures also play a role. Prior experience has an important impact, especially driving reactions like neophobia and disgust. At a fine grain, these factors mean that no two taste experiences are exactly alike, but even at a coarse grain, we can see that any particular taste experience is a confluence of factors and that it is highly sensitive to idiosyncrasies of past experience.

It would be unduly radical to claim that you can be wrong about a particular taste-experience. It rightly seems like any taste-experience (including all the factors discussed above) you have is what it is: if you found the brussels sprouts you ate last night unpleasant, then you really had an unpleasant experience with them. What I dispute is the leap from there to the further claim that you do not like brussels sprouts, or to the claim that brussels sprouts taste bad, or to the future action of avoiding or refusing brussels sprouts. While you may not have enjoyed *those* brussels sprouts, and there may be many biases to break down and tastes to develop before you could ever like them, it may be that you could come to like brussels sprouts very much. Indeed, there are good reasons to think that many people could do so. And even if you never could like them all that much, there are reasons why refusing to eat them might still be the wrong choice.

I have had very different experiences from a Japanese man the same age, and this in part accounts for our tastes inevitably being quite different. I can never gain his perspective, because of all this accumulated experience. Nevertheless, I can expand my horizon in order to come to appreciate more of what he appreciates, allowing our horizons to partially overlap. That this process is possible we know from countless examples in our own lives: seven or eight years ago there would have been very little Japanese food that I would enjoy. Today, while there is surely much Japanese food that I still would not like, I take pleasure in many kinds of Japanese cuisine. (Though, I still have not accumulated the gumption to develop a taste for *uni* (sea urchin), I am sorry to say. But I feel rather bad about it.) The amount of overlap that is possible may be subject to certain constraints, but these constraints do not account for the morally objectionable cases of picky eating.

The considerable degree of overlap that exists between experts, at least at a coarse-grained level, is also evidence that cultivated taste experiences will overlap. While it is possible that among a community of experts, unwarranted biases may accrue, a large, lively, and critical community of experts can minimize these effects. Areas of wide overlap provide reliable tips about food experiences that one should learn to accommodate. For example, sauces that do not have enough salt in them will taste too bland. A certain type of red wine goes better with red meat than a white wine, while the reverse is true for dishes of a more delicate flavor. These old culinary saws are general rules that tell you how to find a better culinary experience. Each of them can be explained, either in more basic culinary terms, or even in psychological and physiological terms. Violations of these rules are met with skepticism, and there are routes for certifying the validity of a claim to an exception, ideally, both in theoretical explanation and experimental testing (tasting).

We must be careful with the role given to experts, however. It would defeat the arguments of this essay if we exchanged an untutored version of picky eating for the picky eating of a snobby gourmand. Indeed, it is quite imaginable that someone with a gourmet palate might themselves be exceedingly picky, that they might reject certain kinds of foods, not because they taste bad, but because of their association with status, refinement, sophistication, and so on. Culinary experts can be helpful when they pave the way for us to find new and more enjoyable gustatory experiences. They are vicious when they work to close us off to experiences that we would have otherwise found valuable.

Pickiness is the practical side of the belief that matters of taste are entirely subjective. The picky eater is not open-minded to new taste experiences, and they see no reason to be fallible about their own preferences or try to understand their reactions to food. They see no reason they should have to accommodate food they do not like, and they often react to food in a way that lacks grace and respect. Picky eating is thus not so much a matter of which foods you eat, but your approach to eating, a matter of attitude and behavior. We have seen reasons to believe that one does not always know what is best for oneself with respect to gustatory experiences, which would make these attitudes a mistake. But how does all this tie into ethics? In the next three sections, I will provide three foundations for the ethical evaluation of picky eating.

First Course: Openness to New Experience and Duties to Self

The first foundation of an ethical evaluation of picky eating is the duties you have to yourself.[4] Picky eating is a violation of your duties you have to yourself because of the way that it closes you off to new experiences and because of the habits it produces in you that tend to decrease your capacity to have further experiences. It violates the duty you have to develop you own capacities and excellence. Picky eating is by no means a *special* moral concern in this area, but it is both an instance and a symptom of a larger problem.

Before defending the kinds of duties you have to yourself and the importance of new experiences therein, I will talk a little about how picky eating closes you off from new experiences. At this point, you may want to say, "Look, I do not want to eat this thing, so what? It has very little effect on my life or my capacities." But not so fast! Let us look at some examples of the sort of effects I am concerned about, meant to be exemplary of the effects of being picky or not. Hopefully, these stories will suggest very similar experiences of your own.

Most people find piquant food aversive at first,[5] though for some, that experience might be so long ago or at so young an age that its memory has dimmed. Suppose you have a few bad experiences with spicy-hot food, and you formulate a couple of maxims for yourself: "I do not like piquant food" and "I am not going to eat anything with chiles." Now, you may well go through life not eating piquant food, and there will be a few cuisines, where piquancy is a major component, that you never learn to like.

The problem here is not so much in the end results by themselves, but on what has been given up. My own case has some representative features: I was slow to warm up to piquant foods, and I came to enjoy them through some foods that I enjoyed independently of how hot they were: Mexican, Tex-Mex, and barbecue. After a while, and partly due to eating with people who already liked piquant food, I developed quite a taste for heat. This opened up new avenues of experience. For instance, I used to have little taste for Thai food; it seemed unremarkable and not as good as Chinese. Then I started going out for Thai with friends who liked their Thai food hot, learned about the spiciness conventions, and started to see it as a distinct and interesting cuisine. What piqued my interest is that Thai food, especially curry, is served extremely piquant, and many of the flavors in Thai food are much more appreciable when the food is spicy-hot. Served very mild, a red curry seemed fairly unremarkable. Turn up the piquancy, and the whole flavor landscape changes for the better.

I had a similar experience with Vietnamese food. I found my first tastes of phó to be quite jarring and initially a little bit unpleasant, due to the unfamiliar combination of flavors. Finally, I decided to go crazy with the Sriracha (a piquant sauce) and the lime. In addition to making the taste a bit more familiar (the mix of spiciness and lime is common in many cuisines, including Mexican), I also sweated my way through the meal, which itself can be a pleasant experience. Now I enjoy phó quite a bit, and I do not make it nearly as piquant as I had to at first. Now I experiment with the different combinations of the condiments they give you, and generally enjoy the mix of flavors.

And it does not just stop with new food experiences! Food is a natural entreé into curiosity about a culture at large. To take a minor example, contrary to what some Americans think, most Thai food is not traditionally eaten with chopsticks. Most food is eaten with a spoon, while a fork is used like Westerners might use a knife. Sticking a fork in your mouth in Thailand is a lot like sticking your knife in your mouth in Maryland! In Thailand, chopsticks are only used for a few dishes like noodles and noodle soups and dishes imported from China. Interestingly, their use of chopsticks has increased with commerce with China. In this way, one can move from food to eating customs, to cultural and political interactions in the Southeast Asian region. The particulars of the example are somewhat idiosyncratic, but the phenomenon it exemplifies – the way that food opens up new possibilities for experience – is quite general. Open-mindedness and curiosity about food can go hand-in-hand with open-mindedness and curiosity about culture generally.

Food can encourage not only an interest in gaining general knowledge of other cultures, but also with new personal experience. An interest in the cuisine of the region might beget an interest in traveling there. It would be a barrier to having a meaningful interaction with someone of another culture if you refused to sit down to a traditional meal from their society's cuisine with an open mind. It would be difficult indeed for someone to integrate well into a society, to get the flavor of the people and their customs, without developing a taste for their food.

Furthermore, the more often you balk at new and unfamiliar food, or food that you do not expect to like, the more you ingrain a habit of avoiding these types of new experiences. A conscious decision to turn down something unfamiliar and thus a bit frightening at one time becomes a habitual refusal. Decisions become a pattern, and a pattern becomes a habit, and habitual behavior is done without considering the consequences, and can be quite difficult to overcome. And why think that this habit will confine itself to food preference?

Could many of the good experiences that go beyond food be gotten in other ways? Can I compensate for the loss of pleasure from good foods with finding pleasure elsewhere? That this is possible there should be no doubt. But cutting oneself off from new culinary experiences closes one such avenue, making it that much less likely and that much more difficult.

Current experience is connected with future experience in such a way that current activities can widen or restrict the potentialities for future experience. Pickiness in one case can contribute to a general habit of pickiness, which in turn restricts your ability to enjoy new experiences in the future.[6] It can cut off opportunities for expanding your horizons. In turn, it can make you a more parochial, less open, less democratic, and ultimately less valuable person. It prevents you from developing and reaching a greater state of human excellence and self-realization. The harms you can cause towards your future self in this manner are no less serious, no less ethically poignant, than such harms done unto others.

Open-mindedness is a morally valuable attitude to have when approaching unfamiliar situations, or situations in which your natural reaction is quite different from those around you. It is natural for many people to react to such situations with distrust, fear, or distaste. Neophobia *and* xenophobia are altogether too common. They make sense as general tendencies on an evolutionary scale – in a dangerous world, stick with habits that you know work, and avoid the unfamiliar. But today, these tendencies are easily taken to the point of parochialism and irrationality.

Being open-minded towards new things, exploring them, and trying to understand them are good means to finding what value there might be in things. Coming across an unfamiliar group of people, you may initially find things about their way of life distasteful, or perhaps even morally objectionable. It would be wrong to leave matters at the level of this immediate reaction. An open-minded exploration of the practice, its effects, and its internal justification might show you that it has real values that your way of life is missing.

There are obviously limits to open-mindedness. I will not explore a cultural practice that involves killing humans for fun. Not only does it violate reactions of disgust probably too fundamental for me to overcome, but I think I have considered this thoroughly enough to know roughly the value involved. Likewise, I would not explore a cuisine that served up fresh human fecal matter. Again, there is extreme disgust, and I have also sufficiently thought through the consequences to know that it is probably not worth it (in this case, the risk of contracting a terrible disease is quite salient).

One of the most important families of duties you have to yourself is to self-development or growth.[7] A lack of openness to new experience frustrates this duty. Your actions ought to be evaluated in part in terms of whether they further your development, helping you realize greater excellence. These excellences include both intellectual and aesthetic excellence. On the one hand, being closed-minded can decrease your ability to appreciate many aesthetic experiences, and it can also decrease the number of pleasing experiences you actually have. Your capacities for pleasure and appreciation remain underdeveloped. Your intellectual capacities suffer as well: a closed-minded person is less curious and inquisitive. They have less drive for and will tend to attain less knowledge about themselves and the structure of their preferences, as well as knowledge about other foods, other cultures, and other people. And, as we will see below, their capacities for social relationships are hampered as well.

Another way in which your intellectual capacities are hampered by picky eating is the attitude towards knowledge and judgment that it involves. A picky eater does not consider their judgments of taste to be open to revision. If taste is not completely subjective, if there are things to get wrong about it, then picky eating amounts to a kind of unbending and inappropriate dogmatism. It is like saying, "I know this to be true, and nothing could ever convince me otherwise." That such an approach to knowledge is problematic and epistemically irresponsible is perhaps too obvious to merit much attention. This kind of inflexibility and infallibilism tends to frustrates progress with respect to *any* kind of judgment or knowledge.

Because of the continuity of experience, the sorts of experience one has now affect the kind of experience you can have later. We grow and develop when we gain access to a wider range of experience, when we are able to engineer a wider variety of situations to our benefit. The importance of growth is most obvious in education: it is the duty of the teacher to see to the growth of their students. The paradigm example of retarded growth is the spoiled child, who demands from others that they cater to his desires, who seeks out situations in which he can do whatever he feels like at the time, and who fails to cope in situations that require effort and intelligence in the face of difficulty. The spoiled child is unable to take responsibility for his life, to be the author of his own fate. The child's development and self-realization have suffered. Just as parents or teachers that spoil children have failed them by retarding their growth, you fail yourself when you act in way that is detrimental to the realization of your own capacities.

Instead of being distrustful of new taste experiences or deciding to permanently cut yourself off from them, you should approach unfamiliar foods and foods that you have yet to develop a taste for with open-mindedness. You should explore the food, trying to understand why others enjoy it and why you might be reacting to it in the way that you are. You should try new approaches that can make it easier at first, like using a sauce that you know you like, or by beginning with dishes in the cuisine that are not as far out. It may be that, after approaching some food with an open mind, learning about it, learning about yourself, and trying different ways of enjoying it, you still just do not like it. As we know, not everyone is capable of exactly the same taste experiences, so we should expect some disagreements. But this differs from picky eating, which is characterized by neophobia, quick judgment, and willful ignorance.

Second Course: Picky Eating in Social Situations

An important part of ethics concerns your relationships with other people. It should be no surprise, then, that the impact that picky eating might have on others gives us further reason to see it as a moral concern. In several ways, large and small, picky eating is harmful to others and to your relationships with them, and thus is a morally problematic way of behaving.

Picky eating harms others by inconveniencing them. When trying to coordinate meals with other people, whether you are going out or cooking together, a picky eater constrains the choices and makes the decision that much more difficult. Sometimes the inconvenience is small: for example, if Amanda is picky about onions, it is pretty easy to go somewhere she can order something without onions, or to prepare a meal without onions in it (though it may make some meals less enjoyable for others). Sometimes it is more difficult, as when someone is picky about a great many foods or rules out entire cuisines. When your pickiness is known, it means that anyone cooking you a meal will have to compensate for it, or make special exceptions when preparing your food. When it is not known, you host may feel the need to do something at the last minute to compensate.

In cases in which someone is serving you a meal, being picky is an inappropriate response, as it is whenever someone gives you a gift. When someone does something nice for you, you ought to accept it with grace, you appreciate what there is to appreciate in it, and you accommodate the ways in which it might differ from your ideals. To do less, to complain or be picky, is hurtful and disrespectful to the gift-giver. Thus, if someone serves you a meal, you do not turn up your nose at it, or tell them that you do not like onions, or ask them to make special exceptions for you, unless you have a very good reason. It would be appropriate for someone who is lactose intolerant to politely refuse ice cream. It is inappropriate to sneer at a carefully prepared meal because it has something in it that you have not particularly enjoyed in the past. That does not mean that you have to be disingenuous, or pretend to like it. But you should try it, appreciate it, and be gracious about it, even if you cannot find a way to enjoy it.

When someone shares a meal with you, they are often sharing an important part of their lives. Sometimes they are sharing a favorite meal, one that they enjoy and want to share. Sometimes it is an experiment, trying a new recipe. They hope to do well, and they want someone to go on this adventure with them. Even when the meal is simple, they are still sharing food with you, seeking some communion with you. When you refuse, you make it difficult for them to share this part of their lives with you. It makes things difficult for you with your friends, and it can be hurtful to the person trying to share something with you. Again, you do not have to pretend to like it, but you should not approach the situation with a picky attitude.

Picky eating also cuts you off from avenues for shared experience with others, and thus makes it more difficult, perhaps impossible, to fully understand other people and other cultures. We have seen the different ways in which food forms an important part of culture and social life, and how it is one way of gaining new experiences, even ones that go far beyond food. Perhaps one of the most important types of experience, both morally and in terms of personal meaningfulness, is the experience we share with others. When you refuse to share food with others and make it a positive experience, you close off one of the most central ways of connecting with other people in everyday life.

Being a picky eater does not just violate etiquette and custom. While violating customary, polite norms of behavior can indeed be insulting or shocking to those around you, and is itself to be avoided, picky eating consists of more than just conventional rudeness. Meals are a universal social event, and their gravitas is nearly ubiquitous. Picky eating really hurts other people, though admittedly the hurt is often small: an inconvenience, or hurting someone's feelings. Furthermore, it hurts your relationships with those people, straining personal relationships, closing you off to shared experience, preventing you from widening your social horizons. A small harm is still a harm. While you need not like every food that others try to get you to eat, it is important to approach shared meals with an open mind, self-knowledge, grace and respect, and to try to accommodate the circumstances as best you can.

Salad: Vegetarians, Supertasters, and Other Hard Cases

A few problematic cases present themselves against the claim that picky eating is immoral. I will deal in-depth with two: vegetarianism and supertasting.

Vegetarianism

Vegetarianism is the practice of restricting one's diet by not consuming any meat or fish.[8] This almost always takes the form of a strict maxim; the dietary restriction is adhered to in all circumstances.

Vegetarianism is often undertaken for ethical reasons, whether they are primarily related to animal rights, environmental issues, or religious ideals. What sometimes gets left out of the picture when someone is considering vegetarianism is that there are moral reasons *against* being vegetarian. Most people will admit that there are costs: vegetarianism (especially strict varieties) tends to be inconvenient, and they may lose some pleasure when denied meat products. But these personal, egoistic, or hedonistic reasons would be usually recognized to be superseded by moral reasons.[9]

On the other hand, thanks to the arguments of this chapter, we can now recognize that there are moral reasons that tell against vegetarianism. Vegetarianism has the problematic features of picky eating. Vegetarians (with some exceptions) categorically refuse to eat meat. They will spurn restaurants and cuisines that have poor or no vegetarian options. They will refuse food with meat in almost any situation. They are not willing to try new foods with meat in them. Once committed to vegetarianism, they will not approach meat dishes with an open mind, they will not explore them, and they will not make an effort to appreciate what is being offered. The extreme few will not even be gracious about it, unapologetically asking to be accommodated and ungraciously rejecting anything that does not fit their food preferences.

As such, there are a number of moral reasons that tell against vegetarianism. It cuts you off from new experiences, standing in the way of your development and self-realization. It cuts off avenues of broadening one's horizons and gaining new understanding. It is an inconvenience to others. It can involve the rejection of a meaningful gift that makes it difficult for others to share parts of their lives with you, and it can make it difficult to have shared experiences with others, cutting you off from one avenue of under- standing with other people and cultures. In the worst case, it may make it difficult for you to get along with others who do not share your food preferences, leading to an increase in the parochial- ism of your life.

For all their weight, however, these reasons against vegetarianism are merely *pro tanto* reasons, reasons that could be outweighed by more important considerations against them. Vegetarianism might well be the best option, but that judgment must come from a balanced consideration of the reasons on either side. But the necessary sort of consideration cannot be undergone unless the significant weight on both sides of the equation has been addressed. I will not take a stance on the substantive question of whether veg- etarianism is the right choice or not, as this goes beyond the bounds of this essay, but I do wish to underscore the importance of some often ignored considerations. Vegetarianism may be the right choice; rather than being an objection to the view of this essay, my view can better explain the proper way to arrive at it.

Supertasters

One physiological axis of variation of taste has to do with the number of taste buds. Supertasters are (roughly) the quarter of the population who have the highest concentration of taste buds. The extra taste buds mean that supertasters have an unusually strong sense of taste. Supertasters will be far more sensitive to the basic flavors that are perceived through taste buds (sweet, salty, sour, bitter, and umami), especially bitter flavors. This makes supertasters far more sensitive to some foods, which they will probably not come to like. Supertasting is probably responsible for a lot of picky eating. Supertasters (and their opposite, non-tasters, who have an uncommonly weak sense of taste) may seem to pose a significant challenge to the arguments of this essay. After all, if there is that much variation in taste, and it is genetic, does not that work in favor of taste-subjectivism?

At first blush, the existence of supertasters might make it seem like the hope for making taste out to be anything but subjective is misplaced. But remember, we were not asking for universalism in the first place! All along, I have admitted that there are variations in the way people taste, some of which are due to innate factors. And, in the case of taste-bud concentration, we can see the variation as smooth and nearly linear. Supertasters may, on consideration, come to different conclusions than the majority, but that is okay, so long as they have adequate self-knowledge about their tastes and their condition, have given a fair chance to certain foods, and have striven to understand them.

The treatment of supertasters should make an important feature of picky eating, as I have been using it in this essay, clearer. Picky eating is not so much about what foods you eat as the way you approach eating. I have argued for four gustatory obligations: openness, self-knowledge, accommodation, and grace. You should be open-minded about new taste experiences. You should try to understand the food you are eating and the reasons for your current preferences. (Are you a supertaster, or do you just need to get used to bitter foods?) You should attempt to accommodate new experiences and the gustatory needs and desires of others, and you should do so with grace and respect.

Other hard cases can be treated in much the same way as vegetarianism and supertasting. Perhaps you have moral, health, or safety reasons that lead you to avoid certain foods. This is okay, so long as you have considered all the sides of the issue, and so long as you decline the food with respect and grace.

Dessert: Food and Morality

It has probably occurred to you in reading this essay that none of the points it makes are particular to food. There is no *special* ethics of food, no additional obligations that accrue by way of culinary experience. But the consideration of food nonetheless has considerable value for ethics. On the one hand, picky eating has allowed for the exemplification of some important moral principles, showing certain moral values at work. Furthermore, the case of picky eating, the reactions we have to it, and the things we learn when we look at its details, help us to *interrogate* the structure of morality in a new way. I hope we have learned more about ethics by looking at eating, especially the way that ethics and aesthetics intersect, rather than just having learned about eating by looking at its ethics.

Notes

My thanks to Jon Johnston, who inspired this essay, Amanda Brovold, who made it possible, and Dale Dorsey, who read many parts of it and discussed them with me at great length.

1 See Rozin, P., "Food Preference," in *International Encyclopedia of the Social and Behavioral Sciences*, ed. N. J. Smelser and P. B. Baltes. Oxford: Pergamon Press, 2001: 5719–22.
2 Most often four are listed: saltiness, sourness, sweetness, and bitterness. A fifth basic taste is now gaining recognition: savoriness or umami, which has long played an important role in Japanese and Chinese cuisine in particular.
3 A tingly-numbness sensation is the main sensation provided by the Sichuan (or Szechuan) pepper.
4 Duties to self are a controversial category. Some ethicists would only recognize moral concerns in interpersonal matters.
5 See Logue, A. W., *The Psychology of Eating and Drinking: An Introduction*. New York: W. H. Freeman, 1991.
6 Such experiences are what John Dewey called mis-educative. See *Experience and Education* in *The Later Works of John Dewey*, vol. 13, ed. Jo Ann Boydston. Carbondale: Southern Illinois University Press, 1988. They retard growth in the sense used below.

7 The duties discussed here rely on a form of Moral Perfectionism, which emphasizes development, perfection, or self-realization. See Hurka, Thomas, *Perfectionism*. New York: Oxford University Press, 1995. A similar concern with growth is a central concern of Dewey's ethical and educational thinking. See *Experience and Education*, especially ch. 3.

8 There are many variations: vegans also do not consume any animal products, while pescetarians will eat fish. A fruitarian will not eat anything, plants included, that kills the organism. Vegetarians who do consume dairy or eggs are sometimes called lacto-vegetarians, ovo-vegetarians, or lacto-ovo-vegetarians.

9 That does not mean that everyone who thought about it would choose vegetarianism. It only means that, given moral reasons of significant weight, eating meat would be the morally wrong thing to do. But moral reasons are not the only considerations that actually determine action, probably no one is a total moral saint and, if Susan Wolf is right, it is probably best that no one is, See Wolf, Susan, "Moral Saints." *Journal of Philosophy* 79/8 (August 1982): 419–39.

14

Shall We Dine? Confronting the Strange and Horrifying Story of GMOs in Our Food

Paul B. Thompson

The short answer to the title question is, "Sure, why not?" The long answer probes the subtitle along with some of the reasons why *not*, but readers beware! Like the boor who insists on reciting the allowable limits for fecal matter over a feast of bread and cheese or notes the number of insect parts allowed in a box of corn flakes, this essay sits awkwardly among more celebratory philosophical musings on food. Wanting to fit in, I had proposed a pleasant reflection on food and identity, but the editors have insisted, "No, we want you to write about GMOs." Thankfully, I am limited to 5,000 words, so the tedium and disgust cannot last long. But you may learn some things that you would rather not know about food.

For example, revolting as it may seem, almost everything that people eat (salt and ice crystals are among the exceptions) either is or was recently alive. The plants and animals that become steaming plates of delicious foods are living organisms. Furthermore, every cell of all living organisms contains DNA, the so-called blueprint of life. DNA is itself a sequence of chemical bases. Some bits of the long sequence that exists in any part of any living thing allow cells to make specific proteins, other bits control those bits. Both kinds of bits are commonly called genes. Some other bits in the DNA sequence may not do very much at all other beyond taking up space, but taking up space itself may be important to ensuring that the whole, long sequence of genes and other bits works the way it has to for the organism to live.

So I begin with the sad and depressing news that all of us have been eating genes, organisms, and living things all our lives. Public opinion surveys reveal that many people do not like to eat organisms and believe that ordinary tomatoes do not have genes, so on the one hand, perhaps these things are worth pointing out. The surveys do not probe how people feel about eating proteins but, terrifying as it may be, your feel-good attitude to high-protein energy bars really doesn't translate into a widespread endorsement for eating proteins. The word 'protein' refers to a huge class of biologically active substances, including many toxins. Cobra venom is a protein. Perhaps, on the other hand, you dear reader, do not believe that you really needed to know all that in order to eat healthily and happily. If that is indeed what you believe (and, by the way, I agree with you), turn back now, before it is too late!

For those who insist upon reading further, I am obliged to report that, along with the external environment, the proteins that cells make according to instructions in their DNA go on to make the plant or animal what it is. This means that, at bottom, that wonderful acidity of a summer tomato, the tart sweetness of a spring strawberry, and the chewy texture of artisanal bread each owes something to DNA. What is more, the growth rate, flowering time, and response to water or sunshine of the tomato, strawberry, and wheat – things you may not care much about but that are really important to the farmer who grows them – owe something to DNA. At first farmers and then later scientists and seed companies have been cross-breeding plants to get varieties with the taste or texture that consumers want, and even more so to get the plant characteristics that they want. When they did this they were manipulating DNA, whether they knew it or not.

Lest you think that I am being patronizing with my biology lesson here, I will cut to the chase. GMO (an acronym for genetically modified organism) is a popular term for a plant or animal that has had its genes (i.e., its DNA) manipulated using some methods that have emerged over the last two decades. These methods – called genetic engineering – involve insinuating new bits of DNA into the plant's genome using microbes, as well as simply blasting it into the genome with something very much like a shotgun. Farmers and seed companies have seen this as fairly consistent with what they have been doing for a long time, but perhaps you demur. Couldn't slipping some new bits of DNA into a plant or animal genome mess up the way that the genome works? Couldn't it accidentally make nasty proteins that might not be good for us, or screw-up the way that cell processes are regulated with similarly unhealthful results? These are very reasonable, if somewhat unappetizing, questions, and the answer is that indeed it could. So here we have a big "why not": GMOs may not be *safe*.

There is a problem with the reasoning leading up to this "why not," but I warn once again you might prefer to remain ignorant about exactly what this problem is. To wit, the screw-ups that can happen in genetic engineering can also occur with the kinds of plants and animals that farmers, scientists, and seed companies have been developing for a long, long time. When one farmer decides to cross one of his squash or apple trees with a squash or apple tree that he got from another farmer, thousands of new genes get incorporated in the genome. The only reason this works at all is because, for the most part, the genes for a trait like flowering time (that is, under what climatic conditions or at what point in its growth cycle does a plant blossom in preparation for reproduction) occurs at roughly the same place in the sequence for both squash plants or apple trees. Hence, it is possible that the flowering time gene from the male bits of one farmer's squash can be transferred (along with a lot of other genes) to the female bits of another farmer's squash as a result of the cross. (I am sorry to inform you that plants tend to be bisexual.) But this reproductive trading of male and female DNA *can* also mess up when genes interact in unexpected ways. Ordinary crosses *can* and *have* produced progeny that are dangerous to eat.

Now you might say, "Yeah, but isn't it much more likely that there will be a mess up with modern biotechnology?" And I would say, "Yes, it *is* much more likely." But we need to recognize that plant breeders went far beyond the above crossing scenarios more than 150 years ago. Plant breeding involves crosses between plants from distant parts of the world whose genetic blueprints *do not* actually match up all that well, and that would be unlikely to produce viable offspring without human help. It involves techniques such as cell culture and embryo rescue (things that would bust my 5,000-word limit to explain). Suffice it to say that these techniques do, in fact, allow them to breed across species lines (though subject to some limitations) so, when critics say this is what is new about GMOs, they are simply wrong. Plant breeders have also bombarded seeds with chemical treatments or high doses of radiation to stimulate spontaneous mutations, types of genetic sequence that have never occurred in nature before. Plant breeders have been using all these methods except genetic engineering for between 50 and 150 years. In comparison, genetic engineering came on line about twenty years ago.

With this startling picture in mind, one can put the likelihood that there will be a screw-up on a scale that looks something like this (* means "cross between"):

Type of modification	Chance of a screw-up	
	Unlikely	Likely
Close relative * Close relative	✓	
Close relative * Distant relative	✓	
* Two sexually incompatible plants	✓	
Genetic engineering	✓	
Radiation or chemical bombardment		✓

As frightening and nauseating as this information is, one must admit that it shifts the question a bit. Given that plant breeding is not the happy tea party that we thought it to be, why aren't we all dead already? The answer to this question is that, after plant breeders do all these heinous things to get new seeds, they try them out. They plant them and watch them very carefully in lab settings and test plots. In fact, lots of attempts are losers. They produce weird or simply non-viable offspring. There is a big chance of a screw-up *at the point where a new gene gets put into the plant* (whether by breeding or biotechnology). But this is *not* the same thing as saying that there is a big chance of a screw-up in the plant that you and I eat.

After culling out the promising plants where the gene transfer seems to have worked (scientists like to call these "events"), there is a further testing and back-crossing (e.g., breeding the modified plant back into some stable plant lines). So plant breeders are pretty confident that the DNA has landed in a place that does not mess things up before they develop a product of cross breeding *or* genetic engineering into a crop anyone will eat. There is also some testing to make sure the plant does not make people sick, but do not get your hopes up. This might not be very elaborate. After doing some lab work to see if the chemical make-up of their new potato is pretty much like the chemical make-up of an old potato, they might just throw some to the hogs, and if the hogs do okay, they will take some home and fry it up themselves. So just when you might have been starting to breathe easier, here is another "why not": even if they are probably safe, GMOs are not adequately *tested*.

Before I let myself in for nasty letters from Monsanto and Dupont, I should point out that biotechnology companies spend a lot of time and money doing the testing that they do on GMOs, and I have no reason to think that they are not very serious about it. They do extensive chemical analysis of the GMO to determine whether the amount of this and that in the GMO is comparable to the amounts of this and that in non-GMO varieties of the same plant. This costs so much money that only big companies can afford to develop genetically modified varieties. And when they do go out and throw it to the hogs, they keep impeccable records. They send all this information to folks at the United States Food and Drug Administration (FDA), who take a look at it and then send a letter to the company that says, in effect, "Yep, you sure did take a look at a whole lot of stuff." They post the letter on the FDA website, along with advice to the public stipulated in mind-numbing bureaucratic prose which states in effect that although the new crop has not been proven to be safe, the FDA has accepted the industry's claim that it is substantially equivalent to a non-GMO (more on this later). This process is very impressive to the biotechnology industry, but critics have made numerous complaints about it. So perhaps whether the testing is elaborate is in the eye of the beholder.

As a trained philosopher (be careful not to try this at home), I am inclined to shift this argument away from the scientific questions. The awful truth is that while we do a pretty good job of testing the chemicals or other miniscule ingredients that get *added* to food, we really do not have a very scientific ways to test *any* whole food. The trouble is that one can only eat so many watermelons, and either eating enough watermelon or getting enough people (or mice, for that matter) to eat watermelon under circumstances that would provide statistically significant evidence that watermelon is safe is a daunting task. So instead the FDA has a list called "Generally Recognized

As Safe (GRAS)." Watermelon, squash, wheat, soybeans, and corn are on this list, and nobody complains. But this does not eliminate the possibility that for some small segment of the population, eating watermelon everyday will cause stomach cancer, or allergic reaction, or a brain aneurism, or the heartbreak of psoriasis. We have no way to know.

A GMO squash, papaya, wheat, soybean, or corn variety (all of these and more exist) gets treated as GRAS if the protein that the modification produces is either also GRAS (comes from a GRAS food) or has been subjected to thorough toxicological tests for safety. How do we test to be sure that something weird has not occurred? Other than making sure the "this and that" in GM squash, corn, or soybeans occur at roughly the same levels as the "this and that" in non-GM squash, corn, or soybeans (that's what "substantial equivalence" is) and throwing some to the hogs, there is not much that *can* be done. But the truly appalling fact is that we are in exactly the same boat for all the crops produced the old fashioned way (and I will repeat, the old fashioned way *can* and *has* gone wrong). So the upshot here is that biotech companies can truthfully say their products are tested thoroughly, while opponents can plausibly say they are not tested enough. As a philosopher, I can point out that *none* of our foods are, on this basis, tested thoroughly *or* insufficiently, but you will have to decide for yourself how you feel about that.

But enough on this depressing topic. Public opinion surveys reveal that many people who oppose GMOs do so not because they believe that they are unsafe to eat, but because they believe that they are harmful to the environment. Environmentalists have argued that transgenes (a fancy word for the genes that have been introduced through genetic engineering) can spread via pollen to other plants. If the GMO is "herbicide tolerant" (i.e., when you spray it with Round-up™ or similar weedkillers, it just sits there and keeps growing), this characteristic can be spread to other plants. They have also argued that the toxins produced to kill insects in GMOs can also kill "non-target species" (e.g., other insects we might not *want* to kill). Colloquially, GMOs might become "superweeds" or else kill monarch butterflies. So here is another "why not": GMOs may be *environmentally risky*.

At the unfortunate peril of becoming repetitive, I must here inter-ject a familiar refrain: *all* agricultural crops can be environmentally risky. In fact, conventional crops, which have been bred so that they ripen and flower at the same time for convenient harvesting, tend to be very risky because the same things that make them attractive to farmers make them vulnerable to insects and plant diseases. Farmers are currently using a lot of pesticides to grow these crops, and using heavy, environmentally damaging equipment to plant and to harvest them. I am not being facetious when I say that these environmental risks are the result of conventional plant breeding. I am not kidding when I say that from an environmental perspective, industrial agriculture is so badly broken that we should be willing to try just about anything to fix it. If the concern that GMOs may be environmentally risky is meant to suggest that what we are doing now without GMOs is hunky dory, then it is flat out crazy and needs to be beaten down with a stick.

It is possible to go on *ad nauseam* about relative environmental risks. It is something I love to do, so feel free to invite me to your garden club to talk about it. All I ask is a big fat honorarium (or at least a delicious dinner) and expenses. But I am halfway to 5,000 words already and there is still more to say. For now, this summary statement will have to suffice: there *are* substantive environmental risks for GMOs, and some of them are much riskier than others. Among the most risky are those being tested for their ability to produce drugs, industrial products, and biofuels. Sadly, the industry is turning to these products in a big way because they have not been able to make enough money on GMO food crops. But you will not be eating *these* crops because they are not intended for use as food (or at least you will not be eating them on purpose). So let's stay on point, hope our regulators can keep the nasty bits out of the food supply, and continue thinking about GMOs like the corn, squash, soybeans, and papayas that you are probably eating right now. It is very questionable that the GMO versions of *these* plants are more risky than the agricultural production methods being used to produce conventional varieties, though there is every reason for people involved in agriculture to watch this issue very carefully.

But perhaps you have heard that the problem here is that GMOs are being developed by the same clowns who *gave* us chemical pesticides or fertilizer, mechanized harvesting equipment, and hybrid monocultures that deplete our environment. Why shouldn't we be suspicious of them on those grounds alone? We hear further that these guys (not all of them *are* guys, by the way) want to spread their way of doing agriculture to the developing world. If our agriculture is broken, wouldn't that be a bad thing? So now we get to yet another "why not": the companies and university scientists developing GMOs are not to be *trusted*?

Now 'trust' means many things, but we can take this "why not" to mean that we should worry about GMOs because the companies and research institutes that develop GMOs are the same companies and research institutes that gave us synthetic fertilizers and pesticides. "Fool me once, shame on you. Fool me twice, shame on me." It is certainly true that the major industry players in agricultural biotechnology have been in the agrichemicals business for many years. Yet at the risk of being very pedantic indeed, I want to point out that we have arrived at a point in our little adventure where we have concluded that the guys who developed the agricultural technologies from which something in the neighborhood of 95 percent of our food is produced are not to be trusted because of evident problems in industrial agriculture. From this, we seem on the precipice of inferring that while it is okay to eat industrially grown crops that are *not* GMO (and produced by these same jokers), the fact that we cannot trust them provides a good reason for refusing to eat industrial crops that *are* GMO. I am sorry. Maybe it is all that symbolic logic I took when I was a graduate student, but this just seems wacky, an example of willful self-deception if I ever saw one. And so I repeat for emphasis: the reason you are producing for "why not eat that" as applied to GMOs actually applies to virtually everything we eat!

It would be more reasonable to turn in the direction of that last 5 percent or so that is not produced by industrial agriculture. You might think that this means eating organic, but things are, I boorishly report, not quite that simple. Although the availability of organic food is fast increasing, and although I will happily testify to the fact that I eat organic foods whenever I can, not only are there some very good reasons for *not* eating organic sometimes (you'll have to invite me to your garden club to hear them), but a fairly large chunk (maybe 50 percent and growing) of the organic foods that *are* available are produced by the same companies that we usually associate with industrial agriculture. However, if you *do* decided to go organic, you can be assured that you will not be eating GMOs. Whether produced by big industrial farmers, mega-corporations, hippie communes, the Amish, or some other traditional family farm, organic certification rules stipulate that foods labeled as organically produced may not be products of genetic engineering. It's still not altogether clear that you are getting food from *people* you can trust, but let's not lead a dead horse to water in the vain hope that we can make him think.

But now maybe we are getting somewhere. Maybe we should see the anti-GMO campaign as a *political* movement. The hope is to reform the food system, to encourage the good guys, the little guys, the Norwegian bachelor farmers, Marin County hippies, former linguistics professors, fifth generation Texas High Plains ranchers, and retired insurance executives who are once again hoping to forge an agriculture that connects us to the land, that protects and stewards nature, that nurtures us and makes us native to the places that we live. Although my 5,000-word limit is now really starting to pinch, maybe I can get by simply by saying that there are lots and lots of social, cultural, and aesthetic reasons why we might want an agriculture that looks like *that*. Maybe I can wave my hands a bit as the string section swells up in the background and assert that we have identified yet another big "why not": GMOs are not *sustainable*.

While I'm filling out the forms to sign up for the sustainable agriculture action army here, let me make just a few rude noises on the side. Notice that we've gotten to a point where "sustainable" doesn't mean more safe, more tested, less environmentally risky or even more trustworthy. We have defined it in terms of certain social and political ideals, and it would be disingenuous of me to omit mention of places like my book *The Spirit of the Soil: Agriculture and Environmental Ethics* where I have pretty blatantly said that this is something we should not do. Nonetheless, we live our real political lives under conditions in which we have to tolerate a fair amount of vagueness in our political ideals. So despite the fact that I know plenty of molecular biologists who think that they can develop GM crops that meet all the criteria, vague as they are, for sustainable agriculture as we have defined it here, let's rest content with this. If you see resistance to GMOs as a form of political protest against rampant capitalism, globalization, corporate greed, or the decline of rural communities, more power to yuh, bud. That is a good enough "why not" for me.

In fact, I will go further. If you think genetic engineering of all kinds is ungodly, inconsistent with Christian, Muslim, Jewish, Buddhist, Hindu, or other religious principles, or if you believe that we were not meant to eat GMOs for some other reason that you have difficulty telling me about, that is *also* a good enough "why not" for me. To what extent *do* these religious traditions provide a basis for thinking that GMOs violate religious principles? Well, it is obvious enough that ancient religious texts tend to omit straightforward religious commands that refer to genes. There is no scripture saying, "Thou shall not partake of those transgenic foods that are likely to turn up around the beginning of the third millennium," at least not that I know about. So it would be difficult to argue that GMOs are strictly proscribed. Most rabbis who have addressed this question have concluded that Jewish dietary law permits genetic transformation, and relatively few imams have taken the trouble to apply the traditions of *hallal* to GMOs, at all. But mainstream religious traditions provide plenty of support for incorporating one's vision of social or environmental justice into one's religious practice, so it is fairly easy for the concerns just listed under the heading of sustainability to attain a religious underpinning.

But I want to go farther still, to suggest that while this wrangling over dietary law deserves attention and respect, it is not as if you need to have a religious authority to sign off on a simple dietary preference. We started with a bunch of risk-oriented considerations and found that none of them really provide reasons for being more concerned about GMOs than we should about virtually everything we eat. But I assuredly do not think that people should have to produce a risk assessment to justify their dietary preferences. In fact, I'm happy if you tell me, "Well, I just don't like the idea of eating GMOs." I'm not even going to pull the standard philosopher's trick of saying, "Well, okay, just be consistent." I think it is totally okay to be wildly inconsistent about your food choices. If on Tuesday you will not eat maccaroni and cheese because you are a vegan, then on Wednesday you chow down on chicken, *I do not care.* There is absolutely no reason why we should police each other's food choices. That is my view.

Now this is a view that may get me into trouble with some fair-traders and ethical vegetarians out there, but at present we are talking about GMOs in our food. So cut me some slack and stay with the program. In this context, the importance of my libertarian attitude to food choice is this: *any* reason "why not" for refusing to eat GMOs is good enough when it comes to personal dietary choice. Have you read this essay down to here and you still think that GMOs might not be safe? Okay by me. Still think you cannot trust Monsanto and Dupont? Good enough. Pass the organic cabbage, please. Now lest you think I am being facetious or relativist, I am *not* saying that your reasons are good enough for *me*. If we sit down at table together, I am willing to eat what you eat (I draw the line at bulgur). I might eat something else when I am on my own, and it might even be a tasty plate of Flav*r Sav*r™ genetically engineered tomatoes (if I could get my hands on some). But I am *not* going to get in your face telling you that *you* should eat them.

Sure, if you come to me saying, "Paul, you've done a ton of work on agricultural biotechnology. Is it okay to eat?" I'll turn around and say "Sure, why not?" I hope I have not been so boring and tedious since the beginning of this essay that this now sounds unfamiliar. But if you have any reason at all for *not* wanting to eat GMOs, even if that reason seems totally arbitrary from my perspective, I will stand up in front of the US Congress (like bulgur, I draw the line at Parliament) and defend your right to eat whatever you like. And here we come to a fine philosophical point, one that has made me just as unpopular with many in the pro-biotech crowd as my dismissal of the food safety and environmental risk arguments has made me among its critics.

GMOs need an opt-out for those who have any reason at all for not wanting to eat them. Your right to eat what you want to eat is not explicitly mentioned in the US Constitution, and there would clearly be problems if we interpreted this as a *positive* right. A positive right to eat what I want would mean that someone, presumably the government, is obligated to meet my dietary preferences. The actual right we are speaking of here is a *negative* right, technically, a right of *exit*. No one should be able to coerce me into eating something I do not want to eat, whether by deception or force. I should have a way out of any situation where I could find myself eating something I feel is dangerous, repulsive, irreligious, politically incorrect, non-vegetarian, tragically un-hip, made in New York rather than Texas (this list goes on and on, as I hope you can see).

As applied to GMOs, the protection of this right is exceedingly tenuous in the United States food system, and for an interval in the late 1990s it was not protected at all. Although the FDA has promulgated rules for labeling foods as containing (or not containing) GMOs, these rules are voluntary and are almost entirely unutilized by the US food industry. Your only choice, your only means of exit, is the refuge of the organic label. This is also pretty much the situation in Canada, although the rules for voluntary labeling are a little more flexible. In Europe, by contrast, foods containing GMOs are subject to mandatory labeling requirements, a policy that has resulted in almost no GMOs being sold in European supermarkets. I am not at all sure that the European result is what we want.

Although I fear that I am now getting altogether too serious to be tolerated, I will note that, as I have intimated above and argued for elsewhere,[1] there are a number of reasons why we really should use biotechnology to improve agriculture. If a labeling policy leads people to be needlessly frightened by GMOs, then that is a bad outcome. Not surprisingly, the biotechnology industry agrees with this judgment, and has used this argument in blocking all attempts to impose mandatory labeling policies in the United States. Yet at the same time, surely we could have a more straightforward and transparent system for enabling those who, for whatever reason, want to avoid GMOs to do so. Surely we could, for example, at least have a significant number of products labeled as "non-GMO." I'm not entirely sure why we do not, but I suspect that the FDA rules for this kind of labeling provide legal and economic disincentives for any company that would be inclined to try it. If you started the essay looking for a reason to write a scathing letter to your congressperson, then this is it.

So now you have heard both the short and long answers to the question "Shall we dine?" and you know the strange and horrifying story of GMOs in our food. You also know why I don't want you to write to me with angry justifications about why you do or do not want to eat GMOs, in spite of what I say. *I do not care! Eat what you like!* I am tired of playing the boor. When it comes to myths and self-deception about our food, let a thousand flowers bloom! Let us believe what we like, then live and let live. Let us not *lie* to one another, however, so ask me again and I will tell you even more things

Paul B. Thompson

you probably do not want to know about dinner. Just do not turn me away from the table afterward.

Note

1 Thompson, Paul B. "Why Food Biotechnology Needs an Opt Out." In *Engineering the Farm: Ethical and Social Aspects of Agricultural Biotechnology*. Ed. B. Bailey and M. Lappé. Washington, DC: Island Press, 2002: 27–44; "The Environmental Ethics Case for Crop Biotechnology: Putting Science Back into Environmental Practice." In *Moral and Political Reasoning in Environmental Practice*. Ed. A. Light and A. de-Shalit. Cambridge, MA: MIT Press, 2003: 187–217; and *Food Biotechnology in Ethical Perspective, Revised Edition*. New York: Springer, 2007.

15

Taking Stock: An Overview of Arguments For and Against Hunting

Linda Jerofke

Introduction

Hunting camp is the most important event for many people in the United States, whether they are from a small, rural town or the big city. It is often equated with a group of men going off to have fun, with a lawn chair in the back of a pickup, a beer in one hand, and a rifle in the other. These are the same people who wantonly hunt without a license as well as out of season. Stories are commonly told in rural communities about the brazen hunter who enters onto private property in order to follow his right to hunt wild game. When approached about illegally entering private property, he uses a wide variety of strategies to get out of the situation, from indicating that he is a longtime friend of the family to "the state fish and wildlife told me that I could hunt here." Of course, this rarely turns out in the favor of the miscreant hunter set on fulfilling his dream of bringing in the big one. The ultimate outcome is a date in court explaining foolish actions that often ends in the loss of money, and forfeiture of rifles or even a vehicle.

The stereotypical hunter is also the target of non-hunting proponents who focus on multiple issues, including the obtainment of a trophy to display back home, only wounding an animal without putting it out of its pain and suffering, as well as the encouragement of youth into the dwindling ranks of the hunter. During the fall, you are almost guaranteed to see a proud hunter heading back home with a large deer draped across the hood of his car or truck. The proud hunter wants to share his glory with everyone else the entire way home. Unfortunately, there is usually one significant problem with this scenario: the meat is ruined before the hunter even makes it home. The bloated belly of the deer, due to the continued presence of internal organs and an insulating blanket of hide and hair, causes the meat to spoil. The proud hunter is often left with a rotted carcass with little to show for it except – if he is lucky to have shot a buck – a head or antlers that can be mounted on the wall. A few hundred dollars later, the hunter is able to boast about his great hunt, conveniently forgetting that there was no meat left to consume. Anti-hunting organizations focus on this scenario because it is wasteful and a tragic waste of life. According to them, no animal should be killed to become a future ornament.

The perspective that focuses on the misleading image of the stereotypical hunter does not consider that game meat is seen as a necessary part of life for many people living below the poverty level in rural communities, as well as for Native Americans. They supplement their diet with game meat; in some cases, it may even be a major food source. Hunting can be done economically, from their point of view, and game meat can be an important protein source for a family for a good portion of a year, especially those that find the purchase of commercial meat to be outside of their budget.

Hunting season is also seen by a segment of the population as an important event that individuals, families, and friends start planning for as soon as the previous year's hunt is over. They consider what went wrong, what strategies would work better, as well as divide up the long list of tasks that must be completed for next year's camp. In "lottery states" (i.e., states where not all hunters can hunt every year), it is important to consider the strategy of putting in as an individual or as a hunting party, since the group could easily be thrown out of the running for receiving tags for the year. Individuals who would not normally talk about everyday activities come together to share their experiences regarding hunting. This stereotypical person is usually the exception, and a hunting camp can include anywhere from a group of dedicated hunters all the way to extended families with children and grandparents present. It is a time to bond and form lifelong friendships.

In contrast to the perspectives of hunters, animal rights activists focus on the belief that the positive aspects that may come with hunting do not outweigh the negatives. They do not consider hunting to be a moral activity. Animal rights activists strongly believe that hunters do not have the right to take the life of a wild animal for the purpose of sport or sustenance. In many cases the value of animal life is considered to be more important than these human activities.

This essay will focus on a wide variety of perspectives on the practice of hunting for large and small game in the United States. Arguments for and against hunting will be explored, as well as the viability of game meat as an important food source for the American public. It is important to note that, due to the breadth of belief systems regarding hunting, I will focus on central positions rather than provide an exhaustive survey.

Arguing for Hunting: The Hunter's Perspective

Hunters are at the top of the food chain. They believe that this gives them the right to participate in hunting for sustenance, sport, and familial relationships, despite the apparent rights of animals. Humans are able to out-compete game animals through the use of technology and cultural belief systems, such as laws, that give them the right to hunt. Animals are viewed as subservient to human ends; thus, hunting rights outweigh the moral consideration due to game animals.

According to the hunter, it is his or her right to be out pursuing game animals within the limits of the laws of the state. Each state, through permits, controls animal populations within its borders. The hunter is a valuable commodity in this multifaceted relationship existing between game animals, state government, and residents of the state. As long as hunters are following state laws by getting a permit and following other related regulations, then they have every right to follow their desired pursuit of hunting wild game. There is the expectation that they will go about fulfilling this right without interference from outside parties. Each hunter is required to be able to identify himself with some type of identification. As an example, in Oregon, a hunter is required to carry a hunting license as well as the tag that indicates that they are lawfully hunting for the animal they are seeking within the area they are permitted to hunt.

It is also within the right of every hunter to find fulfillment in his or her chosen recreational activity. Many hunters believe that their right to hunt contributes to a sense of wellbeing, as well as other exclusively human goods, which overshadows moral deference for animals. The fact that hunting contributes to these human ends justifies the activity. Thus, hunters believe that anti-hunting perspectives are misguided. For example, humans are social animals that seek satisfaction through interaction with people sharing common interests. Hunting, as a social venue, has a long established history that is well supported by the numerous stories that are told around assorted dinner tables and camp fires. It is a time for fun as well as serious discussion. Detailed strategies are worked out around the campfire that consider the actions of other hunters, the weather, the health of the hunting party, animal movements, and a dash of dumb luck. Each hunter can put his own twist on the bonding they experience through the act of hunting, and many stories come down to the simple desire to be with friends. It is not all that uncommon to find that hunters have been returning to the same camp for decades. They find trust in the companionship of friends. Hunting buddies know each others' strong and weak points. It is a time to get together, to tell old stories and, hopefully, to make new ones, too. Some of the best times are in the evening, sitting around the campfire with well-fed bellies, talking about the excitement (or else lack thereof) of the day.

Hunting is also justified as a time to celebrate life and as with any other important event, food is present. A great deal of planning goes into the type, variety, and amounts of food at each hunting camp. A snapshot of one camp's provisions of food is quite telling. The foods reach the most basic needs of humans because fat, sugar, and salt are well represented! Donuts, muffins, juice, pop tarts, candy bars, and chips are readily available to fill any snacking need. The rest of the menu is carefully planned, with emphasis on the evening meal after a long day's hunt. Protein is of primary concern, with the focus on that of the pursued game animal. Rituals around game animals are common and usually include some of the finest cuts off of the animal. To some hunters, the finest cut is the tenderloin, while others focus on the back strap. Fond memories are created through companionship that is enhanced with the presence of food.

Companionship extends to the sharing of meat between family members and friends. A successful hunt is not guaranteed. The social structure of the hunting camp ensures that everyone comes away with some meat, even if they did not get an elk. No one goes home empty handed; the meat is always shared with the other people in camp. This is an important part of elk camp because there are good and bad years. Eventually everything equals out over time.

Families are an important component of many hunting camps. It is not uncommon to see three or four generations present at a camp. Everyone has an important role to fill, from gathering firewood to helping to take care of younger family members. It is a valuable educational experience, especially for younger members of the family. Younger family members have the chance to learn outdoor survival skills, which can help them build self-confidence. Children have the unique opportunity to learn to value game animals and to treat them with respect. Game animals are viewed as an important part of the food chain. It is not uncommon for children to participate in many aspects of the hunt, even before they physically start hunting themselves. Children want to be a part of the hunt and it is a learning experience that they will not forget. Animals are not to be taken lightly, since they provide valuable meat for the family. Both parents and grandparents often take the opportunity to give their children biology lessons when an animal is brought down. The biology lessons are often detailed, focusing on all parts of the animal's anatomy. At a recent elk camp, I observed each child paying attention to every action taken by the hunter as she carefully field dressed the animal. This experience connects the children to the circle of life and death. Each hunter knows that his or her children understand how meat gets to the grocery store.

Personal responsibility is also an important concept acquired at the hunting camp. Hunters see this as a vital concept to teach the younger generations, especially when it appears to the general public to be sadly missing in many aspects of some people in society. Each child learns hunter safety because they are handling a potentially dangerous weapon that can injure or kill another person if handled irresponsibly. Also, one of the basic hunting ideas is that you eat what you kill. The goal is to develop a responsible child that will in turn become a responsible adult.

There is personal satisfaction in the ability to successfully track down an animal that is considerably bigger than you are and will contribute valuable food throughout the year. As an example, an elk is a big animal, with an average weight of 600–700 pounds; a bull elk can be as much as 1,000 pounds. A hunter will eventually be left with a couple hundred pounds of meat after the butchering is done. All of the hard work getting an animal back to camp and then on to home is worth it. If hunters are lucky, then they have a four-wheeler that can be driven to the elk and can be used to haul the animal out. If they are not so fortunate, then they are left to packing out each quarter strapped to their back on a frame, sometimes for miles. It can be a long, tiring, and painful journey back to camp this way. After packing the quarters out, each part of the animal is hung up in the camp on a "meat" pole strung between two trees. To allow for proper cooling, it is important to make sure that the meat is completely clear of the ground and not touching any other pieces. Some hunters save the hide to be used in antler or head mounts, while others take theirs to commercial tanners or private individuals who process their own hides for personal purposes. Others may donate their hide to an elder from one of the nearby Native American Tribes for traditional use, or to veterans' organizations as a money raiser. It is important to use as much of the animal as possible, including the meat and the hide.

Many hunters prefer to butcher their elk themselves, while others take their animals to a trusted expert for handling. Butchering is time consuming, but to a perfectionist, it must be done right. By being self-reliant, one gets the cuts of meat the way one wants them. It can be a family ritual, sometimes factory-like, with everyone being involved from the basic cut, finishing cut, cleaning, wrapping, and taping. Everyone, no matter the age, has an important role that binds them to the meat. They can proudly say that they helped to bring in an elk for the family.

Game meat is considered by many to be the best tasting in the world, a delicacy not to be ignored. It has a rich, wild flavor that is satisfying to the consumer. There is also relief that the meat is not filled with synthetic hormones and chemicals that are rampant in commercially sold products. Game meat is an excellent protein source that is low in fat. It is a healthy alternative to the consumption of highly processed foods upon which a majority of the American public relies. Ultimately, there is satisfaction in the fact that you provided the meat for your family.

Trophy hunters who just hunt for the antlers, head mount, or hide are considered to be a minority in their chosen sport. They are not necessarily well-respected by their peers, but, at the same time, the average hunter is somewhat envious of them. Hunters who do obtain an exceptionally large animal may end up in the top hunting record book, the *Boone and Crockett*. Scoring of the animals is based on antler width, number of tines, symmetry, diameter of the beams and points, and other measurements. This form of measurement, developed by the Boone and Crockett Club, was initially started to keep track of game herds and their success rate.

In addition to the competitive measurement of game animal antlers, the Boone and Crocket Club promotes an ethical hunt, also known as the Fair Chase Code. The concept of honor is central to a hunter's perspective towards hunting. In direct contrast to the perspective of anti-hunting proponents concerning hunting, which is presented later in this discussion, the Fair Chase Code is the "ethical, sportsmanlike, and lawful pursuit and taking of any free-ranging wild, native North American big game animal in a manner that does not give the hunter an improper advantage over such animals."[1] As an example, activities that would break this code include aerial reconnaissance or scouting, use of laser sites, shooting across public right of ways, hunting on closed animal refuges, hunting within the limits of a town, hunting outside the designated area, hunting without a tag, and hunting with dogs. Great emphasis is placed on the honorable practice of hunting and the morally suspect activities described are widely condemned by the majority of hunters. Hunters are expected to follow all state laws, and to act in a manner appropriate to societal norms.

There are a number of different attitudes toward trophy hunting. On one hand, there are the hunters who follow the Fair Chase Code and openly display the head and antlers of the animal they have killed. These are commonly seen in the homes of hunters and proudly displayed as evidence of their hunting ability or success. This is in direct contrast to the trophy hunter who purchases a canned hunt on private land and has to expend very little effort in getting an animal. Trophy hunters also feel they have the right to hunt in their chosen manner because they are doing it within the limits of the law and can afford the often high cost of participating in a trophy hunt. However, an action being legal does not mean that it is necessarily moral. For example, someone may buy a hunt where a wild animal is let out of a cage to be shot. Few hunters would consider this a moral action even though it is legal.

The type and manner of trophy hunts can vary greatly. Some trophy hunts are held on private land, where game animals are raised for the sole purpose of the landowner selling the right to hunt to individuals. It is a money making venture that can be good source of income for a private business or landowner. There is some level of chance, which minimally relates to the Fair Chase Code, in these types of hunts because tracking and hunting knowledge is an important factor.

Arguing for Hunting: The Native American Perspective

Native American communities consider game hunting to be an integral part of their culture and as sovereign nations they have the right to develop their own laws regarding hunting that will take place on their land. This right is also spelled out in a number of treaties that the US government entered into with numerous tribal governments, including, as examples, the Confederated Tribes of the Umatilla Indian Reservation and the Mille Lacs Band of Chippewa Indians. Treaty language can vary greatly, but the ones that do include language concerning hunting present information on the rights of tribal members to hunt off reservation land. Tribes can assert their right to hunt off the reservation on state, federal, and sometimes private land that is not posted.

This right to hunt for food and spiritual purposes was also fought for in court by the Alaskan Athapaskan Indians of Minto, Alaska in 1975. In 1975, a cow moose was taken out of season as part of a funeral potlatch (i.e., a traditional ceremony for these Native Americans). Minto villagers made the argument that the moose meat was to be used for a significant religious ceremony – their funeral potlatch – and that the State of Alaska was denying them their religious rights. The lower court found against the plaintiff, and he was sentenced. A higher court later overturned this decision, citing that the moose meat was an essential part of the ceremony. Funeral potlatches are still a vital part of that culture today. This is but one example of the rights of Native Americans in the United States, and the right to hunt both on and off reservation land is a vital to these communities.

Hunting is also considered as a rite of passage for younger tribal members. Younger tribal members, under the tutelage of family members, learn to respect the animals they hunt, pray for the giving of an animal life, and learn important tracking techniques. A first kill is valued because the child may now be considered to be a young adult. This change in status is highly valued. I had the opportunity to see an example of this while conducting research in Alaska. A highly respected elder had died and the village expected hundreds of people to travel to attend the funeral potlatch. Village residents were concerned that there might not be enough meat for everyone attending the potlatch. One brave young man decided to honor the elder who had died and took a boat out by himself to get a moose without any assistance. A little over a day later he returned to the village with his moose. Everyone was in awe of his ability. On the last day of the potlatch he was respected for his desire to obtain a moose for the potlatch and was given a great honor: the family of the deceased gave him a rifle.

Hunting for food and spiritual reasons are not the only reasons why Native Americans participate in this activity. A great deal of cultural activities are linked to hunting. The hides are used for the construction of drums that are used in many aspects of cultural life. Individual hand drums are used for spiritual purposes and during dancing. Larger, multi-person drums are used by musical groups or "drums" that perform at the many pow wows that are held throughout the US. It would be difficult to create a drum without the use of an animal hide.

Hides, and other animal parts, are also used for the construction of traditional dress, jewelry, and ceremonial items. They are used to construct both male and female clothing for personal, everyday use by tribal members and for sale to the general public. The processing of animal hides is an integral part of the cultural life of many Native Americans. Individual tribal members often learn the process of tanning hides from an older relative. It is an important opportunity for younger tribal members to bond with family as well as a chance to gain valuable cultural knowledge. One of the most common forms of clothing that the general public identifies with Native Americans is the moccasin. Tribal members of all ages can be seen wearing moccasins for everyday use, ceremonies and at pow wows. It is an important clothing item as well as an art form that is highly valued by all. Besides the construction of moccasins, hides are used to create other clothing, such as dresses and pants. The other animal parts are used in a variety of situations, such as for ceremonial fans. Ceremonial fans often include animal hides, teeth, bones, bird talons, and feathers. They can be used in the blessing of a house, prayers, and spiritual or medicinal healings by medicine people. It would be impossible, from a Native American point of view, to conduct these ceremonies without the items given by each animal. So, for the Native American, hunting is a multifaceted activity that provides them with food, clothing, and art as an important part of the process of the continuation of their individual cultures.

Traditional foods, such as game meats, are a vital part of tribal communities and their individual member's wellbeing. Native Americans developed a symbiotic relationship with the foods from their unique environments, which included game meats. This relationship developed over thousands of years. It is believed that Native American populations used to be some of the healthiest in the world due to their lifestyle that included a high amount of physical activity, as well as a diverse diet. After contact with Euro-Americans, they experienced drastic dietary changes. These changes included a dependence on processed products, such as refined wheat flour, sugar, coffee, and alcohol. Unfortunately, this dependence led to numerous health problems, including diabetes, heart disease, and obesity. Many Native Americans believe that their path back to physical health is through a more traditional diet. This has been substantiated through first-hand experiences by tribal members and scientific research. One of the best examples is that of the Pima Indians, who have one of the highest rates of diabetes in the United States. Tribal members have found great success in reaching a healthy status through the incorporation of a traditional diet. Individuals who have suffered with diabetes have been able to reverse the effects of this devastating disease through a healthier, less-processed diet.

The type and variety of game animals varies greatly, depending on the environment. It is important to note that Native Americans do not only focus on large game animals, but also consider smaller animals to be significant food sources. As an example, the Wadatika, a Northern Paiute Tribe, strongly identifies with the consumption of "groundhog" or yellow-bellied marmot. This food source is highly valued and is almost always served at important cultural events. Traditional foods, such as game meats, are a vital part of their cultures and Native Americans strongly feel that access to these foods is their right.

Arguing Against Hunting: The Anti-Hunter's Perspective

Anti-hunters present a mosaic of perspectives concerning hunting – including the beliefs that animals have inherent rights that must be respected, that animal life is intrinsically valuable, and opposition to the ownership of guns that are used to kill animals – and that these values ought to prevail over those espoused by hunters. In contrast to hunters who feel that it is their right to continue hunting, opponents of wild game hunting are adamant that the practice be abolished because it is unnecessary in today's society. According to animal rights activists, we have outgrown the barbaric practice of killing wild game animals for sport and sustenance. People have easy access to food, whether it is handed to them through the drive-thru window at their fast food restaurant, farmers' markets, grocery stores, or gardens. Why would someone need to hunt to get food in this land of abundance? Hunting is seen as multiple violent acts against other living things, which should not be tolerated. Rifle hunting is seen as having an unfair advantage over animals, and bow hunting is viewed as cruel because the kills are not swift. Opponents point to the number of game animals that are seen wandering around residential neighborhoods with arrow shafts sticking out of their bodies during and after hunting season. Hunting opponents feel it is their duty to stop hunters based on these convictions.

There is also objection to the terminology used to describe hunting because it diminishes the fact that animals are sentient beings that are being killed for the pleasure of people. Objectionable terms and phrases include 'take,' 'harvesting,' 'population control,' and 'conservation.' All of these terms are used by federal, state, and private agencies and organizations to describe how they control animal populations within their jurisdiction. Both federal and state agencies are involved in the continued existence of wild animal populations within their jurisdiction and consider hunters as one way to control population levels. Hunting opponents disagree with this methodology and strongly believe that conservation or herd management policies directly benefit hunters over other interested parties using public lands. They strongly believe that herd populations would come to a homeostatic state without the intervention of human controls. Animal rights activists are at war over the issue of hunting. They disagree with the use of hunting in the United States, hunters themselves, organizations promoting hunting, and state and federal agencies that allow hunting on the lands they manage. Objections to state and federal policies towards hunting are demonstrated in a wide variety of ways by hunting opponents. One less confrontational method is to comment on all published state policies towards hunting, as well as changes in the state language. More confrontational methodologies include blocking hunters from entering designated hunting areas, interfering with hunters by making a lot of noise in order to scare off animals, standing between hunters and animals, and physically attacking hunters. Opponents believe that their intervention is permissible on the moral basis that no one has the right to kill defenseless animals. Animals are seen as having rights that human agents must observe; animal rights activists believe that they are following a basic moral code when disrupting hunting activities.

Opponents may also feel a sense of obligation to harass hunters in order to dissuade them from killing animals. Harassment takes the form of anything from general conversation, yelling, and blocking the line of site of a hunter, to scaring off wildlife. Despite a majority of the states having outlawed this behavior, anti-hunting proponents continue with their actions in order to stop animals from being killed. An example of one of the state laws is that of Massachusetts, which states:

> Section 5C. No person shall obstruct, interfere with or otherwise prevent the lawful taking of fish or wildlife by another at the locale where

such activity is taking place. It shall be a violation of this section for a person to intentionally (1) drive or disturb wildlife or fish for the purpose of interrupting a lawful taking; (2) block, follow, impede or otherwise harass another who is engaged in the lawful taking of fish or wildlife; (3) use natural or artificial visual, aural, olfactory or physical stimulus to effect wildlife in order to hinder or prevent such taking; (4) erect barriers with the intent to deny ingress or egress to areas where the lawful taking of wildlife may occur; (5) interject himself into the line of fire; (6) effect the condition or placement of personal or public property intended for use in the taking of wildlife; or (7) enter or remain upon public lands, or upon private lands without the permission of the owner or his agent, with intent to violate this section. The superior court shall have jurisdiction to issue an injunction to enjoin any such conduct or conspiracy in violation of the provisions of this section. A person who sustains damage as a result of any act which is in violation of this section may bring a civil action for punitive damages. Environmental protection officers and other law enforcement officers with arrest powers shall be authorized to enforce the provisions of this section.[2]

Animal rights activists believe that this is an attack on their free speech and religious rights and are fighting such laws in the court system. Rutgers University School of Law has published information concerning civil disobedience for activists fighting for animal rights in order to assist them in their fight against hunting and against limits put on their behavior directed towards hunters.[3] They believe that even though hunting is considered legal, it is not moral, which gives them the right to break the law and hinder or stop hunter activities.

Hunting opponents also object to canned or trophy hunts. These types of hunts give hunters an unfair advantage over the animals they pursue. Some types of trophy hunts are considerably less challenging than more traditional pursuits. The animals have little chance to get away and the person almost always comes back with a trophy sized animal to display in their home. The focus on this type of hunt is not the meat, it is the status that comes from the hunt. This type of trophy hunting is outside of the realm of most hunters due to the high cost of the hunts. The high costs of guided hunts are well demonstrated and can range from $2,500 to $20,000 for one animal. You can have a "monster elk" for as little as $5,000 that would be in the range of the records books; an antelope would cost $1,300 and a bison around $2,200. So, ultimately, trophy hunts are for the wealthy hunter who can purchase the animal of their choice and opponents feel they should be abolished.

Many animal rights organizations and groups assert that animals are no longer seen by a large segment of US society as game that is to be used in human consumption. Most people have a different relationship with animals in the wild that does not involve killing them for food or sport. The general public goes into the wild to view, enjoy, and interact with wild animals and hunting activities are in direct opposition to the goals of wildlife enthusiasts. Wild game animals must be protected from human predation.

Conclusion

Diametrically opposed belief systems exist in the United States concerning hunting. On one side are the people who feel it is their basic right to engage in the act of hunting. They are acting in a legal and responsible manner as they hunt. Hunters also assert that they are raising children who will eventually be responsible adults due to the wide variety of things they learn while growing up in a hunting family. Native Americans also fall within the category of the population that consider that they have the legal right as sovereign nations to hunt both on and off reservation lands. As sovereign nations, they can enact their own laws as well as monitor the hunting behavior of their tribal members. Many Tribes also have the legal right to hunt off reservation land as negotiated with federal and state governments. In contrast, hunting opponents argue that it comes down to basic morality. It is not right to kill, and animals have rights equal to those of humans. Animal hunting is no longer needed in modern society, especially since food is widely available.

Ultimately, individuals must decide where they stand on the issue of hunting. Sorting this out involves considering the claims of the opposing value systems. Do humans have an authority over animals that gives them the right to kill for sustenance and sport? Hunters would argue that we have this right because animals exist for our use as human beings. We need them for food, the building of familial relationships, and to use as a tool to teach responsibility. Anti-hunters argue that this perspective is wrong and that humans have no right to take any life needlessly. Animals deserve to be treated with respect; they are seen as having value beyond their instrumentality to humans. How one chooses which position to adopt will depend upon what one believes about these fundamental questions.

Notes

1 Boone and Crockett, 2006, Fair Chase Code and Hunter Ethics; at: www.boonecrockett.org/huntingEthics/ethics/_fairchase.asp?area=huntingEthics.
2 Massachusetts, State of, Part I. "Administration of the Government, Title XIX. Agriculture and Conservation, Inland Fisheries and Game and Other Natural Resources, Chapter 131: Sections 5C, Obstructions or Interference with Lawful Taking of Fish or Wildlife; Remedies, General Law of Massachusetts," 2006; at: www.mass.gov/legis/laws/mgl/131-5c.htm.
3 Francione, Gary L. and Anna E. Charlton. "Demonstrating and Civil Disobedience: A Legal Guide for Activists, Rutgers University School of Law, Animal Rights Law Project," 2006; at: www.animal-law.org/index.html.

Petits Fours

Compliments of the Chef

The true cook is the perfect blend, the only perfect blend, of artist and philosopher. He knows his worth: he holds in his palm the happiness of mankind, the welfare of generations yet unborn.

Norman Douglas, Irish writer

16

Food and Sensuality: A Perfect Pairing

Jennifer L. Iannolo

Glorious sensuality. That perfect counterpart to cuisine, which turns each bite into an opportunity for satiety, and each meal preparation into a lovemaking session. Certainly, there are some who treat food as mere nourishment – one's fuel for the day – and though I see such an approach as misguided, it would be unfair to chastise those individuals. I will admit to attempts at converting some, however, in which I have asked them to step into my world, where the quest for sensual enjoyment in cooking and eating is paramount – and where each of those provides nourishment for the mind and soul, as well as the body.

But what of the "food porn" addicts? There are armchair chefs who rarely cook, but who continuously watch cooking shows; or those who live to dine at the latest, greatest restaurant simply because it has become *de rigueur*. These well-meaning souls, while still exploring the pleasures of the palate to some degree, are unfortunately missing out on the true glory of the bounty at their fingertips. The shallow pleasures they seek do not last long, and no matter what the level of consumption, cannot provide the sweet moment of satiation to be found in deeper sensual engagement. To be clear, there is nothing inherently wrong with pleasure for pleasure's sake (as anyone will tell you after a "quickie" before heading to work), but there is so much more joy to be had with a comparatively small amount of effort if one brings one's mind to the table (or into the kitchen) with one.

You see, I have found that my own journey of sensory development has heightened the entirety of my life experience, and this path toward satiety has introduced me to a world that was quite unexpected at the start. Knowing this, I now have a fervent desire for every man and woman to arrive here, right alongside me – not only to embrace food on a deeper sensual level, but also to savor each heartbeat we have left. If you have already come to this Garden of Eden on your own, I salute you, and though I am preaching to the converted, I hope you will join me in this salutation to sucking the marrow from life's sweet bones.

For those not yet on that road, I will let you in on a little secret: in awakening your senses, you will find that it is not only food which takes on new meaning and inspiration in your life. Suddenly, treasures are to be found around every corner, whether in the hue of a perfect orchid, the sound of sweet violins, or a woman's delicate, dewy complexion; this is not the stuff of fairy tales and poetry, but what is possible *right here and now*. If that does not convince you, perhaps you will be intrigued to know there are depths of sexual pleasure to be discovered that will make any truffle or oyster pale in comparison. Oh yes. No two acts are as similar in their effect on the senses as eating and making love, and by understanding the roots of each you will amplify the sensations of both. Let us take a look at the groundwork, shall we?

The complementary pairing of food and sensuality is proper to humans as rational animals, for the deep enjoyment of both goes beyond the immediate visceral gratification of feeling good, as might be experienced by a toddler or a dog, and enables us to make a higher connection with the world around us. That is not meant in a mystical way, but in one that is much more tangible and discernible *on earth*. Such a connection is not automatic, however – it requires thought and introspection to arrive at a place of knowledge *within* so we can gain pleasure from the world outside. Every experience we have in life is conditioned by our state of mind at that moment, so what we "bring to the table" is more than just a catch-phrase; we can move from whim to whim, looking for the next thrill, or we can savor what is right here before us, and reflect on the pleasure we receive. That reflection may happen in a barely discernible instant, but it deepens the pleasure when one knows *why* one is pleased and can articulate it. As psychologist Nathaniel Branden states:

> The emotional quality of any pleasure depends on the mental processes that give rise to and attend it, and on the nature of the values

involved. For the rational, psychologically healthy man, the desire for pleasure is the desire to celebrate his control over reality.[1]

For centuries, from Epicurus to M. F. K. Fisher, philosophers and writers have extolled the virtues of sensual food pursuits, and their words remind us that such an approach indeed applies not only to the culinary realm, but also to existence itself. If one trains the mind and senses to appreciate the value of aesthetics, it is almost impossible to refrain from seeing the rest of the world with the same passion as one does the plate. Such gratification fulfills an inner need we develop during our first days on earth, and for this type of pleasure there is no substitute. Like the sexual act, it cannot be faked with any satisfactory results because to be truly enjoyed, it requires us to have a deep level of self-knowledge and understanding. Only then can we free our spirits to savor the pleasure we gain from looking outward.

When we are in a heightened sensual state, nothing in our life experience can surpass it. We are able to completely lose ourselves in an ethereal moment of bliss as our senses are overcome with anticipation, then heightened arousal, and at last the sweet reward of complete gratification. The sensations reverberate through our being as we take everything in, allowing ourselves to be engulfed in a moment of pure beauty. And though this description may sound very much like the phases of a sexual interlude, the process can be experienced in different forms as we go from kitchen to bedroom to out of doors.

This beauty we notice outside ourselves is a reflection of our inner state, though we may not be consciously aware of it; when we are internally at peace, we are able to focus on beauty for its own sake, and the pleasure it brings to our person. We may see the same level of glory in a perfect tomato as we do in a five-star meal. If you have ever been in the presence of a sensualist, you will note that his eyes twinkle, or he seems like someone who is truly *alive*. What you are seeing is the purest of spirits – that person free of inner turmoil who is free to enjoy without restraint; it is a person greedy for the full experience of existence. The road to achieving such a state is a long one, and can be arduous, but it is critical to note that we *need* these sensual moments as human beings; they make our existence sweeter, freeing us to soar to the other side of bliss. In order to begin the process, however, we must truly understand its foundations.

Sensuality's Roots

If we look at sensuality very simply, it is a state we encounter before any other kind of knowledge is even possible. We form our first impressions of the world in purely sensual fashion by virtue of necessity. Our surroundings are interpreted by a series of impressions recorded by our lips, fingers, ears, eyes, and noses. A mother's breast provides our first sense of comfort and nourishment, when we are not yet in possession of formal language skills; we cannot articulate what it is we sense, but we know what brings us pleasure and pain, and we pursue that which comforts.

Our senses also protect us before our minds have integrated concepts like "boiling hot tea," and our instinctual physical makeup – our taste buds, for example – warns us of potential poisons. We must rely on all of these until our minds develop to the point where our senses are not our only means of interpretation.

As we age, our minds integrate concepts to form language, and we rely less on our senses to survive – we are no longer in a primitive state where the validity of our sensory perceptions can mean the difference between life and death. In *The Physiology of Taste*, food philosopher Jean-Anthelme Brillat-Savarin captured well this phenomenon, stating that man's increasing level of intelligence compels him to pursue "new heights in experiencing life on earth. In such a quest for satiety, once survival has become more assured, man's senses become a powerful tool of enjoyment." By use of man's mind, "he has made all nature submit to him; he has bent it to his pleasures, his needs, his whims; he has turned it upside down, and a puny biped has become lord of creation."[2]

What is necessary to earn this state of lordship, however, is the use of thought to integrate why and how the senses are stimulated, and at what depths. In order to put those senses to good use, man must understand *himself*; his mind is at the root of it all, so he can choose to bypass thought and coast through existence in the pursuit of whimsical, shallow pleasures, or he can exercise his mind to see how deep the pleasure can go.

Given the close relation of food and sex, the philosophical and physical parallels involved in taking shortcuts or using substitutes

242

in either has the same overall result. Man can be titillated with a quick thrill, or he can savor a lengthened moment of soulful, intense gratification.

Sensuality vs. Titillation

There is no question that food is sexy. One need only see the delicate skin of a peach or savor the onset of an "eye roller" when tasting a bite so sublime: one could die on the spot having lived fully. I have personally experienced a heightened state of arousal brought on by a truffle-flecked potato soup, so by no means do I dismiss or discount the pleasure to be found in such moments. Where this can become problematic, however, is when the state of arousal becomes the end instead of the means to the end, when the lust-induced momentary high of visceral stimulation replaces a profound depth of pleasure yet to be discovered.

We can see these surface-level thrills all around us in the form of pornography, both sexual and food-oriented. The phenomenon proliferates everywhere, from our computer screens to television, where one merely has to tune in to see it in action: chefs moan and roll their eyes with every bite, tempting an audience that is more likely to make reservations than the recipes they demonstrate. In fact, an August 2006 *Details* magazine article asked readers to distinguish between screen shots of porn stars in the throes of "ecstasy" and television chefs, and the audience (myself included) had difficulty discerning which was which.[3]

This is titillation – the idea that such visual stimuli make the food erotic somehow, rather than the food providing us with the means toward a sensual journey of our own. In similar fashion, aphrodisiacs are touted as the ingredients du jour: *the catalysts for a sensual food experience.* Like olden-day carnival barkers the "sensual cooking" experts appear on camera extolling the erotic properties of sexy little avocados and bites of chocolate that will unveil *your true path toward relationship bliss.* Much like a curing tonic, the placebo effect is powerful – and it has taken our culture by storm. Of course, little is mentioned in all of this about the mind's role in sexual stimulation, as that would not only hurt sales, but would also require the delayed gratification that comes with introspection. Instead, the pleasure has become an end in itself, with no connection to the why of the pursuit – aside from getting one's partner into bed.

It is important to note that in and of itself, there is nothing wrong with porn in any form, whether it is of the sexual or food variety. Anyone who has used it as an element of stimulation in a relationship knows how it can enhance the sexual experience. Where the problem occurs is when it replaces all other forms of stimulation, or when we find ourselves watching porn instead of pursuing a real relationship. Similarly, if we do nothing but watch "foodtainment" instead of doing the actual cooking, and learning to savor the process, we are missing out on scores of opportunities to enhance our lives.

Sadly, as our cultural attention span gets shorter, it seems that foodtainment has taken hold and is slowly replacing the real joy to be found in cooking and eating. Star quality now takes precedence over the food, and gastronomic inquiry is second to a good push-up bra or catch-phrase. Like the consumption of sexual porn, the motive seems less about consuming the food than it is about consuming the entertainment.

The Joy of Cooking

When one is fully engaged in the act of preparing a meal, one is offered a journey of the senses that brings pleasure in numerous forms; and such enjoyments are not merely left to those who dine. For the passionate cook, each step of the planning – from carefully choosing a menu to hand-selecting each ingredient – is an act of love, a desire to satiate and nourish another. If all goes well in the cooking, each of these small steps builds to a crescendo of smiles as guests offer their sincere thanks and praise. The power to be found in such a moment cannot be discounted, and any chef will tell you so. As James Beard Award-winning chef Jean-Louis Gerin so eloquently put it, "Each night I make love to my guests. They are presented with the best I have to offer, because they are in my home."

244

When we are able to provide this incredible service for another human being – no matter how simple the meal – we are making a statement of caring. We have put such time and effort into ensuring the happiness of these welcome guests as they sit at our table, those whom we have taken into our care for a short time. Sometimes the love comes in a to-go package as well. When I assemble my ingredients for Christmas baking, I anticipate with great excitement the smiles to come from my recipients. I know exactly who likes which cookies, and how they wait all year to receive that little tin from me. Talk about a power trip – to know that my gifts incite such anticipation is a soulfully enriching feeling.

If I am preparing a meal for a lover, the intensity is magnified tenfold. Here is a man I wish to satiate in every way possible, and my act of seduction begins with his palate. I carefully choose the right flavor to heighten his sensual experience, balancing texture and flavor with deft hands to demonstrate my skills, and more importantly to excite his mind. I carefully watch his face as he tastes each dish, eager to see a reaction. When it is a positive one, my soul does a little dance as I step ever closer to receiving the physical expression of thanks for my efforts. It is one long dance of foreplay that arouses, then satiates, and repeats again until there is but one measure of music left before the final step.

Contrast these scenarios with that of assembling a series of take-out containers on the table and see how the message changes. Such an act makes a statement that says, "Here is the quickest thing I could find." Granted, in our modern culture it seems we are all pressed for time, and even I do not prepare a home-cooked meal each night; I understand what it means to feel rushed and hungry. However, I still make the time to cook as often as I can, and especially on the weekends, because it is my way of reinforcing what is important to me. I am committed to treating myself well, and to savoring the sensual pleasures inherent in food. Even if my meal is as simple as a garden-ripened tomato drizzled with olive oil and some large basil leaves, I am comforted by the perfection I have tasted, and am satisfied knowing I have done something wonderful for my senses. The fragrance of the basil soothes me, and the delicate flavor of the olive oil grounds me to the earth as the juiciness of the tomato's flesh excites me with its tart punch.

When we, as a culture, increasingly turn to others to feed us, we lose an important layer of personal involvement that enables us to nurture ourselves and one another. Where once Mother (or perhaps Father) prepared a meal served around the table with the whole family present, now it is more likely that someone in the family (whoever happens to be home) assembles food from a packet and throws it in the oven, or calls the take-out place for delivery. Nutrition and obesity issues aside, many children have never learned what it is like to receive the comfort of a meal crafted by a parent who loves them.

The irony is that homes are being built with ever-larger kitchens stocked with the latest in kitchen technology, and professional-grade ranges stand lonely and unlit while microwaves heat take-out meals. (If one has the income to hire a personal chef to come into the home, at least that magnificent kitchen is put to use!) This modern quandary has no easy solution – surely it is difficult to abandon our modern conveniences and change our lifestyles, but what has progress cost us? If we continue in this way, we may one day be left with generations who know nothing of the sense of pride and pleasure that comes from crafting a meal.

But perhaps – just perhaps, if they were encouraged to embrace the true beauty to be found in eating itself, they would find their way back to the kitchen.

The Art of Eating

To elevate eating to a form of art is to turn all of existence into a radiant canvas, where all that is wonderful in nature can be embraced in one sitting, as our eyes and nose take in the first hints of the pleasures to come. Our salivary glands respond, eager to take the first bite. As the texture of that bite coats our palate, we are engulfed with fragrance and hints of sweet or savory, then the full rhapsody of flavor and its aftertaste.

The desire to devour in this way – with what philosopher Ayn Rand referred to as *radiant greed*[4] – is to engage one's entire self in that moment of pleasure. We want to consume to the brink of ecstasy, and then a little bit more. Eating becomes a dance of the senses, where our heightened state of arousal takes on a heady, other-worldly feeling.

The same could be said of lovemaking, as the approach is what is most important. Do we wish to go through the motions, or do we want to experience that heightened sense where the rest of the world disappears? This is why I find the idea of aphrodisiacs troublesome, for they are mainly a placebo; any well-prepared meal becomes an aphrodisiac when savored in the right way. The aphrodisiac does not make you sexy – your own sensuality does.

As we pay more attention to sensory stimulation and gain a greater appreciation for our inner mechanisms, our senses become more acute, enabling us to reach such heights. Suddenly, we notice things that seemed to pass us by, and we might find ourselves stopping in mid-step to admire the crisp air and bright stars of an autumn sky; we feel as if some sort of inner poet has been unleashed, eager to see ever more beauty in our surroundings. And sex – a person never knew such heights, where the pleasure caresses us in gentle waves, enabling us to sustain a height of passion we might not have thought possible outside the realm of fantasy.

Such is the state of existence of the sensualist. For those unaware of this sublime state of reality, I cannot convey emphatically enough what a pleasure it is to arrive at such a destination.

The Road to Edenism

If my musings have inspired curiosity in you, or an eagerness to make your way toward the spot where I am now standing, take that as a very good sign: your inner sensualist has awakened, and is tickled with curiosity to know what lies ahead.

To get here, however, you must first plant your feet firmly on the path that heads this way, and the journey is comprised – as is any – of small but important steps. Most importantly, you must get to know who you *really* are, for it all begins in the mind. Do you know what makes your inner engine hum? What triggers a sensual response within you? If not, there is no better time to get to know yourself; take some time to be still and ponder quietly as you reflect on the things you value. What brings you true happiness of the kind that moves your soul?

As you get to know yourself better, it is time to start exploring the wonders that cuisine has to offer, to make a deeper connection with the foods you eat. Rather than going through the motions of eating what an anonymous person has created thousands of miles away – or worse yet, in a laboratory – develop an intimate familiarity with your food. To use that porn metaphor once again, think about the difference between watching the sex and *having* it. One is stimulating, to be certain, but the other eclipses it in comparison. The latter enriches us physically, mentally – and soulfully.

Instead of watching those cooks on television, learn to prepare that meal yourself, and present it to someone you love, even if the person is yourself. Learn to distinguish the difference in flavors and fragrance when you use fresh herbs in place of dried. Better yet, drive right by that supermarket parking lot and head for your local farm stand, where you can meet the farmer who lovingly grew the fruits and vegetables you are about to consume. All of these efforts build upon each other until the sight of a perfect plum is a source of inspiration instead of mere sustenance.

As with anything, of course, it is important to take your time, and moderate your actions. If the senses are constantly over-stimulated, they begin to dull, which will slow your progress. Remember, we all need a breather, as anyone can tell you after a marathon of great sex or delicious four-course meals. We need to give our senses time to recuperate so we can entice them once again – and that is the fun part, after all.

This entire journey is one of self-exploration, so there is no formulaic approach I can give you. Simply start by thinking, and act on those thoughts. See what results from your actions, and commit to exploring further with an endless state of curiosity. Find out what Brussels sprouts look like on the stalk, and put your hands in the dirt of a farm. If you are really into the adventure, go and milk a cow. Each of these experiences contributes to our holistic view of what we eat, and the earth it comes from – and to soar toward the sky, we must first know the ground on which we stand.

We may be born sensualists in a primitive sense, but it is as thinking, rational adults that we can elevate ourselves to a more evolved state of sensuality. I cannot recommend the voyage highly enough, and I implore you to try it for yourself. I will put aside a fig leaf here in Eden for your arrival.

Notes

1 Branden, Nathaniel. "The Psychology of Pleasure." *The Virtue of Selfishness*. New York: Penguin Books, 1964.
2 Brillat-Savarin, Jean-Anthelme. "Meditation 1: On the Senses." *The Physiology of Taste, or Meditations on Transcendental Gastronomy*. New York: Counterpoint Press, 2000.
3 "Food Network or Spice Network?" *Details*, August 2006.
4 Rand, Ayn. *Atlas Shrugged*. New York: Penguin Books, 1957.

17

Duty to Cook: Exploring the Intents and Ethics of Home and Restaurant Cuisine

Christian J. Krautkramer

Introduction

What I hope to demonstrate in this essay is how the food served in a home and the food served in a restaurant are each prepared by a cook with specific duties, derived from their unique stations, that should aim to meet certain expectations of both the cook and his diners. With each set of duties, the respective kitchens of amateur and professional chefs should abide by certain ethics to achieve the intent of each type of cuisine.

While certainly there are lessons that the home cook can learn from the professional chef, and vice versa, the idea that one type of cook should create food in the style of the other is contrary to the spirit of each unique cuisine. Specifically, there are unique qualities to home and restaurant cuisines because each: is created by cooks with different values; puts different emphasis on an end result; and is produced in environments with different rules. In my essay, I will draw upon personal experience in both home and restaurant kitchens to expand and discuss the following examples.

A restaurant kitchen, and those who produce its food, in the absence of a direct and personal relationship with the diner, have a specific duty to cook "to the food." This means that they should intend to create food that is artfully made using expert techniques, drawing out optimal flavor, texture, and color, and in which the ingredients often produce complex, original, and stimulating cuisine. The ethics of the restaurant kitchen both emphasize honoring the abilities of the ingredients to create something greater than when they stand alone and, in order to achieve that emphasis, promoting an exclusive fraternity of the kitchen where the work of the kitchen can only be accomplished by the chefs themselves. Perhaps an appropriate analogy is that of the professional musician: each chef, like career musicians, must execute his individual effort impeccably, but just as the musician must be in sync with every other player to give proper treatment to a great symphony, so too must the chef work in tandem with the rest of the kitchen to produce a great meal.

The home kitchen and the home cook, on the other hand, have a duty to cook for the diner out of love and friendship. Their relationship is direct, personal, and unmediated – an emotional connection is present. The home cook's intent values a fostering of comfort, providing abundance, and creating a dining atmosphere of conviviality. The ethics of the home kitchen place emphasis on honoring the diners first (and the food itself second) and accomplishing this by promoting an inclusive fraternity of the kitchen where cook and diner interact either at the stove or *à table*. Here an appropriate analogy might be a church choir, where although good singing is certainly desired, the primary goal is not perfectly hitting each note as paid singers might desire, but rather to enhance a worship service and promote fellowship.

A Short History of Home and Restaurant Cuisine

The preparation and consumption of food is, by all accounts, the human activity that most frequently and fully marries utility and artistry. Food is necessary to sustain and energize us. All people eat (and this is almost always done several times a day) and most are frequently, if not daily, involved in the making of a meal, either by simply gathering different foodstuffs together on a plate, or by combining them as ingredients of a recipe. Unless faced with starvation, we generally will not eat something that does not look, smell, or taste good. That is where art and craft come into play; one uses his or her ability to create a dish that is pleasing to the senses, and when fully realized, make something that becomes valued for more than simply its sustenance.

Food is the basic component of cuisine, the creation of a style of cooking, and the related study of cuisine, gastronomy – the part of society that Brillat-Savarin said

> is the intelligent knowledge of whatever concerns man's nourishment. Its purpose is to watch over his conversation by suggesting the best possible sustenance for him. It arrives at this goal by directing, according to certain principles, all men who hunt, supply, or prepare whatever can be made into food. Thus it is Gastronomy, to tell the truth, which motivates the farmers, vineyardists, fishermen, hunters, and the great family of cooks, no matter under what names or qualifications they may disguise their part in the preparation of foods. Gastronomy is a part of . . . natural history . . . physics . . . chemistry . . . cookery . . . business . . . political economy . . . It rules over our whole life . . . It concerns also every state of society, for just as it directs the banquets of assembled kings, it dictates the number of minutes needed to make a perfectly boiled egg. The subject matter of gastronomy is whatever can be eaten; its direct end is the conservation of individuals; and its means of execution are the culture which produces, the commerce which exchanges, the industry which prepares, and the experience which invents mean to dispose of everything to the best advantage.[1]

The home is the primary place where food has been prepared and consumed since the beginning of civilization. Unless you were wealthy or of high status, you raised or bought your food to prepare it yourself or with your family. If you were of high status, then you perhaps had servants who performed a similar function; those of particularly elite status had the privilege of eating well-crafted dishes prepared by skilled cooks in elegant settings. Unless you were traveling, you generally did not "eat out" – the only places which served meals outside of a home would have been an inn or tavern where meals were generally reserved for lodgers.

But something happened in the eighteenth century that changed the course of cuisine: the modern restaurant came into being, the profession of chef was created, and the foundations for *haute cuisine* were set. *Haute cuisine* is a style of food preparation and service that puts a premium on high-quality ingredients, expert technique, and refined service in an elegant setting.[2] Much of this can be attributed to the work of Auguste Escoffier, who, through teaching and writing, trained more chefs in the techniques of *haute cuisine* than anyone of that time (and perhaps of anyone since). Escoffier elevated the status of chefs beyond common laborer to that of an artisan. Many servants of French aristocrats (e.g., cooks and valets) lost their jobs in the years during and following the French Revolution and some, seeking gainful employment in a new social climate, gravitated to Escoffier's kitchens for training. There, they frequently spent many years under the Master's tutelage. When ready (and, more likely than not, when Escoffier himself felt they were prepared), these newly minted chefs graduated to helm a kitchen of their own.

It was at this time that the production and consumption of food became divided. While eating for pleasure is almost as old as cooking meat over an open flame, the possibility that one could eat something that in addition to being delicious was prepared with an artistic touch, would be only afforded to the very wealthy or elite prior to the invention of the restaurant. Along with the restaurant came the profession of chef and new ways of thinking about food and cuisine. Professional chefs developed their own set of techniques and methodologies, and the practitioners of *haute cuisine* in particular spent time thinking about how human reaction to cuisine could be raised beyond that of comfort and simple enjoyment. Ever since, we need not have households that support servants and lavish dining rooms and the finest china to enjoy an exceptional meal – we can simply go to a local restaurant and purchase that experience.

The *haute cuisine* experience in Europe remained confined to the cities for most of the nineteenth century and into the twentieth century. A few chefs saw opportunity in the United States, moved there, and opened restaurants of their own. Opportunities were greatest in major urban centers, specifically New York, where the wealthy and well-traveled gravitated, and these French-trained chefs established it as the center of fine dining in the US, with restaurants like La Caravelle, La Côte Basque, Lutèce, and Le Cirque. But the techniques and recipes of the chefs in such kitchens remained part of a secret language known only to those willing to devote their lives to the culinary arts. In the 1960s, however, home cooking in the United States was revolutionized by Julia Child and her co-authors, Simone Beck and Louisette Bertholle, when *Mastering the Art of French*

Cooking was published.[3] The book provided a methodology and technical repertoire for home cooks to bring *haute cuisine* to the home. Recipes for fish preparation, baking, and pastry demystified what was previously known only to those trained in restaurant kitchens or culinary school. *Mastering the Art of French Cooking* sparked a gradual revolution: the home cook could now create meals with the complexity and artistry of the *haute cuisine* chef.

Since the publication of *Mastering the Art of French Cooking*, the evolution of cookbooks has been drastic. Julia Child, while trained in a culinary school, was not a seasoned professional cook but was able to distill the techniques and recipes of French high cooking into an approachable book for home cooks. Gradually, cookbooks came into the purview of professional cooks, and became a way to introduce their personality and the signature style of their own cuisines to the home cook. Particularly since the late 1980s, the most popular cookbooks have been authored by professional chefs such as Alice Waters, Thomas Keller, Wolfgang Puck, Paul Prudhomme, Charlie Trotter, and Mario Batalli. Home cooks who buy the books frequently seek wisdom from the professional chef, hoping to tap into his or her experience and artistry, and perhaps even hoping to replicate the cuisine that emerges from his or her restaurant, thus capturing for a moment the feeling of what it means to be a world-class chef.

This desire of home cooks – a wish to distill the essence of great chefs into easier recipes with equally stunning results – however well intentioned is usually misguided. Restaurant cuisine and home cuisine, in their most fully realized forms (that is, high-level cooking), are distinct styles of food preparation and presentation often at odds with one another. While certainly both types of cuisine have shared values, they can differ significantly from one to another in the aims of the cooks, the ethics of the kitchen, and the aesthetics of the cuisine itself.

Assumptions, Limitations, and Definitions

Before I delve too deeply into comparing the foods produced in home and restaurant kitchens, allow me to set some assumptions and limitations for this essay. First, when I use the word "cooking" I mean to include all forms of food preparation, regardless of whether or not the food is actually prepared by combining various ingredients and, possibly by heating, creating a new dish. Second, I will be exclusively discussing kitchens in the United States. Third, because of my own background and experience, I am less qualified to speak of the aesthetics and ethics of Eastern kitchens, specifically Chinese, Japanese, Indian, Thai, and other major continental Asian and South Seas cuisines. The cuisines of these cultures might have very different purposes for different types of cooks and diners, but I do not have the experience to properly reflect upon them. Fourth, I will only be referring to restaurant and home cooking in the present day.

Also, a note about aesthetics: when creating a food, dish, or meal, a cook desires something that stimulates the senses in the manner desired regardless of experience or employ. The aesthetics of cuisine, however, go beyond the plate itself. An aware cook knows that the setting of the food and the way in which it is served often significantly contributes to the overall dining experience. When speaking of culinary aesthetics, therefore, we have to consider elements beyond the taste, texture, and design of a dish: how it is served, how it interacts with the other dishes during a meal, and how it fits with the overall dining environment. Additionally, I would like to take a moment to clarify some terms.

Intent: The *intent* of cuisine depends largely on the goals of the cook and how those goals fit into his or her role as amateur or professional. The cook comes into a kitchen with a given set of cultural and personal experiences that inform his or her cuisine. Generally, he or she shapes the intent depending upon the diners for whom the food will be prepared – is the diner a family member, a friend, or a paying customer? Second, the cook takes stock of the reasons for which she is cooking, considering what sorts of food are appropriate for the time of day or occasion. Third, a cook accounts for the setting in which the food will be eaten. Is it a restaurant with a formal dining room, or a home where the food will be eaten informally? These factors jointly shape a cook's intent.

Ethics of the kitchen: This essay is not about the ethics of eating – what and why we put something in a pot, on a plate, or into our mouths. What I mean by the ethics of the kitchen is simply the set of acceptable and desired standards according to which a kitchen operates.

Finally, before discussing the intent and ethics of restaurant and home cuisine, I feel I need to establish what exactly restaurant and home cuisine are at their most fully realized. Restaurant critics make a living by judging the quality of a dining experience, keeping in mind concepts such as the specific intermingling of flavors, the presentation of the dish, the ambience of the dining room, and the élan of the wait staff. In much the same way, I believe the best way to judge the quality of a dining experience is to examine your own expectations as a diner. Is the experience below, meeting, or exceeding what I had envisioned it to be? If I am in someone's home, or even my own, I ask whether the meal has satisfied its purpose, be it to provide a tasty, simple lunch or a more elaborate and rich dinner for friends and relatives during a holiday celebration. These are the questions that need to be asked before anyone can judge the merits of cuisine.

In many cases, however, the diner's expectations need to be tempered against unreasonableness by adopting an understanding of process – a way of thinking whereby one believes that the process of achieving, or journeying towards, a goal is as valuable as the goal itself. This attitude is exemplified in the traditions of Taoist or Roman Catholic teaching. Grant Achatz, a leader in the so-called "molecular gastronomy" movement, has said that once he has perfected a dish in the kitchen of his Chicago restaurant, Alinea, he retires it and moves onto another challenge.[4] We can assume, therefore, that almost every time a dish is offered to a diner at Alinea, it is not up to the chef's expectation. Yet, by most accounts, Alinea is one of the most exciting and perfected dining experiences in the US. Most seasoned diners of outstanding restaurant cuisine would likely be very impressed by their meal. So sometimes, if diners are expecting perfection from a restaurant, perhaps it is best if they moderate the standards and expectation a chef has for his cuisine with what the diners expect of the chef. Ultimately, fully realized restaurant cuisine is born when the chef uses all the tools at his disposal to perfect flavors, textures, and colors, creating something that will delight, satisfy, or challenge diners' expectations.

My conception of fully realized restaurant cuisine, however, is most likely be found in a restaurant that most would consider as 'fine dining,' where highly trained chefs create food in a restaurant that puts a premium on service and quality. Most of this sort of food is being created in or near major US cities, where dining, without factoring in the cost of drinks, tax, and tip, can run between $100 and $300 a person.

What I envision as fully realized home cuisine, however, is a bit more difficult to capture in a simple description because the circumstances in which food is prepared in a home vary more than those in a restaurant. In a restaurant, expectations are fairly consistent – you know that you would not be served a burger and fries at an Italian restaurant, just as you would not expect to be served Eggs Benedict at a pizza shop. So, for sake of consistency, let us confine a fully realized home cuisine experience to times when cooking is done for an occasion. That occasion might be as simple as trying out a new Kitchenaid mixer, or having a friend over for dinner, or cooking Christmas dinner for ten. By applying this standard, we can define fully realized home cuisine as when the cook has applied some amount of thought and planning into the meal and has expended a reasonable amount of effort to prepare a good meal.

Duty and Intent

Before exploring the intent of home and restaurant cuisine, we should ask if there are any common intents between them. An argument might be made for nourishment; because all food is seemingly meant to provide the eater with sustenance, all cooks must be interested in producing nourishing food. Twenty years ago, I would have agreed that this might be a common intent. Today, I am less certain. While no chef worth her salt would want you to leave her restaurant ready to go out and eat another meal, the primary intent of some of the most innovative chefs is not to nourish, given that chefs now create dishes which seemingly disappear in your mouth – so-called "foams," "airs," and their variants – without making a discernable dent in your appetite. I believe that cuisine is moving in a direction where nourishment will become less and less an aim of the highest of *haute* dining.

The basic job of the professional cook, especially the head chef of any kitchen, is to produce food which fits the style set by the restaurant and lives up to a minimum expectation of the diner. Chefs often attend a culinary school, and then spend years training in modern-day apprenticeships, joining a kitchen to hone their skills under a more learned chef. If ambitious, a young chef might aim to ride the coattails of a star chef known for being on the cutting edge of restaurant cuisine, and whose kitchens serve as a breeding ground for future head chefs with kitchens of their own.

If we move beyond nourishment as the intent of cuisine, it becomes more difficult to find shared aims. This is largely because of *who* is cooking and *for whom* the cuisine is being cooked. In the case of restaurant cuisine, the chef or the kitchen staff generally cooks for anonymous restaurant diners. Ultimately, these two factors determine intent, for the chef is trained in the culinary arts to raise simple ingredients to a higher level without (in all but a few circumstances) having any meaningful relationship with his or her diners. The chef can only cook to the expectations of the diner and in service of the food itself – his is a duty to the food itself, and through it, a duty to nature and to art.

In Thomas Keller's *The French Laundry Cookbook*, the chef/author describes a seminal moment in his tutelage in cooking, taking place before he would journey to France, where his apprenticeship at several world-class Parisian restaurants would set the foundation for the rest of his career. He had already become somewhat of a seasoned kitchen worker, having spent much of his twenties in his mother's restaurant in Palm Beach, Florida, and in the resort areas of Rhode Island and New York's Hudson River Valley during the busy summer season. At one such Hudson Valley restaurant, La Rive, he was given latitude in designing a cuisine that focused on local ingredients, including livestock unusual for menus at that time – pigeon, offal of pigs and fowl, and rabbits. It was in the presence of these rabbits that he became aware of how significant cuisine truly is:

One day, I asked my rabbit purveyor to show me how to kill, skin, and eviscerate a rabbit. I had never done this, and I figured if I was going to cook rabbit, I should know it from its live state through the slaughtering, skinning, and butchering, and then the cooking. The guy showed up with twelve live rabbits. He hit one over the head with a club, knocked it out, slit its throat, pinned it to a board, skinned it – the whole bit. Then he left.

I do not know what else I expected, but there I was out in the grass behind the restaurant, just me and eleven cute bunnies, all of which were on the menu that week and had to find their way into a braising pan. I clutched at the first rabbit. I had a hard time killing it. It screamed. Rabbits scream and this one screamed loudly. Then it broke its leg trying to get away. It was terrible.

The next ten rabbits did not scream and I was quick with the kill, but that first screaming rabbit not only gave me a lesson in butchering, it also taught me about waste. Because killing those rabbits had been such an awful experience, I would not squander them. I would use all my powers as a chef to ensure that those rabbits were beautiful. It's very easy to go to a grocery store and buy meat, then accidentally overcook it and throw it away. A cook sautéing a rabbit loin, working the line on a Saturday night, a million pans going, plates going out the door, who took that loin a little too far, does not hesitate, just dumps it in the garbage and fires another. Would that cook, I wonder, have let his attention stray from that loin had he killed the rabbit himself? No. Should a cook squander anything, ever?

It was a simple lesson.[5]

Keller goes to the extreme, describing a moment where he wanted to be so in touch with the foodstuffs he used every day that he would even butcher his own meat. He feels beholden to the food; that he has a duty to "ensure those rabbits were beautiful." I am sure that today Chef Keller does not regularly kill his meat and fish, or go out into the fields and harvest vegetables, but this gave him the insight that preparing food transcends normal labor because there is a weight, a responsibility, that chefs bear to honor the food. Keller seeks greater communion with the food. Through that communion, he seeks a better understanding of our own humanity and our relationship with nature and art.

These sorts of professional cooks – the ones who seek to produce fully realized cuisine – seek to honor their duty to the food with a set of specific intentions. First, they seek to perfect a technique. Most chefs want to be able to make any dish they want. In order to do that, certain cooking techniques need to be practiced and honed, either through repeated practice of a technique or by duplicating a recipe many times over. For example, the great steakhouse is known not only for the highest quality cuts of meat, but also for its chefs' abilities to duplicate a rare-to-medium-rare steak to taste. Second, chefs seek to create a signature style. To be called great, most chefs know that they need to set themselves apart from others. The most significant way to do that is to create their own style of cooking, one that gets noticed by diners and critics. Third, chefs aim to challenge, dazzle, or surprise a diner's senses. This may be an offshoot of a chef's intent to produce innovative food, but many chefs actually want diners to be surprised by what will be put in front of them, realizing that at the right moment, the unfamiliar can delight. Finally, a chef seeks to divine the true flavor of the food. Creating cuisine also means preparing food in such a way that the flavor of any ingredient is full and apparent. This may mean doing very little to an ingredient, or it may require extended, complex cooking methods. A great chef wants each ingredient to be served at the peak of its intended flavor.

Home cooks, I believe, have a very different set of aims; although preparing tasty and aesthetically pleasing food is important, it is secondary to the direct relationship with the diner. Home cooks are not paid for their work; their cooking is not an occupation which affords them days of studying and working in a kitchen. The home cook, in contrast to the restaurant chef, has a special relationship with his or her diners that supersedes a moral or spiritual calling to honor the food. True, creating outstanding food is not exclusive to a restaurant kitchen, but ultimately the reason the home cook creates cuisine is not payment, a sense of responsibility to the food, or the satisfaction that comes with expert craftsmanship. Rather, it is out of love for the diner. Further, the home cook has a very different audience for her food. In almost every case, home cooks know the people for whom they are cooking and hope that the act of cooking will maintain a longstanding relationship (cooking for family) or strengthen a newfound one (cooking to impress an evening's date). The home cook has a personal relationship with her diners that the professional chef does not generally have with his patrons. There is an affection the home cook has for his or her diners, because of personal history, that with rare exception the professional chef will never have.

Think of the last great meal you had in a restaurant and try to recall the feelings that it invokes. The food likely serves as the center of that experience. Contrast that by thinking of the last great meal you had in someone's home. Now, it is more likely our feelings center on those with whom we enjoyed the meal. The home meal is less about the food/diner interplay and more about a shared experience among diners and between cook and diner. The home cook, while hopefully trying to produce something delicious, cooks directly for the diner in a spirit of love and friendship.

Therefore, the home cook must have the following set of intents. First, the home cook must produce comfort. Home cuisine has the ability to invoke memories, strengthen relationships, and make the diner feel good in a way which restaurant cooking cannot. The concept of 'home cooking' fosters love and good will. Second, a home cook intends to produce abundance. Abundance is not the same as gluttony; instead, it is a way of sharing yourself. Restaurants are tempered in the amount and frequency in which they serve their food for cost reasons. The home cook sacrifices time and money in the name of love for the diner. Furthermore, the home cook seeks to foster an atmosphere of conviviality. The professional chef seeks recognition for the food they create; the centerpiece of the meal is the dish itself. The home chef hopes that the food significantly contributes to an atmosphere that promotes joyful interactions among diners.

Ethics of the Kitchen

I have already visited the ideas of duty to food and diner. The ethics of the kitchen reflects these duties depending on the circumstance of place. In the restaurant kitchen, because honoring the food is paramount, the atmosphere the head chef of a kitchen must promote is one where hard work, diligence, and creativity are valued. I will not rehash what others have already said about the pressures, trials, and rigors involved in both training to become and working as a chef.[6] Needless to say, there is a certain mentality that most who work in the kitchen of a restaurant either develop or possess prior to joining a kitchen. From my experience, professional cooks tend to be bold, opinionated, and determined in their drive to create great food. These are necessary qualities which create an *exclusive* fraternity of the kitchen. Chefs must seek to know what good food really is and they must work together to produce good food. This means that those who do not follow the aforementioned tenets will quickly find themselves excluded from the fraternity. Ruhlman relates in *The Making of a Chef* how important it is that a chef show up each time, every time, and on time when they are supposed to be in the kitchen. This is because not only are the other chefs dependent on them, but they are, in a vital sense, beholden to the food they are to make.

On the other hand, the home kitchen is one which fosters an *inclusive* fraternity. The good home cook seeks to share the kitchen experience by becoming more participatory in the dining experience. The person who dines in the home rarely sits *à table* waiting to be served. Instead, they join the cook in the kitchen and either help to produce a meal, or simply join him or her in conversation in the spirit of conviviality. The home kitchen is not off-limits – it is not a place where secret wisdom is kept to be unleashed when the plate is put in front of the diner. Instead, it is an *inclusive* fraternity, where the shared experience of creating cuisine is key to the duty to the diner. Instead of searching for communion with the food, as the professional chef does, the home cook searches for communion with the diner; a communion between individuals rather than a communion with nature and art.

Conclusion

This essay has explored some duties in cooking – how those who prepare and serve food do so for different reasons. The professional chef has chosen a life where purpose comes from the creation of great food. He does not have a personal relationship with the diner, so his duty derives from the profession itself – to follow aims that make a chef great and to adhere to the professional ethics of the kitchen – in order to become closer to nature and to art. For the home cook, their duty is to the diner, with whom they have relationships, and to follow intents and create an ethic of the kitchen that brings them closer in a spirit of love and friendship.

Notes

1   Fisher, M. F. K. (trans.). *Brillat-Savarin's The Physiology of Taste*. New York: Knopf, 1971: 51–2.
2   Trubek, A. B. *Haute Cuisine: How the French Invented the Culinary Profession*. Philadelphia: University of Pennsylvania Press, 2001.

3 Beck, S., L. Bertholle, and J. Child. *Mastering the Art of French Cooking.* New York: Knopf, 1961.

4 "America's Top 50 Restaurants." *Gourmet.* October 2006: 131.

5 Keller, T. *The French Laundry Cookbook.* New York: Artisan, 1999: 205.

6 See Ruhlman, M. *The Making of a Chef: Mastering the Heat at the Culinary Institute.* 1997. New York: Henry Holt, 1997; Ruhlman, M. *The Soul of a Chef: The Journey Toward Perfection.* New York: Viking Adult, 2000; Buford, B. *Heat: An Amateur's Adventures as Kitchen Slave, Line Cook, Pasta-Maker, and Apprentice to a Dante-Quoting Butcher in Tuscany.* Toronto: Doubleday Canada, 2006.

18

Diplomacy of the Dish:
Cultural Understanding
Through Taste

Mark Tafoya

Introduction

How do food and culture inform one another? Is it possible to gain greater insight and understanding of a culture through its food? We live in an increasingly multicultural and global society. We come into contact with people from vastly different backgrounds, and we may not have had any direct experience of them. Our individual and cultural food tastes and choices say much about who we are and the cultures from which we come.

As a chef, I explore many ethnic dishes and micro-regional cuisines, and present them to my diners, many of whom are discovering these tastes and flavor combinations for the first time. As the availability of products and cuisines opens up, Americans have begun to sample an increasingly wide variety of ethnic cuisines, often without a previous understanding of the root culture.

When we try a new dish that comes from another land, we have a visceral experience of foreignness brought into our bodies, which begins the process of familiarization which can lead to great understanding of our shared tastes and values. The act of consuming new dishes can be a powerful leap into the culture from which these dishes come. I explore the notion that one of the best ways we can learn to understand, and indeed celebrate, each other, is through our cuisines. Something as seemingly small as our approach to food can transform the world in ways both small and vast, opening up new paths of understanding between even rivals.

Familiarity

Regardless of who we are, we have been raised with a relatively limited range of familiar foods. With few exceptions, the local produce, animals, and specialties, as well as our ethnic heritage, dictated what we ate as children. Like our core beliefs, morals, religion, language, and clothing, what we eat is generally inextricably tied to our family heritage. Not only is this cuisine familiar and comforting, but it actually informs our personal definitions of food. In adulthood, the slightest whiff of particular aromas can evoke strong memories of food we ate as children, and remind us of family members long gone. Conversely, as a child, who has not had the experience of visiting a friend's house and smelling the aromas coming from the kitchen, only to be shocked at how strange they seem? Even among people who grow up in the same broad culture, it can be an odd experience at first to discover how unusual other people's food seems to us.

Yet it is fair to say that in the so-called "melting pot" of America, we have a core set of familiar foods. The modern American palate is defined by a general set of foodstuffs that have traditionally been grown here. We think of these foods as comforting. They tie us to our heritage, both within the family and with our country as a whole. We even have a core group of dishes that despite their origin are now considered "All-American." We have even enshrined expressions into our lexicon which attest to this. The phrase "As American as apple pie" springs from an erroneous assumption that apple pie is an American invention. We know that some form of apple pie was made in many cultures long before it made its way into the American ethos. Just ask the Tatin sisters, who invented their famous upside down apple tart in France! It might be more appropriate to say "As American as scrapple, hoe cakes, or molasses baked beans," but that does not have quite the same ring. Pizza, roast turkey, hamburgers, and mashed potatoes are now part of our American culinary landscape, and they all have distinct connections in our collective memory.

This culinary familiarity is not limited to the United States, nor is it new to world culture. In the ancient world, people were largely limited to the foods that could be foraged or grown within a radius of about 20 miles. Far from being a trendy and eco-conscious fad, the concept of "local and seasonal" was a fact of life for people worldwide until as recently as the last century. The foods people grew up eating were simply whatever they could grow themselves or trade for with others. The spices, seasonings, and methods of cooking were all dictated by environmental, political, and religious circumstances. In many cases, religious and tribal strictures dictated what was permissible to eat, and what would be restricted or forbidden. The Jewish laws of Kashrut and the Muslim Halal strictures are perhaps the best-known examples of this. They remind the people who they are and where they come from, binding them in a covenant which dictates what goes into their bodies.

Melting Pots

While the familiar brings comfort and even ties us to our heritage, it can be limiting to us. This is especially true in an increasingly global society in which we have interaction with people from many different cultures. There is economic and cultural exchange between nations, as well as direct personal interaction with "the other" in our daily lives. Very few places on the planet are untouched by this aspect of contemporary life. Will we be faced with these cultural differences and turn away, retreating into the familiar, and isolating ourselves from "the other," or will we embrace the differences, seeking out novel experiences, and discovering the familiar within the unusual?

Our modern world, seemingly small, brought together by advances in technology, is not the first era to see a melding of traditions and cultures. It has happened frequently throughout history, when great advances in technology, and the power which comes with it, bring people from different places and traditions together, willingly or not. Ancient Rome is a paradigmatic example of such a period in history. At one time the saying "all roads lead to Rome" was not simply a hyperbolic expression; it was true. Through its military dominance the Roman Empire conquered many lands, and as a result, Rome itself was among the most cosmopolitan and diverse cities ever known. At its height, Rome had a population of nearly 5 million people. No modern city would even come close in size until London's population boom in the Industrial Revolution.

Rome's population was largely composed of slaves from the far flung regions of the empire, people of widely divergent backgrounds. Along with the tribute, gold, and riches, Roman soldiers brought back with them the foods and animals of conquered lands, and surely the slaves brought with them the cooking methods and traditions of their homelands. Romans were voracious for the exotic, made evident by tales of coveted plants and animals being transported at great expense from North Africa or Gaul to the city for special feasts for rich citizens. Likewise, Rome had great influence on the places it conquered, and the commerce that came with empire increased the movement of interesting foodstuffs throughout the Mediterranean and Middle East. This commerce started a long tradition of trade between East and West which over time influenced cuisine worldwide. The great food traditions of Europe would arise from the marriage of these various styles and cultures.

The practice of sitting down together at table and breaking bread is one of the most ancient forms of contract negotiation, sealing a deal, or promising a betrothal. Long before the Roman Empire, and before the written word and courts of law, humans used food to cement a bond. The taking of another's food into one's body is a symbol of accepting their offer, or signifying that you trust their word. In Ethiopia, the practice of "giving gushta" entails wrapping morsels of food in *injera*, the sourdough flatbread, and placing it into the mouths of your fellow diners, who in turn feed you to honor the connection between people.

This sharing of food at table has ancient origins. Most cultures have traditionally held hospitality in extremely high value. In fact, there is evidence that one of the most egregious sins of the people of Sodom was in refusing hospitality to guests and foreigners passing through their lands. Jewish folklore from the *Haggadah* has accounts of Sodom being a place where hungry strangers were cruelly given gold, but no food or lodging. When they starved to death, the gold was taken and the bodies desecrated. Most Near Eastern cultures require protection of guests under one's roof. In the biblical story, Lot was visited by two angels in disguise, and when the mob attacked and insisted on "knowing" the guests, Lot offered his own virgin daughters instead, so great was his felt duty to protect his guests.

A Personal Culinary Journey

Of course, any analysis of cultural culinary discovery must spring from personal experience. Surely, to attempt to understand the new, one must examine the familiar, and why it influences our lives so deeply. Our personal experience, whether we grow up with abundance or penury, adventure or the comfort of safety, forms a layer of assumptions from which our food psychology springs. Most people grow up assuming that the way their mother cooks is simply the way it must be done. Going to a friend's house and smelling the aromas of unfamiliar foods on the stove can be a challenging experience for a young child. New smells, textures, and tastes give our palates completely new sensations which we can either embrace or reject. The degree to which a person can break through this early imprinting to be open to new tastes determines how he will take to the foods of different cultures.

My own food epiphany came early in my life, and through a childish curiosity which has stayed with me into adulthood. I grew up in central New Mexico, which has a distinctive regional cuisine, a blend of ancient Pueblo foods, Spanish and Mexican dishes brought by the *conquistadores*, and of course, the ubiquitous American foods. We always had a pot of red chile on hand, and special occasions saw dishes like *posole*, a pork and hominy stew served around Christmastime, and *carne adovada*, another pork dish marinated in a chile/vinegar sauce and slowly baked until the cubes of pork are tender with a light crust of chile on the outside. The holidays also brought *biscochitos*, little cinnamon and sugar dusted cookies made with copious amounts of shortening, and dozens of *tamales* would steam on the stovetop while we kids filled paper bags with sand and candles to make *luminarias* to line the walkways. We would come in from the cold to find a hot mug of *atole*, a drinkable blue corn meal mush cooked with milk and sweetened with honey.

These and other New Mexican dishes were as familiar to us as pizza, burgers, and hot dogs, or a roasted turkey with gravy, corn bread stuffing, green beans, and all the trimmings. For many Americans, our New Mexican dishes would seem strange and even foreign, although several of these dishes really are the native foods of the very first Americans. Yet for me, the exotic usually meant

"Chinese" food (a catch-all phrase for anything remotely Asian, whether authentically Chinese, or otherwise).

My epiphany came one afternoon at the age of eight when I joined my aunt Ruth and older cousin Beverly (already an 18-year-old culinary adventurer) for a daylong project of making Chinese egg rolls. I had never seen such an array of strange ingredients: water chestnuts, bok choy, wood ear mushrooms, oyster sauce, and egg roll wrappers. The smell of these ingredients, even raw and unprepared, invaded my nostrils like an army of imperial terra cotta warriors and transported me far away from the Rio Grande valley to an imagined fantastical China.

I learned how to chop, shred, julienne, and combine these strange flavors, watching Beverly stir fry them in a wok. Once it had cooled, my job was to place the filling onto the oddly pliant and cool, yet silky-smooth wrappers coated with cornstarch and roll them up into a neat cigar-shaped package ready to be frozen or fried. As the afternoon went on, I imagined what it would be like to be in China, surrounded with these aromas and flavors, and what it must look like. My childish image was pretty far removed from what I actually discovered twenty years later, but the pleasure of the exotic kept my imagination fueled and my hands moving all day. After making about six or seven dozen egg rolls and freezing them in plastic bags, our hard work was rewarded when Aunt Ruth heated up a pot filled with oil and deep fried a few of our egg rolls to be immediately devoured. I can still taste the too-hot outer wrapper (which I could not wait to bite into) and the crisp, vegetal interior flavored with garlic and oyster sauce, and I re-member thinking how lucky Chinese kids were to get to eat like this every day.[1]

My taste buds had been activated, and I was off. Over the next few years, I tried to experience as much foreign cuisine as possible, given the sparse choices available in Albuquerque in the late 1970s. One particularly memorable event occurred on a family trip to Santa Fe when I was about twelve years old. I learned that Santa Fe had the only authentic Japanese restaurant in the area at the time. I strong-armed my family with constant and overly plaintive pleas to go to this strange place and try the sushi I had heard about. They acqui-esced when they learned that the Japanese also serve cooked food, and that there was a *teppanyaki* table at the restaurant. Benihana had just hit it big in the Southwest, so they figured that they could at least eat rice and chicken.

I was the only one who wanted to try the sushi, and yet even I was stricken with fear when I smelled and saw the odd parcels and small bites lined up on the sushi plates. My brother laughed at me as the wooden tray was laid before me with an array of raw fish lying atop balls of rice, some of them wrapped in a strange green paper. The waitress, a beautiful Japanese woman, noted my look of panic and the strange inquisitiveness of the rest of the family and spent time explaining what each piece was, and the way to enjoy it. She called the octopus slice *tako*, which made me laugh and intrigued me, since we had eaten tacos all our lives. I thought it strange that the Japanese would also have something called *tako*, which was so different from the familiar crunchy shell filled with meat and cheese. I carefully placed the cold white octopus in my mouth and was shocked by its chewy texture. It was not rubbery, as badly prepared octopus can be, but it had a texture that was so foreign to me. The waitress suggested I dip it into the soy sauce flavored with *wasabi*, which nearly blew out my ears. I must admit that my first venture into sushi was more an experience of asserting my culinary independence than of gustatory satisfaction. It was simply the most foreign experience I had yet discovered, and I would need a few years and a more developed palate before returning down that path.

Yet something shifted after that experience, and I learned that things which were so odd to me were mundane for other people. Granted, I would not have access to these people for many years to come, but the time the waitress spent explaining to me the customs and intricate eating rituals of the Japanese helped me to recognize that tasting foreign foods is a fast track to understanding. Like the egg roll experience, the décor of the restaurant helped me to imagine myself in Japan, wearing their clothes and exploring the pagodas and wooden walkways. It awakened in me a thirst for knowledge, and actually provided a base for further exploration. Because I now had some familiarity of the food, I was able to integrate new knowledge about Japan and its traditions into a coherent whole, based in a visceral experience, not just in a theoretical or visual one.

These early experiences would form the basis for a desire to add to my knowledge about other cultures and cuisines. I chose to learn French in high school, and through that study, became enamored with all things French. In fact, I even started to become quite francocentric, at least as much as is possible for an American who had not yet traveled to France. French was one of my majors in college, and in my junior year abroad, I finally had my first experience of living in another culture.

I learned that many of the assumptions at the base of my worldview were not shared by others living halfway around the globe. This was most clear in the European tradition of shopping for each day's staples every morning, making a circuit of different specialty purveyors. Growing up in the late twentieth-century United States, my only context included weekly trips to the supermarket, convenient yet devoid of the vitality and sense of community commonplace in European markets. I was unaware that one could have fresh produce, fish, dairy, meat in different places, often brought to market by the farmers themselves, and of the highest quality. This is happily becoming a strong value here in the United States.

Bringing New Tastes to the Table

While not everyone has the luxury or inclination to travel the world in search of deeper cultural and culinary understanding, today Americans are blessed with a multitude of world cuisines here at home which are becoming increasingly more authentic. Gone are the days of ketchup in marinara sauce, or Chop Suey passing for authentic Chinese food. We have fallen in love with couscous, eat chiles with abandon, and most of us are even brave enough to eat sushi. We have shed our fear of the foreign in a way that entices us to taste of what we might once have considered exotic. In the past twenty years, the proliferation of ethnic restaurants throughout America, even in places far from urban centers of immigration, has brought us many new tastes. This is most assuredly a good thing, as Americans who might never have had the means or desire to travel the world are being introduced to new worlds, and embracing them.

The native familiarity and comfort of what we have known as children gives way for some to the desire for the next hot trend, and for others the desire to explore what might not have been available to them before. The upshot of this is that as Americans develop a palate for the taste of world cuisines, the people serving them can develop progressively more authentic versions of their native dishes, and are in turn increasingly beholden to avoid cutting corners.

In order to help people to get in touch with the deeper layers of world cuisine, I have developed a series of classes introducing people to the international cuisines that have most inspired my own cooking, and I have presented these classes throughout the country. Four of these classes are *A Taste of Vietnam*, *A Taste of Umbria*, *A Taste of Persia*, and *Small Plates Around the World*.

Much has changed since my early forays into eating sushi and egg rolls. True, in the past twenty years, it has become much easier to find food from other countries, and unusual tastes are no longer derided as weird. However, when it comes to cooking ethnic foods at home, we have generally not ventured beyond the usual suspects: red sauce-based Italian foods, Mexican night, and perhaps the occasional stir fry. As more ethnic haunts pop up just about everywhere in the US, we find ourselves eating sushi, *pad thai*, *arepas*, *tagines*, and *gyros*, but we are not always crafting these same dishes at home.

My desire is to delve deeper, moving beyond the typical and better known dishes of world cuisines, and focusing on micro-regional dishes from the cultures I love. Thinking of these cultures and cuisines like an onion, the typical – or more to the point – stereotypical dishes are that first layer of onion. When you begin to peel back the layers, you discover the nuances and varieties, special dishes that come from particular towns, brought over and adapted from others with a unique lineage. Discovering these micro-regional specialties helps to tell the story in more detail than just broad strokes.

Rather than focusing on generic "Italian" food, I saw an opportunity to introduce people to the foods and ingredients of Umbria, the landlocked region of central Italy and neighbor to both Tuscany and Lazio. Most Americans know and love the food of Tuscany, and rightly so. Florentine cooking, the wines of Chianti, and the lavender fields of Tuscany deserve their place in the hearts of anyone who has had the good fortune to travel there. But I have always been a fan of the underdog, and love to promote lesser known, yet fabulous, cuisines. This is why I am a champion of the cuisine of Umbria, the "Green Heart of Italy," which is known for its truffles, wild boar, wood pigeon, and lake eel, and is the production center of as much as 40 percent of all pasta made in Italy. With dishes like wild mushroom bruschetta with polenta, *Tegamaccio* (a fish stew from Lake Trasimeno in central Umbria), and poached pears in Sagrantino wine, this cuisine focuses on the simplicity and purity of its core ingredients. Many of these dishes have evolved from the early cuisine of the Romans, as mentioned before. My own visits to Lake Trasimeno, Perugia, and Assisi have etched the flavors into my sense memory, and I hope that tasting these dishes encourages people to discover Umbria for themselves.

Ancient Persia was a crossroad of history and culture; once the center of the known world, Persia influenced most other Mediterranean and Middle Eastern cultures. Many of the principles of Persian cuisine were developed during the height of the Islamic golden age, when much European cooking was still rather primitive. Using more subtle herbs and flavorings than many other Middle Eastern foods, Persian cuisine is based on ancient principles of "hot" and "cold" foods, and strives to balance body and soul through diet; saffron, sumac, fenugreek, pomegranates, and rose water figure prominently. The building block of Persian cuisine is rice, which is best expressed in *polow* and *kateh*. The intricate ritual involved in making a satisfactory *kateh* gives us great insight into the culture. Time is spent picking over and repeatedly washing the rice, which is gently steamed over very low heat with a towel over the pot to prevent steam from escaping. The bottom forms a crisp caramelized crust, which is overturned onto a serving platter and enjoyed separately from the fluffy steamed top rice. *Kuku Sabzi*, an herbed egg dish, combines eggs with a healthy mix of herbs, ground walnuts, and saffron, and likely influenced the *frittata* seen in Italy and the *tortilla española* in Spain. *Khoresh*, a method of braising almost any meat or vegetable, is much more than simply stewing. The subtleties of Persian herbs and flavorings come through in these special dishes. *Sohan asal*, a honeyed almond brittle made with saffron and rose water, is a simple and easy dish which is the touchstone for candied nut sweets of other cultures.

The food of Vietnam is influenced by its geography and history, by both native and European foods. Learning how to handle rice paper, thin translucent sheets made from a pounded paste of glutinous rice, forms the base skill for making an assortment of Vietnamese summer rolls. This staple of Vietnamese cuisine uses fresh vegetables, herbs, ground meats, and shrimp, as well as *nuoc cham nem* dipping sauce, redolent with lime juice and fish sauce.

In the class *Small Plates Around the World*, we explore the concept of *tapas* from Spain, *dim sum* from Southern China, and *mezes* from Greece, all small plates and hand snacks found in diverse cultures. I lead the class on an exploration of *Albondigas*, stuffed grape leaves, *kataifi*, *bruschetta*, and potstickers. As with other explorations, we see that many cultures have similar ways of enjoying snacks, whether wrapped, as sandwiches, small pies, or meatballs.

What strikes me most each time I teach one of these classes is how eager students are to learn about the tastes and techniques of different countries. In some cases, students sign up for every class, so eager are they to learn for themselves how to make food from around the world. There is a culinary renaissance going on in the US; we are eager to learn not just how to eat, but also how to make foods from many different places.

It seems that once people get a taste of new foods, the floodgates open, and they cannot be satisfied. It helps that many specialty products are readily available in shops around the country, not to mention the ethnic restaurants which are ever more commonplace. One might assume that the preference for comfort foods would drive people's culinary choices, but the more people learn about world cuisines, the more they seek out these new tastes and incorporate them into their lives. Though the sense memories of the foods of youth inform our desires, our food choices are equally driven by wanting to recapture a feeling, taste, or smell from our travels in other countries or a special meal eaten in a favorite ethnic restaurant.

The current state of the world may appear to some as a battle of opposing cultural forces. On the surface, this may have some basis in history, politics, and religious values that seem contradictory, but I believe that we have more in common than we tend to think. We all sit down at table and share in the bounty of the harvest, and every culture values their culinary expressions, and how those expressions celebrate the path they have taken into the contemporary world. It is important that each culture retain these values, and often food is the most palpable and sensory way in which they are preserved.

However, even cultures which have widely opposing values and historical conflicts can find in their enemy's traditions some aspect which mirrors their own loves, values, traditions, and desires. Arabs and Jews alike share a rich and complicated history of living in the desert, deriving their sustenance from working the unforgiving land, and holding to the dietary laws of their scriptures. Many of their traditions, while expressed in divergent ways, have similar origins.

There is hope for the future when young people sit down together and share a meal. It is encouraging to see that many university dining halls are places where students from different countries and cultural backgrounds break bread together. Larger universities have many students of foreign heritage who can share their experiences with American youths over a meal, and the dining halls themselves are starting to serve a greater variety of ethnic dishes.

Tables in kosher dining rooms in universities all over the country are platforms for culinary summits. Many observant Muslim students eat in Kosher Hillel dining halls, since the food is prepared in accordance with Halal restrictions as well. The ancient practice of meeting at table and breaking bread as a means of sealing contracts can now serve as a way for Arabs and Jews alike to become familiar with one another and build trust. The taking of another's food into one's body is a symbol of accepting their offer, or signifying that you trust their word.

Seeing that young people are willing to share their time and tables gives us hope that new paths for understanding can spring up over the sharing of something simple like a meal. This seems like such a small thing, but it has the power to change the hearts of individual people, and over time, it can change the world.

Note

1 My perspective at the time was rather narrow, and I did not know that there were many regional cuisines with numerous dishes, and that surely there would be at least some variety in their diet. But I was, after all, only eight.

19

Balancing Tastes: Inspiration, Taste, and Aesthetics in the Kitchen

Aki Kamozawa and H. Alexander Talbot

Every great dish is a delicate balancing act. It is comprised of three key elements: taste – which combines flavor and aroma – inspiration, and aesthetic appeal. There are those who would contend that each element is equally important, but as chefs, we have always believed that taste is the dominant partner. An artistic presentation may draw the eye and a great idea or interesting background story will make the dish memorable, but, in the end, food has to *taste* good. The creation of great food entails capturing the essence of natural ingredients and then magnifying the experience into something arresting and memorable. There is beauty to be found in every aspect of the cooking process and inspirations to be found everywhere. Inspiration is necessary to create great food. An attractive plate will do much to seduce diners and bring them to your tables. But if the food does not taste good, the other two elements cease to matter. On the other hand, when these three elements come together, the result can be truly amazing.

Modern science and technology are used to enhance textures and flavors. As we experiment with new ideas, it is essential to try to remain true to an ingredient's original essence. Food should never be manipulated to the point where it becomes unrecognizable. There are those who claim that cooking is an art where chefs create beauty on the canvas of a plate. Some say that cooking is a craft, a set of skills learned through years of experience. Others claim that it a science and that there are set principles and guidelines to follow. To our minds, the art, science, and craft involved in cooking are powered by the three elements of taste, inspiration, and aesthetics, which must be seamlessly woven together. These elements are the foundation upon which great cuisine is created. Food should always appear to be simple, look natural, and taste extraordinary.

Inspiration

Inspiration is a fleeting and powerful motivator. It is the spark that ignites our ideas, causing them to explode from our imaginations; it gives us the impetus required to formulate new creations. Without inspiration, we cannot move forward. We draw inspiration from many different sources. Different perspectives are excited by divergent inspirations. This allows chefs to share their unique perspectives with one another and to expand upon each other's ideas. The information available today allows chefs to draw from an infinite pool of ideas and information. Recipes are no longer the closely guarded secrets of the past. This atmosphere allows individual chefs to create special cuisines that are more satisfying to them than anything they could have conceived on their own. It is the exchange of ideas with our peers that stimulates our imaginations. We all rely on our improvisational skills to bring our culinary fantasies to life. We bounce ideas around like little rubber balls, each catching hold of the ones we are best able to create. One chef may conceive of a tamarind cavatelli, but another will create the tangy dough with a soft chewy texture. A chef may dream up a delicate coconut consommé, but one of his cooks will actually make the broth. It is the relationships in a kitchen as much as the skill of its cooks that allow new ideas to come to fruition.

We must be focused in our approach to food to overcome the expense involved in procuring high quality ingredients. The local products are not often beautiful, but we find inspiration in the intense flavors concealed beneath the mottled surface of an organically grown potato. In the sanitized modern culinary world, food must look beautiful on the plate in order to tempt the palate. Pages of glossy food magazines depict perfect produce and gorgeous presentations, which encourage unrealistic expectations of beauty. Real food is often radically different. Organic apples come from the tree with various bruises and small imperfections. Corn arrives from the farm with fuzzy caterpillar-like creatures edging from their silken wrappings. Heads of lettuce are large with tough outer leaves shielding a variety of small insects within their depths. Berries arrive from the farm in shallow pails, speckled with mud and dust, with the bottom layers slightly crushed, but warm and fragrant from the blazing sunshine. These products require extra care to unearth their possibilities, but we are rewarded by amazing flavors and the knowledge that we support our local economy and our local environment. There is nothing more inspiring than that.

One of the challenges of being a chef is connecting to other chefs and sharing our inspirations. We can all find good food in our different locales, but in spite of what you may read in magazines, for most of us it tends to be relatively simple meat-and-potatoes cuisine. The world of food is slowly evolving. First we educate ourselves and then we try to share our new perspectives with our diners. We constantly search for new catalysts. Cookbooks, television, and the Internet have been invaluable for opening up new horizons. Other people's thoughts can be instrumental in getting us to look at ingredients from a different perspective. As technology creates the illusion of an ever-shrinking world, we are able to reach out to other chefs from around the globe. This exchange of ideas and insights has been very rewarding. Techniques and flavor pairings are shared and then adapted to different palates and locales around the world.

Mistakes are another source of inspiration. We view them as opportunities to discover something new. We strive to utilize as much of each ingredient as possible, so we are forced to turn mistakes into successes. Since we cannot afford to simply throw products away, we must use our imaginations to turn a failed cake into something different and equally delicious. Often these impromptu creations are some of the best things to emerge from our kitchens.

Many of the ingredients used as part of seemingly new techniques in kitchens today have long been employed in the development of both ancient vegetarian cuisines and modern day convenience foods. For example, Asian countries have never shied away from substitutions such as the mock duck found on countless Chinese restaurant menus, and *surimi*, the imitation seafood often seen in inexpensive sushi restaurants. Mock duck is usually produced from *seitan*, a product made from wheat gluten. The *surimi* is made from pulverized white fish bound together with additives, which is then seasoned, shaped, cooked, and frozen for sale. Puffed grains, which are found in many cultures, are the backbone of the cereal and snack food industries. Carrageenan, which is often seen in restaurants in the form of warm savory puddings, is extracted from Irish Moss and other red seaweeds, and has been used as a thickening and stabilizing agent for hundreds of years. Cotton candy is a confectionary that has seen a recent resurgence in popularity, especially in a myriad display of savory flavors. It is simply a fluffy version of spun sugar, which has been around for centuries, which is now being adapted for modern palates and sensibilities. We constantly revisit techniques and ingredients from the past in order to make the leaps needed to create novel dishes in our kitchens.

All of the enzymes and stabilizers used originally to create convenience foods are quietly gaining popularity in restaurant kitchens. Chefs are finding inspiration in the use of additives to manipulate the textures and flavors of their ingredients. This trend has become known as molecular gastronomy, and it is gaining acceptance and momentum throughout the world. An increasing number of chefs employ this modern approach in an attempt to distinguish and establish themselves in an increasingly competitive culinary field. Experimenting with these new techniques and ingredients is yet another way to broaden our culinary horizons.

Other chefs are moving in a different direction. They embrace simplicity, emphasizing local ingredients and a lack of extravagant manipulation in their kitchens. They serve food grown near their restaurants and tout the benefits of using local, seasonal ingredients. There is even a colony of chefs who have embraced the benefits of raw foods. They are proponents of minimalism in the extreme. These can be wonderful approaches, and many of these chefs create exceptional food in their kitchens. Their creativity inspires us to experiment with their ideas in our kitchens.

We have begun to look more closely at the world around us and to seek out local products to highlight in our kitchen. We have realized that part of our responsibility as chefs is to help safeguard our food supply and make conscientious choices for flavor and for sustainability. Unfortunately, for many of us, drawing the bulk of our ingredients from local sources is largely impractical. Both the demands of our clientele and the accessibility of products are prohibitive. However, this is slowly changing as consumer awareness begins to increase and the food supply begins to open up. Diners are embracing a return to organics and sustainability, and small farms are being championed across the country. This will open new avenues for chefs and consumers alike in the constant struggle to find the best possible ingredients. This evolution is a huge boost to both chefs and consumers, as people become more thoughtful about the food they want to eat.

Chefs develop their personal styles based on many different platforms. Although the simple approach and the experimental approach are the most popular, there are countless variations on these themes. Some chefs are cuisine-driven, embracing the techniques and ingredients of a particular country or region of the world. Others base their style on their own version of fusion, skillfully weaving together imaginative cooking techniques and flavor palates from the global pantry. Some chefs are root-based, emphasizing local ingredients and native dishes, while others pride themselves on procuring far-flung exotica regardless of cost. Cooking techniques based on scientific principles are slowly establishing themselves in modern kitchens across the nation. Of course, there will always be a place for old-fashioned American classics embraced in casual restaurants nationwide. It is daunting to find one's niche in this diverse and shifting culinary environment, but chefs are pressured to do so. Modern chefs prefer the approach of a flavor-driven cuisine, where science and style are basic tools employed in our pursuit of flavor. We are equally happy to play with an aged, prime piece of beef, or a crisp and juicy red bell pepper, because we know that each can be coaxed into releasing its secret essences and creating dozens of different, equally extraordinary dishes. All that is required is some patience, diligence, and imagination. We do not limit ourselves to a particular niche, instead choosing to pick elements from each one that work in our kitchen.

Taste

Modern cooking has evolved as a way to make food look stunning; to wipe away any small imperfections and to seduce the eye before a single bite ever reaches the mouth. Meat is no longer identified with the animals from which it comes. Bacon evokes no images of fat, happy pigs, but instead we see sterile, shrink-wrapped pieces. Produce is sold pre-cut, triple washed, and ready to serve in plastic bags on supermarket shelves. Science has evolved alongside this culinary metamorphosis. Companies are constantly generating new methods to speed and to facilitate this transformation from natural products into supermarket convenience foods. As ready-to-serve meals and snacks gained in popularity, so did the technology, which allowed factories to transform food into shelf-stable, ready-to-eat meals and snacks. Unfortunately, all of this technology has stripped food of its essential flavors. People reach for the idea of convenience rather than for what tastes good. The goal of a chef is to bring flavor back to the table. That is the objective that impels us to search for the best products and the best cooking techniques to tease every last atom of flavor out of each ingredient we bring to the table.

Cooking, as Paul Bocuse noted years ago, is truly just a series of small repetitive tasks done with great concentration and attention to detail. As chefs, ingredients often inspire us because the cooking techniques do not really change. Even in the midst of the new craze for kitchen science one of the most popular techniques, *sous vide* cookery, has been around for decades, if not centuries, in more primitive forms. Who does not remember boil-in-the-bag frozen dinners or has not heard of haggis, Scotland's national dish? Certainly, we can take old techniques and twist them into new forms, but it is extremely rare to develop something novel.

On the other hand, ingredients are fresh every day. No two peppers are the same. Each one has a different level of sweetness, thickness, and crunchiness with which to challenge us. A vegetable can be cooked in a variety of different ways. For example, leeks can be roasted or fried, simmered or boiled, baked dry or in a foil package, grilled over coals or charred over a roaring fire, dehydrated or minced and served raw; the possibilities are endless. Each technique or preparation will yield different, and equally delightful, results. Imagine then the world of ingredients and all of the possibilities to be found there. There are innumerable adventures to be explored when the focus is on ingredients rather than on cooking methods. It is no wonder that so many of us consider ourselves ingredient-inspired.

Once you have settled upon an ingredient, the next decision is how it should be prepared. This choice will determine the taste and the texture of the finished dish. One of the big differences between restaurant cooking and home cooking is the number of elements on a plate. At home, food is usually more simply prepared, while, in a fine dining restaurant, you will often see one ingredient in several different forms in a single presentation. This layering of flavors and textures is one of the facets that make dining out a memorable experience. Many people love to explore the intricacy and subtlety of restaurant food knowing they would never go through the trouble of preparing it on their own.

Restaurants have the equipment and the staff to execute more complex recipes and to distill the essence of an ingredient. Juicers are a simple, yet wonderful way to get intense flavor out of a vegetable. Once extracted, the juices can be infused into broths or caramels, thinned with an acidic liquid and oil to create vinaigrettes, or folded into a batter or dough for baked goods. It can be combined with egg whites and sugar to create a delicate, wafer-thin crisp, or smoked and reduced to intense syrup. The pulp that is left behind when the juice is extracted can be dehydrated and ground into a fine powder to be used as a flavorful finishing touch either by itself or blended with sugar or salt. It is very rare to see that kind of utilization for flavor in a home kitchen.

Immersion circulators are the hottest new toys in restaurant kitchens. They are used to cook ingredients in vacuum-sealed bags, in temperature-controlled circulating water baths. Because the food is cooked in a vacuum there is no dilution of flavor. Because we can precisely control the temperatures, it is possible to have perfectly cooked medium-rare meat that is more tender than its more quickly cooked counterparts. The ability to hold it at a specific temperature for long periods of time allows for a gradual breakdown of collagen and connective tissue while still preserving the juicy attributes of rare meat. Vegetables also reap the benefits of these long, slow, hot water baths. Artichokes can be braised with just a small bit of butter and salt, becoming tender and juicy without having to take on the flavors of an entire court bouillon. Portabella mushrooms slow cooked with a bit of olive oil, wine, and fresh herbs become meaty and tender with a rich silky texture and profound earthy flavors.

The vacuum sealer used to prepare ingredients for the immersion circulator can become a cooking medium of sorts on its own. Vegetables sealed with a bit of salt and left in the refrigerator for several hours become cooked in their own juices. The combination of salt and compression helps to break down the cell walls, extracting excess water and "cooking" the ingredients sealed in the bags. This process tenderizes and compacts the flesh of fruits and vegetables, adding density to their texture. This gives them a luxurious toothsome consistency previously missing. The liquid that is extracted becomes an intense flavor medium that can be used to make complementary sauces and vinaigrettes to pair with the original ingredients in a dish. Since there is nothing added to the vegetables in the compression process there is no dilution of flavor. Instead, there is an amplification of the flavors that are already present.

As chefs, we often need to procure ingredients in large quantities simply to have access to them. This has forced us to look to the past for techniques to preserve ingredients and flavors. The freezer has become our greatest accomplice, with the smoker a close second. The reality of having to preserve and smoke foods made us realize how they easily stock a pantry. We have smoked fish and liquid condiments, fruit and vegetable jellies, truffles frozen in their poaching liquid, various delicate filled pastas frozen on trays in the freezer, dehydrated fruits and vegetables ground to a fine powder, and various smoked and confited proteins stocking our larder. The common feature of these preservation methods is their affinity to flavor. It is amazing how many of the techniques evolved to make food last also make them taste better. This allows us incredible flexibility. We can adjust our menus to any aversions our diners may express at a moment's notice and create substitutions that are flavorful and beautiful.

Aesthetics

It is commonly accepted that we use all of our senses to dine. We are first seduced by the vision of a dish as it is placed before us. Its presentation must be appealing to the diner and make them want to pick up their silver and partake of the meal. Slowly, we become aware of the aromas rising from the plate. Food should smell delicious. These scents will set the mouth to watering in anticipation of the meal. The weight of the cutlery and the feel of delicate crystal in our hands will add another dimension to the experience. Sounds also enhance the culinary aesthetic, like that of cool liquid pouring into a glass, the soft music of silver against china, and the bell-like notes of crystal against crystal. These elements all come into play before we even taste a bite. We consider these elements the aesthetics of dining. It is a weaving together of all our senses to magnify a dining experience and transform it into something truly special.

Unfortunately, many of the most beautiful food presentations can be lacking in flavor or difficult to eat. Part of our culinary philosophy is that food should be inviting. You should want to eat your dinner; when it arrives you should want to dive into it and devour it. Culinary architecture should never come at the expense of flavor or accessibility. A plate should be beautiful and enticing, but it must also be functional from the standpoints of the cook, the server, and the diner. It should be easy to plate and send out of the kitchen at its peak, and it should be relatively simple to serve, to avoid its being destroyed. Most importantly, it must be easy to eat. A diner who is contemplating how to approach his or her food is distracted from how wonderful it will taste.

Our ingredients come from nature, which we seek to represent in our presentations. We have noted that sea foam can spark an idea. Replicating it on a microlevel seduces the diner by promising an edible representation of the sea and its essence. Similarly, we draw directly from nature in using fresh spruce tips as a pedestal for our frozen spruce and vinegar martini. The visual appeal and aroma of the actual evergreen adds to the experience of savoring the frozen treat. While it may not be direct representation of nature, the inspiration behind the aesthetic is solid.

Though we generally find aesthetic inspiration in nature, we do not limit ourselves. As we manipulate ingredients, we sometimes come up with ideas that are not found in nature. In these cases, we use a grand juxtaposition of inspirations to play off what is and is not natural. A recent potato dish truly illustrates the way a modern aesthetic develops as we progress from ingredients to a finished dish. Our inspiration began with the caramelized flavors and crunchy textures of grilled potatoes. The grilling process created dark, charred marks on the outside of the slices, the smoky flavor of which accentuated the sweetness of the cooked flesh. The complex, yet sweet and creamy flavor evoked the image of ice cream. So we transformed the puree into ice cream, and then considered classic pairings with potatoes that would benefit from being served cold. A scoop of potato ice cream was covered with caviar and garnished with a few delicate herbs. It was beautiful, deceptively simple, and easy to eat. The idea of ice cream and caviar surprises and disarms our diners with its combination of elegance and comfort. It is a clear example of how the modern aesthetic works on a plate; it had a stunning visual presentation that was functional and approachable.

Functionality is the word that most defines our aesthetic vision. Anything that we create must excite our senses and please our diners. Beauty is in the eye of the beholder and culinary beauty is achieved when people cannot wait to take that first bite. Food should look natural. Presentations are based around the idea that food comes from the earth. We do not create architectural fantasies or buildings of spun sugar. We focus on clear flavors and approachable compositions. As chefs, we never want diners to wonder how to eat our food; we want them to wonder how they can eat it more often. Everything else that we do in the kitchen flows from that basic aesthetic principle.

Conclusion

What if a scale had three arms with which to balance weights and measures? Ours does. Three parts with various levels of influence play an essential role in how we approach food. Taste is fundamental. If food does not taste good, then you have wasted everyone's time. Inspirations are the driving force behind any great cuisine. Without inspiration food is simply a series of ingredients gathered on a plate. They may taste good, but they will never reach their full potential. The aesthetic is what shapes each dish and ties everything together. It is the signature of the chef. It is what draws people to your table and makes them happy to be there. Perfection is the goal that we all strive for and never achieve. In the rare moments when we can almost perfectly balance taste, inspiration, and aesthetics in the execution of our cooking, all of the components weave together seamlessly and the food becomes something extraordinary.

Afterword

20

Thus Ate Zarathustra

Woody Allen

There's nothing like the discovery of an unknown work by a great thinker to set the intellectual community a-twitter and cause academics to dart about like those things one sees when looking at a drop of water under a microscope. On a recent trip to Heidelberg to procure some rare nineteenth-century duelling scars, I happened upon just such a treasure. Who would have thought that "Friedrich Nietzsche's Diet Book" existed? While its authenticity might appear to be a soupçon dicey to the niggling, most who have studied the work agree that no other Western thinker has come so close to reconciling Plato with Pritikin. Selections follow.

Fat itself is a substance or essence of a substance or mode of that essence. The big problem sets in when it accumulates on your hips. Among the pre-Socratics, it was Zeno who held that weight was an illusion and that no matter how much a man ate he would always be only half as fat as the man who never does push-ups. The quest for an ideal body obsessed the Athenians, and in a lost play by Aeschylus Clytemnestra breaks her vow never to snack between meals and tears out her eyes when she realizes she no longer fits into her bathing suit.

It took the mind of Aristotle to put the weight problem in scientific terms, and in an early fragment of the Ethics he states that the circumference of any man is equal to his girth multiplied by pi. This sufficed until the Middle Ages, when Aquinas translated a number of menus into Latin and the first really good oyster bars opened. Dining out was still frowned upon by the Church, and valet parking was a venal sin.

As we know, for centuries Rome regarded the Open Hot Turkey Sandwich as the height of licentiousness; many sandwiches were forced to stay closed and only reopened after the Reformation. Fourteenth-century religious paintings first depicted scenes of damnation in which the overweight wandered Hell, condemned to salads and yogurt. The Spaniards were particularly cruel, and during the Inquisition a man could be put to death for stuffing an avocado with crabmeat.

No philosopher came close to solving the problem of guilt and weight until Descartes divided mind and body in two, so that the body could gorge itself while the mind thought, Who cares, it's not me. The great question of philosophy remains: If life is meaningless, what can be done about alphabet soup? It was Leibniz who first said that fat consisted of monads. Leibniz dieted and exercised but never did get rid of his monads – at least, not the ones that adhered to his thighs. Spinoza, on the other hand, dined sparingly because he believed that God existed in everything and it's intimidating to wolf down a knish if you think you're ladling mustard onto the First Cause of All Things.

Is there a relationship between a healthy regimen and creative genius? We need only look at the composer Richard Wagner and see what he puts away. French fries, grilled cheese, nachos – Christ, there's no limit to the man's appetite, and yet his music is sublime. Cosima, his wife, goes pretty good, too, but at least she runs every day. In a scene cut from the "Ring" cycle, Siegfried decides to dine out with the Rhine maidens and in heroic fashion consumes an ox, two dozen fowl, several wheels of cheese, and fifteen kegs of beer. Then the check comes and he's short. The point here is that in life one is entitled to a side dish of either coleslaw or potato salad, and the choice must be made in terror, with the knowledge that not only is our time on earth limited but most kitchens close at ten.

The existential catastrophe for Schopenhauer was not so much eating as munching. Schopenhauer railed against the aimless nibbling of peanuts and potato chips while one engaged in other activities. Once munching has begun, Schopenhauer held, the human will cannot resist further munching, and the result is a universe with crumbs over everything. No less misguided was Kant, who proposed that we order lunch in such a manner that if everybody ordered the same thing the world would function in a moral way. The problem Kant didn't foresee is that if everyone orders the same dish there will be squabbling in the kitchen over who gets the last branzino. "Order like you are ordering for every human being on earth," Kant advises, but what if the man next to you doesn't eat guacamole? In the end, of course, there are no moral foods – unless we count soft-boiled eggs.

To sum up: apart from my own Beyond Good and Evil Flapjacks and Will to Power Salad Dressing, of the truly great recipes that have changed Western ideas Hegel's Chicken Pot Pie was the first to employ leftovers with meaningful political implications. Spinoza's Stir-Fried Shrimp and Vegetables can be enjoyed by atheists and agnostics alike, while a little-known recipe of Hobbes's for Barbecued Baby-Back Ribs remains an intellectual conundrum. The great thing about the Nietzsche Diet is that once the pounds are shed they stay off – which is not the case with Kant's "Tractatus on Starches."

Breakfast
Orange juice
2 strips of bacon
Profiteroles
Baked clams
Toast, herbal tea

The juice of the orange is the very being of the orange made manifest, and by this I mean its true nature, and that which gives it its "orangeness" and keeps it from tasting like, say, a poached salmon or grits. To the devout, the notion of anything but cereal for breakfast produces anxiety and dread, but with the death of God anything is permitted, and profiteroles and clams may be eaten at will, and even buffalo wings.

Lunch
1 bowl of spaghetti, with tomato and basil
White bread
Mashed potatoes
Sacher Torte

The powerful will always lunch on rich foods, well seasoned with heavy sauces, while the weak peck away at wheat germ and tofu, convinced that their suffering will earn them a reward in an afterlife where grilled lamb chops are all the rage. But if the afterlife is, as I assert, an eternal recurrence of this life, then the meek must dine in perpetuity on low carbs and broiled chicken with the skin removed.

Dinner
Steak or sausages
Hash-brown potatoes
Lobster thermidor
Ice cream with whipped cream or layer cake

This is a meal for the Superman. Let those who are riddled with angst over high triglycerides and trans fats eat to please their pastor or nutritionist, but the Superman knows that marbleized meat and creamy cheeses with rich desserts and, oh, yes, lots of fried stuff is what Dionysus would eat – if it weren't for his reflux problem.

Aphorisms

Epistemology renders dieting moot. If nothing exists except in my mind, not only can I order anything; the service will be impeccable.
  Man is the only creature who ever stiffs a waiter.

Note

From *The New Yorker*.

Notes on Contributors

Fritz Allhoff, PhD. Fritz Allhoff is an assistant professor of philosophy at Western Michigan University; he has held fellowships at the American Medical Association's Institute for Ethics, the Australian National University's Centre for Applied Philosophy and Public Ethics, and the University of Pittsburgh's Center for Philosophy of Science. His research areas are in ethical theory, applied ethics, and philosophy of biology/science. In addition to co-editing this book, with Dave Monroe, Fritz is also the editor of *Wine & Philosophy*. While he enjoys cooking, he lacks Dave's culinary talent, though he does get to pick the wines.

Matthew Brown is a doctoral candidate in philosophy at the University of California, San Diego. He is currently writing his dissertation under the influence of John Dewey, Paul Feyerabend, and lots of coffee. The dissertation defends a pragmatist theory of scientific methodology that emphasizes the continuity of science with lived experience. He runs a monthly soup night at UCSD, where people share delicious soups with each other. Matt also teaches freshmen how to write at the academic level, and how to distinguish science from pseudoscience. Stop by www.thehangedman.com to see more of Matt's projects.

Jennifer L. Iannolo is the founder and CEO of The Gilded Fork, LLC, a new media company celebrating the sensual pleasures of food. The company's online magazine, GildedFork.com, focuses on the roots of culinary passion, including philosophical opinions from some of the world's leading chefs. In addition, the company's Culinary Podcast Network, launched in 2006, is the world's first all-food podcast collection. Jennifer has collaborated with master chefs from around the globe for more than a decade and is the former Director of Culinary Programs for Relais & Chateaux, the leading international collection of luxury hotels and celebrated restaurants.

Jeremy Iggers, PhD. Jeremy Iggers is a staff writer, restaurant critic, and ethics columnist for the *Minneapolis Star Tribune*. The part of him that likes to eat and the part that thinks about ethics are frequently in conflict. Jeremy's books include *Garden of Eating: Food, Sex and the Hunger for Meaning*, *The Joy of Cheesecake* (co-authored with Dana Bovbjerg), and *Good News, Bad News: Journalism Ethics and the Public Interest*. Jeremy briefly held the University of Minnesota philosophy department record for the most years required to complete a PhD, with nineteen.

Linda Jerofke, PhD. Linda Jerofke is an assistant professor of anthropology at Eastern Oregon University; she received her PhD at the University of Oregon with a focus on nutritional anthropology. Linda's research interests have varied over the years and include Native American health, maternal nutrition during pregnancy, hunger, childhood obesity, and North American archeology. Her interests in Native American studies also led her to working for the Burns Paiute Tribe of Oregon as their Tribal Archeologist. She is the co-director of *Haven from Hunger*, a student-centered community development and service learning project.

Aki Kamozawa is a chef unable to leave words alone. She has been able to capture the emotional nature of food and cooking and to deftly transform the feelings into detailed anecdotes, which inspire those who read them. She has published her musings on her website, www.ideasinfood.com. Aki began her career in food as a child, cooking for family and friends. She graduated from the New England Culinary Institute and has experience in all aspects of the restaurant business, having worked front of the house, back of the house, top of the house, and even selling wine in New York City.

Roger J. H. King, PhD. Roger J. H. King is associate professor of philosophy and chair of the philosophy department at the University of Maine; he received his PhD in philosophy from Boston University. Roger has published extensively on topics in environmental ethics, including the ethics of hunting, ecofeminist ethics, issues related to the built environment, and civic environmentalism. Currently, his focus is on articulating the cultural dimension of sustainability as a counterweight to the more prominent focus on economic, political, and technological dimensions.

Carolyn Korsmeyer, PhD. Carolyn Korsmeyer is professor of philosophy at the University at Buffalo, State University of New York. She has published a number of books and articles in aesthetics, which is her main area of research. Among her publications are *Making Sense of Taste: Food and Philosophy* and the edited collection, *The Taste Culture Reader: Experiencing Food and Drink*. Her interest in diverse eating practices and in emotion theory, as well as a few misguided menu choices, have led her to pay special attention to food, taste, and disgust.

Christian J. Krautkramer is a dual-masters candidate in Medical Science and Public Health at the Boston University School of Public Health and the School of Medicine. Before that, he was employed as a senior researcher in the Ethics Group of the American Medical Association in Chicago. He is the recipient of a bachelor's degree from the University of Wisconsin-Madison, where he was the restaurant critic and food writer for the campus newspaper, the *Daily Cardinal*. Christian has worked in many cafes, bakeries, and restaurants – including L'Etoile in Madison, WI – and has held titles as diverse as cook, waiter, barista, sandwich maker, and ice cream scooper.

Glenn Kuehn, PhD. Where other philosophy majors ended up in fast food, Glenn Kuehn is going all the way to "chef." Self-proclaimed "philosopher-chef," he continues to balance a dual life of teaching and cooking. He received his graduate degrees in philosophy at Southern Illinois University at Carbondale and his degree in culinary arts from the Culinary Institute of America. He has published on food and aesthetics and is a co-founding member of *Convivium: The Philosophy and Food Roundtable*. Glenn credits his drive to combine philosophy and food to his undergraduate philosophy professors at the University of Wisconsin at Eau Claire, who repeatedly took him out for pizza at "Sammy's."

Sheila Lintott received her PhD in philosophy from the University of Wisconsin, Madison and is an assistant professor of philosophy at Bucknell University. She works primarily in the area of aesthetics and the philosophy of art, especially in feminist and environmental issues. Her articles have appeared in *Environmental Ethics, Hypatia: A Journal of Feminist Philosophy, Journal of Aesthetic Education*, and the *British Journal of Aesthetics*. Also, she is co-editor (with Allen Carlson) of *Beauty to Duty: From Aesthetics to Environmentalism*. Sheila argues that both philosophy and food define her life, a life she happily shares with her hearty spouse, Eric, their free-range daughter, Sonja, two divine felines, Odin and Freya, and a zesty canine, Vincent.

Dave Monroe was an accomplished chef, restaurant consultant, and caterer prior to pursuing academic philosophy; he is an Adjunct Instructor at the Applied Ethics Institute of St. Petersburg College. Trained by apprenticeship, he has worked with a range of cuisines, including French, rustic Italian, and Pan-Asian. He was employed by notable restaurants and resorts around the United States, including The Pink Door Ristorante and Blowfish Asian Café in Seattle, and Vintage Gourmet in Pensacola, Florida. Although Dave is fully engaged with his career as a philosopher, culinary art remains one of his passions.

Fabio Parasecoli joyfully commutes between Rome and New York City. After working as a correspondent in foreign affairs, he concluded that suffering from mild food poisoning is better than dodging bullets in jungles and deserts. This life-changing insight made him shift to food writing; Fabio also recultivated an interest in philosophy, his high school passion. He is now an editor for the Italian food and wine magazine *Gambero Rosso*. He also teaches food studies at New York University, and communication and journalism in food and wine at the Citta' del Gusto in Rome. Fabio has written *Food Culture in Italy*, and he is currently working on *Bite Me: The Pleasures and Politics of Food in Pop Culture*.

296

Michael Shaffer, PhD. Michael Shaffer is currently an assistant professor of philosophy at St. Cloud State University in Minnesota; his interests are focused on the theory of rationality. Michael has published a number of articles on topics in logic, epistemology, and the philosophy of science. He is an accomplished amateur cook, and a lover of cheese (preferably stinky) and all varieties of offal. Michael is also the organizer and host of the infamous L. E. Bainbridge Society memorial feast held annually at the Eastern Division meeting of the American Philosophical Association.

Kevin W. Sweeney received his PhD in philosophy from the University of Wisconsin-Madison. He currently teaches philosophy at the University of Tampa. His research interests include topics in modern philosophy, ethics, and aesthetics. Recently, he has written on philosophy and literature, film theory, the nature of film horror, and film comedy, especially the silent films of Buster Keaton. A student of aesthetic issues concerned with taste, he is also an amateur chef. Friends say that he makes a respectable shrimp Creole.

Michael Symons, PhD. Michael Symons, after a career as a journalist, became a partner in a restaurant for fifteen years. He instigated the successful series of Symposiums of Australian Gastronomy and gained a PhD in the sociology of cuisine from the Flinders University of South Australia. Michael is presently a Marsden Fund culinary researcher in New Zealand. His publications include *One Continuous Picnic: A History of Eating in Australia*, *The Shared Table: Ideas for Australian Cuisine*, and *The Pudding that Took a Thousand Cooks*, which was republished as *A History of Cooks and Cooking*.

Mark Tafoya is the chef/owner of the ReMARKable Palate Personal Chef Service in New York City. He is also co-owner and executive chef of The Gilded Fork, a New Media company celebrating the sensual pleasures of food, and the founder of the Culinary Podcast Network. Mark is a graduate of Yale University. He has also studied at the Université de Paris III, Censier, and the Culinary Business Academy. He serves as President of the New York Metro Chapter of the United States Personal Chef Association and was honored with the USPCA's Marketer of the Year Award for 2006.

H. Alexander Talbot is working with his wife and co-chef, Aki Kamozawa, on executing the culinary visions catalogued on their website, www.ideasinfood.com. He graduated from Colby College as an English major, but quickly followed his heart into the food business; he is slightly obsessive in his search for perfection in the kitchen. Now, having been an executive chef in various restaurants across the country, from Martha's Vineyard to Pagosa Springs, he is focused on building a venue where there can be a true exchange of culinary ideas and information and of course, great food.

Paul B. Thompson, PhD. Paul B. Thompson, contrary to popular perception, does not spend his time figuring out how to cram yak genes into your potato salad or blinding chickens with Wittgenstein's poker. He is, in fact, the W. K. Kellogg Professor of Agricultural, Food and Community Ethics at Michigan State University. He was a co-founder and former President of the Agriculture, Food and Human Values Society and is the author or editor of seven books and over 100 articles on topics relating to agriculture, food, and the philosophy of technology.

Jen Wrye is a doctoral candidate in the department of sociology and anthropology at Carleton University in Ottawa, Canada. She holds an MA from Carleton University in sociology and a BA in women's studies from the University of Western Ontario. Her current interests center on the social reality shared by humans and animals in modern culture. Jen's dissertation work focuses on Westerners' growing preference for cruelty-free and free-range animal products in terms of the social–spatial nexus of human–animal interaction. She is also currently completing a project on the social relations surrounding pets.

Lydia Zepeda, PhD. Lydia Zepeda is a professor of consumer science at the University of Wisconsin-Madison. She is an agriculturaleconomist by training, but don't hold that against her; she is a foodie by inclination. Her current research focuses on organic and local food. She is particularly interested in women, children, and people of color in the food system as producers and consumers. Lydia has no formal philosophical training, but does have strong opinions about food. As founder of the huitlacoche (corn smut) festival, her alias is the "queen of smut." She is generally a pretty good sport and plays well with others.

Index

Index

aristology 22
Aristotle 124, 150, 151
aroma 276
art, cooking as 276
art, food as 6, 133, 134, 139,
140, 143, 147, 150, 153
formal structuring 138
instrumental value 141
paradox of aversion 150
and the universalization principle
139–40
art objects 134–6, 147
immaterial conditions 136
instrumental value 141, 142
intrinsic value 94, 141, 142,
143
objective judgments about
141–2
persistence condition 137, 138,
139
Athenaeus 19
aversion, paradox of 150, 151,
159

Bailey, Cyril 18
Baker, Janice 65–6
Barthes, Roland 158
Batalli, Mario 254
Baumgarten, Alexander 120
beauty 6, 151
culinary 117, 118, 278, 285
female 59, 67, 68, 69
Kantian account 121, 122
Beck, Simone 253
Berchoux, Joseph 123
Bertholle, Louisette 253
biodiversity reduction 188
biotechnology industry 212, 215,
219
see also fertilizers and pesticides;
genetically modified organisms
(GMOs)

bitter foods 78, 80, 81, 193, 205
Bocuse, Paul 281
bodily/lower senses 146
boil-in-the-bag meals 281
Boisvert, Raymond 28, 170
bonds and contracts, sealing 267,
275
Boone and Crockett Club 227
Bordo, Susan 64, 66
Bourdieu, Pierre 46–7, 48, 94
Bradley, Richard 150
brain 103, 105–6, 111–12
emotional aspect 103, 112
neural activity 110, 111, 112
synaptic connectivity 106, 110
and taste perception 79, 106–7
value systems 106
Branden, Nathaniel 240–1
branding 6, 96, 99–100
brand image 98, 99, 100
branded environments 88–9,
97–8
branded restaurants 89, 91, 97,
98
emotional relationships 97
and tasting scores 99
Brillat-Savarin, Jean-Anthelme 2,
13, 23, 73, 74–5, 85, 123–4,
125, 126, 127, 147, 242, 252
Brown, Matthew 8, 192–207
brute eating 154, 155
bulimia 59, 63, 65, 67
Bunyan, John 94
Burger King 88, 99
Burke, Edmund 151–2
butchering 226

calories
empty calories 31, 35, 36, 43,
66
energy-dense foods 31, 34, 36,
37, 39, 42, 43